The Catholic Answer Book

Peter M. J. Stravinskas

Our Sunday Visitor Publishing Division
Our Sunday Visitor, Inc.
Huntington, Indiana 46750

Most of the text of this book first appeared in *The Catholic Answer* magazine between 1987 and 1990. Most citations from Holy Scripture are from the original *New American Bible*, copyright © 1969, 1970 by the Confraternity of Christian Doctrine, Washington, D.C., and reprinted by permission; all rights reserved.

Our Sunday Visitor Publishing Division
Our Sunday Visitor, Inc.
200 Noll Plaza
Huntington, Indiana 46750

International Standard Book Number: 0-87973-458-2
Library of Congress Catalog Card Number: 90-60986

Cover design by Monica Watts

PUBLISHED IN THE UNITED STATES OF AMERICA

458

Contents

Key to Abbreviations of Biblical Books
(In Alphabetical Order)

Old Testament Books

Am — Amos
Bar — Baruch
1 Chr — 1 Chronicles
2 Chr — 2 Chronicles
Dn — Daniel
Dt — Deuteronomy
Eccl — Ecclesiastes
Es — Esther
Ex — Exodus
Ez — Ezekiel
Ezr — Ezra
Gn — Genesis
Hb — Habakkuk
Hg — Haggai
Hos — Hosea
Is — Isaiah
Jer — Jeremiah
Jb — Job
Jdt — Judith
Jgs — Judges
Jl — Joel
Jon — Jonah
Jos — Joshua
1 Kgs — 1 Kings
2 Kgs — 2 Kings
Lam — Lamentations
Lv — Leviticus
Mal — Malachi
1 Mc — 1 Maccabees
2 Mc — 2 Maccabees
Mi — Micah
Na — Nahum
Neh — Nehemiah
Nm — Numbers
Ob — Obadiah
Prv — Proverbs
Ps — Psalms
Ru — Ruth
Sg — Song of Songs
Sir — Sirach
1 Sm — 1 Samuel
2 Sm — 2 Samuel
Tb — Tobit
Wis — Wisdom
Zec — Zechariah
Zep — Zephaniah

New Testament Books

Acts — Acts of the Apostles
Col — Colossians
1 Cor — 1 Corinthians
2 Cor — 2 Corinthians
Eph — Ephesians
Gal — Galatians
Heb — Hebrews
Jas — James
Jn — John
1 Jn — 1 John
2 Jn — 2 John
3 Jn — 3 John
Jude — Jude
Lk — Luke
Mk — Mark
Mt — Matthew
Phil — Philippians
Phlm — Philemon
1 Pt — 1 Peter
2 Pt — 2 Peter
Rom — Romans
Rv — Revelation
1 Thes — 1 Thessalonians
2 Thes — 2 Thessalonians
Ti — Titus
1 Tm — 1 Timothy
2 Tm — 2 Timothy

Introduction

With the rise of confusion among some of the faithful as to exactly what the Church teaches on certain issues, it has become evident that there is a growing need for a clear presentation on the basics of our Catholic Faith.

It was to achieve this goal that the bimonthly magazine entitled *The Catholic Answer* was initiated. Edited by Father Peter M.J. Stravinskas, this publication by *Our Sunday Visitor* first appeared in March 1987. By using a question-and-answer format, Father Stravinskas has attempted to respond to the many questions raised regarding the Catholic religion.

Since its inception, the response to this magazine has been overwhelmingly positive. The reason: Catholics have legitimate questions about their Faith and they seek informed answers. And now they can get these answers in the form of a well-structured and carefully written book with the same name.

✠Anthony J. Bevilacqua
Archbishop of Philadelphia

1. SCRIPTURE

Double standard?

Q. *Mary Magdalene didn't commit adultery by herself, you know. Why was her male accomplice never even alluded to? Why wasn't he brought before the crowd to be stoned? And why didn't Jesus tell him, as He told her, to "go and sin no more"? Because it was all right for the man to keep on sinning? Why is it a sin for a woman to commit adultery with a man but not the other way around? Does the same putrid double standard exist in heaven that exists on earth? By the way, everybody tells me you'll never have the courage to print this letter since all you men stick together. This comes from an anonymous subscriber who will no longer be a subscriber if you don't answer this question!*

A. I print this letter not for fear of losing a dissatisfied customer, because, very frankly, with nearly 110,000 subscribers, I don't doubt that our magazine is responding to the needs of the vast majority of readers. I do so for two reasons, however. First, to set the record straight; second, to demonstrate what happens when feminism goes wild and becomes angry and irrational.

First, then, the truth. No one has ever doubted that "it takes two to tango," but in Judaism, women were often seen as part of a man's possessions, so that when a woman violated the covenant of marriage, she was diminishing her value in the eyes of her husband and others. It is important to note that our blessed Lord did away with the very double standard you so abhor. After all, have you ever heard a priest even suggest that men could commit adultery with impunity, or that the penalty for such should be different for men and women?

Why doesn't Jesus deal with the man in the affair? Very simply, logic would show that the crowd dragged the woman, not the man, to Him; how could He say anything to one He didn't even see? Why does our Lord tell Mary Magdalene (if that is who it was; cf. the next question) to stop sinning? Because He obviously saw her as contrite and wanted to put her and keep her on the right track, and it just as obviously worked, since she became the first witness to the Resurrection, the Gospels tell us.

To sum up, I use this letter as a warning to all: Do not let your preconceived notions and secular agenda impinge on the truth of the Gospels. It is disastrous personally (both spiritually and psychologically) and communally, since we end up polarizing the whole Church with matters that are best handled in careful study, prayer, reflection, and intelligent discussion — never amid hostile recriminations.

The adulteress

Q. John 8:1-11 is the story of the adulteress whom Jesus forgave. Although John doesn't call her Mary Magdalene, I was always taught that is who she was. Where did the Church get that notion?

A. The Church has never identified Mary Magdalene as the woman caught in adultery, although I think many people have done so. Aside from her being mentioned in connection with the scene at the foot of the cross and as a witness to the Risen Christ, she is named twice in the Gospels (Lk 8:2 and Mk 16:9), in both instances cited as the one out of whom Jesus had cast seven devils.

Perhaps because of Mary Magdalene's reputation as a sinner, the popular mind has tended to collapse several stories about sinful women and attribute them all to one. Some early Christian writers did, however, which also suggests that Mary Magdalene may have been the adulteress of John 8.

St. Paul

Q. Was St. Paul a full-blooded Jew? A friend said he was half Jewish and half Gentile. I thought the Bible said he was completely Jewish.

A. St. Paul, by his own declaration was a "Jew's Jew" (cf. Acts 22:3ff and Gal 1:14).

Your friend may be confused because Paul was also a Roman citizen (cf. Acts 22:25-29). Many Jews had Roman citizenship, and Paul used it to his advantage in a variety of ways: to avoid being flogged by the soldiers; to obtain an imperial trial; to be beheaded rather than crucified.

Establishment of God's Kingdom

Q. What do Luke 9:27 and Mark 9:1 mean?

A. Both passages speak of the fact that some people are standing in Jesus' presence who will not experience death before seeing the establishment of God's Kingdom in power. It would appear that our Lord was speaking about the imminent nature of the coming Kingdom. Indeed, the Kingdom of God came crashing into men's lives with power through the Lord's own paschal mystery; His passion, death, and resurrection reversed the downward spiral of history, defeating the worst enemies of the human race: sin, the flesh, and the devil.

Whoever witnessed those saving events truly saw the beginnings of the Kingdom of God, which will be brought to its consummation at the Parousia.

Sunday Sabbath

Q. I live in a Seventh-Day Adventist neighborhood and am constantly asked how the Church justified changing the Sabbath from Saturday to Sunday. Can you refresh my memory on this?

A. As the Church began, the early Christians went to the synagogue for the Sabbath service and then met in their own homes on the evening of the first day of the week for the celebration of the Eucharist (cf. Acts 20:7), in honor of our Lord's resurrection from the dead on that day. When those first believers in Christ were eventually excommunicated from Judaism and thus expelled from temple and synagogue, they took the Sabbath service with them and simply tacked it onto the Liturgy of the Eucharist. Hence, the Mass in two parts, as we have it to this day.

Lord's Prayer

Q. *How did it come about that the ending "For thine is the kingdom" became acceptable to conclude the Lord's Prayer at Mass?*

A. It should be noted that the doxology mentioned in the question is not used at Mass as the ending for the Lord's Prayer. Rather, it concludes the ensuing prayer for peace.

A quick look at the Gospels of Matthew and Luke will reveal that the Lord's Prayer as recorded in Sacred Scripture does not have this ending. It is a beautiful hymn of praise to God, originally included by a monastic scribe in the margin of the biblical text (technically known as a gloss). Gradually, the Eastern churches adopted the gloss as a concluding doxology for the Lord's Prayer, as did the Protestant reformers.

Although the ending contains no heresy and is surely quite lovely, it is not an accurate representation of Jesus' words and, after all, we do say that we pray "with confidence to the Father *in the words our Savior gave us.*"

Symbolic language

Q. *My father is a Jehovah's Witness and tells me that the Bible says that only 144,000 people are going to be saved. Does that make sense?*

A. Your father is referring to a passage in the seventh chapter of the Book of Revelation.

The 144,000 come from the 12 tribes of Israel and represent the fullness of all the company of the redeemed. If your father were to carry this concept through to its logical conclusion, he would have to argue that not only is the number of the saved limited to 144,000 but that all of them must be Jews, right?

The Book of Revelation is an example of what is technically known as apocalyptic literature, characterized by visions, dreams, and highly symbolic language. Unfortunately, some Christians seek to give the work a literal interpretation, thereby doing violence to the intent of the sacred author and to the message he wanted conveyed.

For a fine discussion of appropriate ways to interpret the Book of Revelation, I would suggest the introduction to that book in the New American Bible.

The two thieves

Q. Please inform me of the names of the two thieves crucified with Jesus. Were they nailed, too?

A. The Gospels do not give us their names, nor whether or not they were nailed or tied to their crosses. Tradition assigns the name of Dismas to the "good thief," and Gestus to the other.

INRI

Q. What does "INRI" stand for on the cross?

A. They are the first letters of the Latin version of the inscription which hung over our Lord's head on the cross: Iesus Nazarenus, Rex Iudaeorum — Jesus the Nazarene, the King of the Jews. St. John tells us this charge was written in the three major languages of that time and place — Latin, Greek, and Hebrew — so that all the passersby would know the reason for the execution. The irony, of course, is that what the Jewish leaders had considered blasphemy and what the Roman officials had regarded as treason was the very truth.

Genealogy of Mary

Q. When they give the genealogy of Jesus Christ, they start with Abraham through David on to Joseph. If Joseph is no blood relation to Jesus, why did they not produce the genealogy of Mary?

A. You will notice that the Gospel according to St. Matthew has a genealogy for Christ, as does St. Luke. There are similarities and differences between them, the most striking difference being that in Matthew (1:1-17), Jesus' origins are traced back to Abraham (as you note) while Luke (3:23-38) throws Jesus' roots all the way back to Adam, indeed to God Himself. Both evangelists had theological considerations in mind when constructing Christ's genealogy. St. Matthew wanted to demonstrate that Jesus was a Jew's Jew and so was careful to highlight this aspect of His identity. St. Luke was intent on showing Jesus' identification with the entire human race and so underscored our Lord's standing among all men, before the development of races and nations.

To answer your specific question now, it must be recalled that in Jewish law inheritance was passed on through the father's line, not the mother's (although Jewishness was — and still is — conferred through having a Jewish mother). Therefore, it was important for Matthew to show Jesus' lineage through Joseph. Even though Joseph was our Lord's foster father, he was nonetheless His legal guardian and was generally thought to be Jesus' father, or as they say more technically, His putative father. We still do similar things today when parents adopt children. Rarely do children consistently say, for example, "I'm going to the movies with my foster father," or "My foster father took me fishing." The evangelist took the same kind of liberty.

Jehovah

Q. Recently a Jehovah's Witness came to our door and said that God's Name is Jehovah. Please comment.

A. The Hebrew name for God, as given in the Book of Exodus, is Yahweh. Ancient Hebrew did not have written vowels; therefore, the name looked like this: YHWH. The four letters of the sacred Name are known as the tetragrammaton. In German, Y can be replaced by J and W by V, so that it would come out thus: JHVH. When certain vowels are inserted, "Jehovah" emerges. However, the substitutions are shaky, and the best proof that the whole process is faulty is that Jews today know the Lord's Name as Yahweh, not Jehovah.

The number 40

Q. How many times is "40 days" or "40 years" used in the Bible? What does it signify?

A. The number 40 is used three times in the Hebrew Scriptures and nine times in the New Testament. Occasionally it reflects an exact count, but usually it is a symbolic number suggesting an indefinite period of time. Frequently, "40" also seems to indicate a time of waiting in preparation. Thus do we read of the 40 days and nights of the flood (Gn 7:6ff) or of the Hebrews wandering in the desert for 40 years (Ex 16ff). In the New Testament, Jesus fasts for 40 days (Mt 4:2), and the Church is instructed by the Risen Christ for 40 days before His Ascension into heaven (Acts 1:3).

The number 40 figures prominently in the liturgical calendar, as the Church has rooted its Lenten observance of 40 days in the Lord's desert experience. Similarly, we celebrate the paschal season with reference to the calculations offered in Acts.

Concordance

Q. What is a concordance? Is it useful for lay people? If so, where can I find one?

A. A concordance is an important resource in biblical study and research, functioning like a word finder. For example, if you are interested in the number of times the Bible uses the word "truth," you look it up in your concordance as you would any word in a dictionary. In the appropriate spot you will find the word noted every time it is used from Genesis to Revelation, with a few words surrounding each citation — to provide context.

It also comes in handy if you cannot remember an exact biblical quotation.

Concordances are geared to specific translations of the Scriptures. The one designed for use with the New American Bible (used in most parishes for the Liturgy of the Word at Mass) is published by Thomas Nelson, Inc.

Say, for example, that you would like to find the place in the Bible where it says, "I am the light of the world." Zero in on the least common word in the citation and look it up in the concordance (entries are listed alphabetically). In this case, your best bet would probably be "light," for which you will find two columns of possibilities. Since you undoubtedly know that this was a statement of our Lord, you can automatically rule out all the Old Testament and narrow your search to the Gospels, leaving you with about twenty-five lines to check, which will lead you to John 8:12.

Teaching Scripture

Q. *When will the laity be permitted to teach Scripture classes?*

A. Any qualified believer — clerical, Religious, or lay — can teach Sacred Scripture. And that has always been the case. In the pages of *The Catholic Answer*, a layman has written on methods of Scripture study.

The charism of teaching is not necessarily tied to the Sacrament of Holy Orders, and the Church has traditionally recognized this. Therefore, we have had many lay people and Religious (both male and female) serve the Church as theologians. Generally speaking, however, most theologians are still priests because of their training, but nothing in Church law or tradition would inhibit a layperson from obtaining the necessary background and credentials.

Lay preaching in a liturgical setting is another story. That is not permissible because of the unity of the eucharistic celebration (ideally, the one who breaks the Bread of the Lord's Body should also break the Bread of His Word) and because of the special nature of the Eucharist in which the one who presides is seen as an *alter Christus*, that is, another Christ.

Lay people may engage in street preaching — once a very popular way of attracting non-believers to the Catholic Faith. In priestless missions, laity may also share their reflections on the assigned Scripture readings during the Liturgy of the Word, which would precede a Communion service.

King James Bible

Q. *What do Catholics have against the King James Bible?*

A. Catholics have nothing "against" the King James Bible, per se. No one could fault this version of the Scriptures on its beauty of language and majesty of expression. Catholic objections would be based on several other concerns, however. First of all would be the incomplete version of the Hebrew Scriptures that it is.

Second is the lack of critical notes to help readers understand troublesome passages or even what might seem to be conflicting passages.

The third objection may surprise many, and it is that it is a rather poor translation, in spite of its high and lofty tone. In the last century, Protestant Scripture scholars convened in St. Louis to work toward a better translation because the King James version had more than thirty thousand errors in it.

No translation is perfect because fallible humans and fallible human languages produce these works.

Catholics in the United States are most familiar with the Jerusalem Bible and the New American Bible. Since Vatican II, ecumenical teams of scholars have collaborated on many translations of great value, including the Common Bible. Such ecumenical cooperation is very desirable since it moves us toward one Bible, to be used as a common point of departure for conversations which have Christian unity as their aim.

Bibles

Q. *I just received a copy of the "New Jerusalem Bible," but cannot find an imprimatur. Is this revision approved by the Church?*

Q. *Will you please tell me who publishes the "Anchor Bible." Is it approved for Catholics?*

A. I have just looked at the 1985 revision of the "Jerusalem Bible" (the only revision of which I am aware), and it does bear an imprimatur — that of Cardinal Hume of Westminster, England.

The "Anchor Bible" series is published by Doubleday. Although it is not an exclusively Catholic production, it is generally reliable. I would caution, however, that the work is of unequal quality; the two volumes on the Gospel of John by Father Raymond Brown, for example, are unparalleled while some others are mediocre at best.

The NAB

Q. *Why is the official Catholic Bible called the "New American Bible"? Is it recognized internationally?*

A. Several English translations of the Bible are approved for Catholic use: Jerusalem Bible, Revised Standard (Catholic edition), New American Bible. The names vary. The one in question is called American to distinguish it from other possible English translations which might be more suited to British speakers of English, for example. If by "recognized internationally" you mean approved by the Holy See, the answer is "yes," since the American bishops have passed on the text and indicated its suitability for study, private prayer, and liturgical use.

Preferred Bible

Q. *I received Bible tapes recently, but they are from the New International Version and not the New American Bible. With so many different versions, which is the best for Catholics?*

A. Any translation of the Scriptures is acceptable if it bears the imprimatur of a Catholic bishop. That having been said, my own preferences are the Revised Standard and New American editions.

A new series has just come to my attention as well: The Navarre Bible, publishing individual books of the Bible in separate volumes. The text is from the Revised Standard Version, Catholic Edition, with the Latin Vulgate text as well. Valuable commentary is provided, including explanations of difficult passages, background information, and practical spiritual applications. The volumes are attractively printed and reasonably priced. To the best of my knowledge, only the four Gospels and some Epistles are presently available for purchase by writing to: Scepter Press, 481 Main St., New Rochelle, NY 10801.

Non-Catholic Bible study

Q. Should Catholics attend non-Catholic Bible study programs?

A. No absolute answer can be given; it will depend on who the teacher is and who the student is. Let me explain.

Studying the Bible with other Christians can be an enriching experience if the course is based on solid scholarship, which takes account of the culture, historical setting, and literary forms of the particular age which produced the work under study. Thus excessive literalism is out of the question. One should also be wary of Scripture study which tries to use the Bible to "prove" the validity of a sectarian viewpoint; Fundamentalists whose principal objective is proselytizing come to mind immediately.

A student who has a poor grounding in his or her Catholic Faith would be ill-advised to join an ecumenical study group for two reasons. First, such a person could make no significant contribution to ecumenical dialogue. Second, that same person will only become confused and risks loss of faith. The solution, of course, is to make up the gaps in one's Catholic education.

The truth of Genesis

Q. Was Adam an actual person? Can the words "original sin" be spoken of as "the sin of our originals" and still keep the same meaning? A freshman high-school religion teacher recently said that the creation stories were just stories to explain a truth. Aren't the stories the whole truth?

A. Let me take both questions together, since they are similar in scope.

When we deal with the early chapters of the Book of Genesis, we find ourselves involved with Hebrew poetry. Therefore, we need to evaluate the literature in that light. Now, we normally do not interpret poetry literally; however, that does not mean that poetry does not contain truth. As a matter of fact, some of the most profound truths of life are best expressed in poetry, hence, the use of that literary form for epics, hymns, and national anthems. Are the creation stories, then, "just stories" or "myths," as is sometimes asserted? If one means by that that they are simply fairy tales designed to inculcate a certain moral, without any basis in reality, the answer is "No." If, however, one understands "myth" as do sociologists of religion, then the reference is apt. Scholars speak of "myths" in the sense of works of literature which communicate cosmic truths. Myths are not synonyms for legends. It seems to me that if Revelation (God's revealing

Himself to us — not the Book of Revelation) is to be taken seriously, it must be grounded in reality. Therefore, the very basics of human existence as described in Genesis must have a historical substratum; otherwise, the essence of the divine human-relationship is rooted in figments of ancient authors' imaginations.

To treat the specific questions raised above, then, I would note the following. In *Humani Generis*, Pope Pius XII taught that a belief in a real set of first parents appears to be the only way to safeguard the very clear doctrine of original sin. Their names, locations, and other such information are matters of indifference, theologically speaking. In fact, the names given them in the Bible are symbolic names (Adam, the Man; Eve, Mother of the Living) to stress their roles as prototypes of humanity. Can one refer to original sin as "the sin of our originals"? Yes, if one means "the sin of the original human beings." If, however, the expression is used to detract from the notion of a historical act of human disobedience or to attempt to identify it with some kind of vague "sin of the world," the answer must be "No."

Hermeneutics

Q. Five years ago I took a CCD teacher-training course, in which I was taught that everything in the Bible is dramatization to help people understand a particular point. So, Adam and Eve, the parting of the Red Sea, and all the stories about the baby Jesus are not really factual. When I began to teach CCD, I found many of these same ideas in the religion text I was expected to use. Is this the teaching of the Church these days?

A. If you have described everything accurately, you have been exposed to some very unfortunate methods and materials, leading to serious doctrinal problems.

The Catholic Church has always had a very nuanced approach to scriptural interpretation. It sees hermeneutics (biblical interpretation) as a special science, requiring specialized tools from the fields of archaeology, linguistics, history, etc. A particular verse cannot be viewed in isolation. First, it must be situated within the broader passage, the passage within the book, the book within the whole Bible. Second, it is necessary to determine a passage's literary form (e.g., history, poetry, drama), for one does not interpret a poem in the same way as a chapter in a history book.

As can be readily seen, this is a complicated and often hard process which does not lend itself to simplistic statements like: "Adam and Eve never existed." Responsible Scripture scholars, therefore, never make such outlandish claims as you cite. Because of the difficulties involved in hermeneutics, the Church at Vatican II insisted on the importance of taking guidance in these matters from the Church, the mother and guardian of the Sacred Scriptures. No less a progressive biblical scholar than Sulpician Father Raymond E. Brown consistently emphasizes the need for a careful interaction between those who would interpret the Bible and the Church's magisterium.

Words of Jesus

Q. I attended a teachers' workshop recently, during which the speaker declared that very few words of the Gospels were truly the "ipsissima verba Christi" (the very words of Christ), but rather are the product of the several evangelists or their communities. This all sounds quite strange to me, and I wonder what the implications might be for Christian faith.

A. You are right to "smell a rat."

First of all, the procedure by which so-called Scripture scholars engage in this dissection of Scripture is hardly scientific. Just the other day I was reading the work of one such individual who cavalierly asserted that "of course, we know that Jesus did not say this." He offered no proof for his position and moved on to make his point, which was to undercut traditional Catholic teaching on the Church.

Secondly, this kind of a process effectively destroys the unity of the Bible and the biblical message. No one verse is any more important or any less important than any other, for the simple reason that all verses are inspired by Almighty God, all are canonical (that is part of the accepted list of biblical books), and all are useful for teaching the truth which God willed for our salvation (cf. 2 Tm 3:16).

Thirdly, such efforts are usually the result of a desire to apply a methodology to the Bible which is alien to faith. This approach to Sacred Scripture arose at the time of the Enlightenment, which tried to highlight and even create an antagonism between faith and reason. Today the best scholars in both the sacred and secular sciences acknowledge the fact that all truth is one, and so there can never be any opposition between "religious" truth and "scientific" truth. Just as theologians should expect scientists to employ the methodology proper to their fields, so too should they operate from a perspective of faith in the pursuit of revealed truth.

Biblical books

Q. Father Leonard Badia, in his article on the Dead Sea Scrolls, stated that every book of the Old Testament has been found in scroll form or fragments, except for the Book of Esther. Did he intend to say that these include the books referred to by Protestants as "apocryphal"?

A. Yes, that is precisely the point of Father Badia's remark. The canon of the Bible accepted by the Roman Catholic Church and the Eastern Orthodox is indeed the Septuagint Canon (that is, the longer one). With this archaeological find and other convincing evidence, many Protestant scholars have indicated a willingness to take a second look at these biblical books. In fact, many Protestant editions now contain these works, at least at the end of the Old Testament.

The disputed books are: Tobit, Judith, Wisdom, Sirach, Baruch, 1 and 2 Maccabees, and Esther. Luther had made the first serious move against these books, largely because 2 Maccabees had always been used by the Church in support of the doctrine of purgatory and prayers for the dead.

God is truth

Q. Does the Bible contradict itself?

A. Contradiction is a facet of falsehood. God, who is Truth, can never partake in falsehood and hence His Word as revealed in the Scriptures can never present contradictory "truths." At times, we are face to face with an apparent or seeming contradiction, but deeper investigation usually uncovers the deeper truth which first eluded us.

At other times, a defective method of biblical interpretation is at fault. For example, if one engages in "proof-texting," one is bound to turn up numerous verses which look as though they contradict one another. However, the use of isolated texts to prove a point is methodologically flawed; one must always place a particular passage in context, so that the true meaning can be perceived.

As Catholics, we believe the Scriptures are God's inspired Word and thus inerrant. History, theology, philosophy, linguistics, and archaeology are all important aids in biblical interpretation. Most important of all, however, is a willingness to benefit from the Church's experience in this area as it has assisted the faithful for two thousand years in coming to an appreciation of the truth of the Bible. The Holy Spirit, who guided the sacred authors in committing the divine message to written form, similarly guides the Church in its interpretation of that revealed Word, which is not always easy to understand but is always true, as God is true.

Knowing the Bible

Q. Why are Catholics ignorant of Scripture?

A. Naturally, to be fair, one would have to modify the question to speak of "some Catholics," for a group indictment would be very wrong and inaccurate.

Many Catholics are ignorant of the Scriptures for the same reason that they are ignorant of a whole variety of faith-related matters: a lack of education. Some of this is through no fault of their own, due to lack of family environment or a lack of Catholic education. Others have a doctorate in physics but a second-grade understanding of their Faith, and so we find a conscious decision to remain ignorant.

Some Catholics know a great deal about the Bible, but they do not have this knowledge arranged in any kind of systematic format. They have obtained this information by osmosis rather than through organized classes. Although they may not be able to cite chapter and verse, as can some non-Catholics (and I stress "some"), they are surely conversant with the characters and themes of both Testaments.

Interestingly enough, recent polls demonstrate that Catholics and Protestants have no appreciable differences among them in being able to name the four evangelists or twelve apostles; all are rather poor. However, the Church since Vatican II has committed itself to "opening wide" the Scriptures to the faithful on the premise that St. Jerome many centuries earlier was correct in asserting that "ignorance of the Scriptures is ignorance of Christ."

The authentic Bible

Q. *Can you suggest an outline for a debate on the authentic Bible?*

A. I suppose you are referring to the differences between the lists of books (called "the canon") accepted by the Catholic Church and the various Protestant communities. If we could modify your question by one word, I would be happy to make an attempt. Let's substitute "discussion" or "dialogue" for "debate"; Christians should not debate each other but should engage one another in conversations which lead to a better grasp of the truth.

This explanation needs to be somewhat historical and technical. Before a word of the Hebrew Scriptures was written, the people of Israel existed for centuries. Gradually, the community came to regard certain writings as reflecting their faith in a unique way, and so they accorded these works a unique status in the life of the people. As the Hebrews migrated to other lands, they took their Scriptures with them. Eventually, they were translated into Greek (the work known as the "Septuagint" because Jewish tradition holds that seventy inspired scholars produced it). The listing of accepted or canonical books was slightly longer in the Septuagint version than in the original Palestinian canon, including the books of Tobit, Judith, Wisdom, Sirach, Baruch, and 1 and 2 Maccabees.

By A.D. 100 the Church was already using the Septuagint version of the Hebrew Scriptures, since it was, by then, operating in non-Jewish environments. As a result, Christianity (in both the East and West) always maintained the longer canon. At the time of the Protestant Reformation, Martin Luther challenged its use and argued for the shorter, Palestinian canon. His position was formulated largely by his desire to evade the doctrine of purgatory and prayers for the dead, clearly taught in the Second Book of Maccabees. Once he had excised those books from the Old Testament, he then questioned the canonicity of several New Testament books: Hebrews, 2 and 3 John, James, Jude, 2 Peter, and Revelation. Again, certain doctrines contained in those books were problematic for Luther.

It should be noted that Eastern Orthodox Christians still accept the same canon as Roman Catholics and, further, that many non-Catholic scholars are now willing to give some acknowledgment to the disputed books, referring to them as "apocryphal" and often reincluding them in their Bibles, usually at the end.

Book of Revelation

Q. What does the Church teach about the Book of Revelation? Does it teach that the Pope is the anti-Christ and that Catholics bear the mark of the beast?

A. The Book of Revelation is the last book of the Bible, perhaps the most discussed, and at the same time the least understood. It belongs to that genre of literature known as apocalyptic because of its concern with visions and dreams. Like the Book of Daniel in the Hebrew Scriptures, it abounds in figurative and symbolic language, which was particularly important to keep its contents from being understood if the work fell into the wrong hands (that is, the authorities of the Roman Empire who were persecuting the Church so fiercely). In other words, it was written in "code," with numbers and animals all assigned a specific meaning.

A favorite section of this biblical book for many anti-Catholics is chapter 17 with its many references to Rome as the whore of Babylon and to the anti-Christ and the beast. Even a superficial reading of these passages would reveal that the Pope and the Church of Rome are hardly intended here, but instead the Roman emperor (perhaps Domitian, who reigned A.D. 81-96), and indeed the entire Roman system which was attempting to destroy the Church at Rome, as it had already killed Rome's first bishop, St. Peter. The irony would be amusing if these Catholic-baiters were not so serious about their alleged scriptural proof for the condemnation of Catholicism. Standard rules of interpretation and an objective view of history, however, will not substantiate their claims.

Babylon

Q. Revelation 18:4 speaks of false religions and the great Babylon. What does the text mean, "Come out of her, my people, that ye be not partakers of her sins, and that ye receive not of her plagues"? Some preachers on television have said this is a warning to the Catholic religion.

A. When the author of Revelation speaks of Babylon, he means pagan Rome, the corrupt and murderous city which ran red with the blood of the martyrs. The language of the entire book is highly symbolic and not to be taken literally. The Book of Revelation stands in the same literary tradition as the Old Testament Book of Daniel and other apocalyptic literature. Since it is not easy to comprehend because of the imagery used, it is good to read at least the introductory material to Revelation as found in the New American Bible or in some other reliable commentary. The notes in the NAB specifically on chapter 18 are likewise valuable.

As far as the assertion of some of our Fundamentalist friends that this passage refers to the Catholic Church, let me simply note that this is the kind of biblical interpretation that occurs when people refuse to study various literary forms and instead insist on bringing their own particular axe to grind to the Sacred Scriptures. Inasmuch as there was only one Church when Revelation was written, doesn't it seem odd to argue that the text was aimed at the only Church in existence? On the other hand, the contention that Babylon symbolizes pagan Rome makes a great deal of sense from every angle — historically, biblically, theologically. Hence, Christians are encouraged to abstain from contact with the institution which is vile and hateful to believers and God alike.

Men over God

Q. My former fiancé left the Church for some pentecostal sect. He now sends me letters about my salvation. His latest is a series of Scripture quotes (e.g., Mt 15:8-9; Jn 4:23-24) which, he says, apply to the Catholic Church since we set the traditions of men over the Word of God. What should I say?

A. The problem of "the traditions of men" being set against "the Word of God" is a false dichotomy created by some Fundamentalists. A brief review of life in the apostolic Church will demonstrate this.

Even after the oral tradition was committed to written form, Scripture was never considered to be the sole source of God's Word and revelation. John's Gospel tells us quite plainly that "Jesus performed many other signs as well — signs not recorded here — in the presence of his disciples" (20:30). The Lord's work and teaching were obviously more extensive than what was recorded in Scripture, for the evangelist also notes with some hyperbole: "There are still many other things that Jesus did, yet if they were written about in detail, I doubt there would be room enough in the entire world to hold the books to record them" (Jn 21:25). The early Church, then, had both an oral and a written record on which to draw, and thus passed on the revelation of God in Christ as Scripture and Tradition.

This assertion is not mere wishful thinking, for it is evident that the early Church accepted various traditions and teachings which were not recorded in writing. In his Second Letter to the Thessalonians, St. Paul exhorts the community there to "hold fast to the traditions you received from us, either by our word or by letter" (2:15). While not enumerating them in his letter, Paul nonetheless advises the Church at Thessalonica to "hold fast to the traditions" it had received from Silvanus, Timothy, and himself.

Behind all the unpleasant rhetoric, the real difficulty is a discomfort with the idea of a visible Church. Christ and His Church are one, as St. Paul noted when he speaks of Christ being the Head and us the members (cf. 1 Cor 12). Furthermore, Jesus shows the identification between Himself and His apostles when He declares that "he who hears you, hears me" (Lk 10:16).

God makes sense

Q. I am forty-three years old and have been Catholic all my life. However, the past two years I have been reading the Bible (for the first time), and wonder why it contradicts so much Catholic doctrine. God's Word makes more sense to me than man's laws.

Q. I am thirty-six, have been a Catholic all my life, have read the Bible all my life and have never found it to contradict Catholic doctrine. Such a contradiction would be impossible because almighty God is the source of all revelation, enlightening with His Holy Spirit both the sacred authors of the Bible and the Church, as Christ promised.

A. Let us recall the order of reality. The Church existed for perhaps as long as twenty years before the first word of the New Testament was ever written and perhaps as long as ninety years before the last word of the New Testament was committed to writing. When the Holy Spirit came on Pentecost, He did not deliver a book; He formed a Church. The Church, in turn, wrote the New Testament. How, then, could the Church's book (namely, the New Testament) contradict the Church's teaching?

The problem surfaces when people lift passages out of context and try to get them to mean what they were never intended to mean. The proper context for a New Testament verse is threefold: the book in which it is located; the total thrust of the New Testament; the Church which gave birth to it. We use this approach in analyzing any literary work, and it is equally necessary in attempting to understand the Word of God which was written in the words of men.

A passage which is apparently difficult to reconcile with Catholic doctrine and life needs to be studied carefully, to be sure. However, when my private judgment calls into question the judgment of the Church, which has been guaranteed the infallible guidance of the Holy Spirit and has lived under that inspiration for two millennia, I need to be cautious. I need to consider whether I am guilty of arrogance or pride, of assuming that my personal grasp of the truth is greater than the collective wisdom of Christ's Church.

Honest and open research into the troublesome passage will reveal one of three conclusions: my understanding of the Scripture was defective; my understanding of the Church's teaching was faulty; the Scripture may not require the doctrine or practice under scrutiny but does not forbid it, either.

The basic difficulty is hit upon when you speak of "God's Word" versus "man's laws," presumably meaning the laws of the Church. Once a believer creates tension between the Church and Christ, he or she is on dangerous ground, because Christ is the head of the Church of which we are the members. Christ has willed to be united to His Church, and so no separation is ever justified. That is, coincidentally, the clear teaching of the Scriptures — especially as we see in St. Paul's theological reflections to the Corinthian Church.

Exposure to Scripture

Q. How are the readings for weekday and Sunday Masses selected? It seems that they are the same year after year. Why not delve more into the entire Bible?

A. In point of fact, the readings are not the same "year after year." The Sundays work on a three-year cycle, while the weekdays operate on a two-year one. Therefore, the Gospel you heard last Sunday will not be read again until that day three years hence:

If a Catholic were to read no Scripture beyond the passages used for Sunday Mass, that person would have been exposed to more than seven thousand verses of the Bible — no mean accomplishment. Bible reading has always formed the first half of the Mass from apostolic times (as the New Testament demonstrates), but the lectionary revised in response to the liturgical renewal of Vatican II opened up even more of the Bible to the Sunday-Mass Catholic. The new lectionary is so extensive in its coverage of nearly the complete New Testament and the most significant portions of the Old Testament over the three-year period that most main-line Protestant denominations have adopted it from us. If a Catholic attends daily Mass, the percentage of Scripture taken in over the two-year span is more than double that of the Sunday figure. Sometimes we just don't appreciate what we have because we are too close to it.

Myths die hard

Q. Why don't Catholics hear about Scripture in the Mass and in their schools?

A. Myths die hard. It seems that once an image is impressed on the minds of some people (regardless of how inaccurate it is), they refuse to be disabused of that opinion. In a sense, they are saying, "Please don't confuse me with the facts."

The Mass is the most biblical prayer imaginable. The entire first half of the Mass is almost nothing but pure, unadulterated Bible-reading and commentary. The second half contains direct quotes from Scripture, as well as biblical allusions. The heart of the Liturgy of the Eucharist is nothing other than a ritual action performed in obedience to the Lord's command on the night before He died — a command clearly documented in the Scriptures.

Catholic education is permeated with the Scriptures, both in direct course work and in an overall meshing of the Word with the study of liturgy, doctrine, and morality, and I would challenge anyone to prove otherwise — so sure and proud am I of this claim.

Reading Scripture

Q. Why weren't Catholics allowed to read the Bible even in the years just prior to Vatican II?

A. They were, and I can speak from personal experience, since I was a schoolboy in those days. As soon as Bibles became more accessible and as literacy rates rose, the Church not only permitted but actually encouraged its sons and daughters to read the Scriptures.

When I was a parochial school student in the 1950s, at least one hour each week was spent on biblical studies. This was in addition to our regular catechism classes, which incorporated scriptural citations to ground Catholic teachings in the Bible. Still more time was spent on studying the Gospel passages used at Sunday Mass. I can distinctly remember receiving the gift of a New Testament for my confirmation at the age of eleven.

All of this autobiographical information is offered to make a point, namely, that the Church's strong endorsement of Scripture reading and study for Catholics did not come out of the blue but was the logical conclusion of a gradual yet determined course of action for which the Church had been preparing believers for decades and even centuries.

Catholics and the Bible

Q. Didn't the Catholic Church for centuries — particularly before the Protestant Reformation — try to keep the Bible from the people?

A. To answer this question calls for a little historical investigation. First of all, Christians did not possess the Bible as we know it until the fourth century. A variety of books claiming apostolic authority were in circulation, and only gradually did the Church come to decide on the precise books which could be accepted as inspired and canonical, in much the same way as did Judaism in the last quarter of the first century of the Christian era.

Second, for the next twelve centuries, even if the Church had given a copy of the Bible to every Catholic, it would have done little good since the vast majority of the world was illiterate.

Third, having personal copies of the Bible only became even a remote possibility with Gutenberg's invention of the printing press in 1456. Interestingly enough, the first book printed by Gutenberg (a Catholic) was the Bible — more than sixty years before Luther's revolt.

Fourth, private ownership of a Bible was still but a "remote possibility" because of the tremendous cost of printing. Some scholars estimate that a Bible would have cost the average person as much as eight thousand dollars.

However, until the advent of the press and of more general literacy, monks preserved the Bible through painstaking hand-copying of the texts. These beautifully illuminated manuscripts (many of which are on display in museums around the world) were then placed in libraries and chained to lecterns — not to keep people from them but to guarantee their availability.

Thread of faith

Q. For whom is the Bible written?

A. The Bible was written by people of faith as a testimony to God's mighty deeds accomplished in Israel and in the person of His Son. Hence, it was intended to arouse others to faith. The Scriptures are also meant to sustain faith in one who already believes. Faith, then, is the thread running throughout.

However, even an agnostic or atheist can benefit from reading the Scriptures as long as he does not consciously block out divine grace or go to the Bible for the wrong reason (e.g., to seek scientific data). The Bible can both console and challenge, and it must be allowed to do both, for "God's word is living and effective, sharper than any two-edged sword" (Heb 4:12).

Increasingly, one finds Protestant scholarship growing more accepting of the Catholic canon of the Bible because it is based on good, reliable, and historical evidence. As a result, many Protestant Bibles now include the so-called "apocryphal books," even if only at the end.

The Church and the Bible

Q. *Why do Catholics place the Church above the Bible?*

A. Catholics do not place the Church above the Bible. As a matter of fact, the Second Vatican Council declared that the Church "venerates" the Scriptures. How does one venerate something beneath oneself?

The Church extends many visible signs of this reverence for the Word of God, especially in the liturgy. The lectionary is carried in solemn procession; the book of the Gospels is flanked with candles, incense, and even kissed. Why is all this done? Because the Church sees in the Scriptures a very special gift of God's revelation to His people. As such, it provides the Church with a clear and definitive norm for it to judge its actions and fidelity.

That having been said, we also know that Catholics do not view the Scriptures as self-explanatory but require the community that formed the Bible to interpret it. After all, we know that were it not for the Church there would be no Bible, for it was the Church that sifted through the many books claiming divine inspiration and came up with the books that now serve as the canon, or definitive list, of works regarded as divinely inspired and worthy of incorporation into what is now considered the Bible.

It is important to recall, however, that this process did not occur overnight. The ancient Hebrews went through this process for their Scriptures, and the Church took nearly four centuries to come up with a standard catalog. This kind of historical background is needed to provide believers with a sense of balance, which avoids the extreme of disregarding the Scriptures as well as the extreme of making extravagant claims for the Scriptures, which even the apostolic Church would reject.

2. DOCTRINE

'Catholic'

Q. When was our Church first called "Catholic"? What about the Orthodox Church?

A. The first record we have of the Church's being called "Catholic" goes back to the martyr-bishop of Antioch, St. Ignatius, who died around A.D. 107. In his Epistle to the Smyrnaeans, he says: "Where the bishop appears, there let the people be, just as where Jesus Christ is, there is the Catholic Church." If it is true that some of the Johannine works of the New Testament were not completed until A.D. 110 or A.D. 120, we can see that even a decade earlier, the Church was called "Catholic."

The Orthodox Church called herself "orthodox" (faithful to true teaching) to distinguish her from Christian groups she considered heterodox or heretical. Among those, the Orthodox Church would traditionally place the Catholic Church!

Organized religion

Q. What kind of an answer is appropriate to give to an Assembly of God member who says "organized religion" is unnecessary and contrary to the Bible?

A. Anti-institutional postures are not new in Christianity. Centuries ago, St. Cyprian reacted to the very same attitude when he wisely noted that "no one can have God for his Father who will not have the Church for his mother."

The Incarnation was a scandal to Jews and Greeks alike; the very thought that God could become man was just a bit much. When Jesus spoke of giving His flesh in the Eucharist, still others found it all too much and so "would not remain in his company any longer" (Jn 6:66).

The Incarnation is continued in the Church, and so it should come as no surprise that people should find this manifestation of God in the flesh just as much a stumbling block. Some people are scandalized by the all-too-human face of the Church; others fear that an embodied presence of Christ in the world might make too many demands on them.

Regardless of the motivation, it is clear that Christianity without the Church is theologically impossible (cf. 1 Cor 12). It is also sociologically impossible, and the best proof of that is that even an anti-institutional Christian such as a member of the Assembly of God is a member of an institution for the simple reason that people need community, a fact acknowledged and accepted by our Lord in declaring His intention to build His Church on the rock of Peter (cf. Mt 16:18).

End of the world

Q. What does the Church teach about the end of the world?

A. The Church teaches what the New Testament teaches on this topic: the day of final judgment is coming (Mt 12:36), although at what moment we do not know (Mk 13:22); Jesus came principally to save and not to condemn, hence there is no reason to fear (Jn 3:17); Christians must prepare for the end by a holy life (Mt 24:42-44), all the while looking toward the final day in joyful hope (1 Jn 2:28; 4:17f).

Some people have made a career out of predicting the precise moment of Christ's return and the exact circumstances surrounding that event. However, the Scriptures are remarkably quiet on those scores. Aside from affirming the above facts, the devout believer simply follows Christ faithfully, unconcerned about the end of time — in the realization that a full Christian life is the best preparation possible for the end, whether that is one's personal end in death or the end of the whole world. Fidelity and confident assurance — not fear or presumption — are the virtues needed to meet Christ when He comes in glory.

Purgatory

Q. I am a convert to Catholicism who has tried to understand the doctrine of purgatory. In my reflection, I often envision purgatory as one painful moment of time when we stand before God and are given the vision of seeing ourselves as God has always seen us. Is this compatible with Catholic teaching on the matter?

A. The Church has no precise explanation of the time, quality, or intensity of the punishments experienced by the souls in purgatory. Once we enter into the realm of eternity, we are operating in God's "time" and not our own; therefore, our own categories and conceptions cease.

Your suggestion seems quite insightful to me and squares perfectly with our notion of purgatory as a place and time of personal purification, for what would better prepare us for the beatific vision than the awareness of the tremendous gap between our sinfulness and the holiness of God? That realization is what can transform a sinner into a saint — the very reason for the existence of purgatory.

More purgatory

Q. I just read an article by Jimmy Swaggart in which he says that purgatory is "that doctrine that gives people a second chance after death." How can he be answered?

A. Swaggart's conception of purgatory does not square with official Catholic teaching. The *New Catholic Encyclopedia* defines purgatory as "the state, place, or condition in the next world, which will continue until the Last Judgment, where the souls of those who die in the state of grace, but not yet free from all imperfection, make expiation for unforgiven venial sins and mortal sins that have already been forgiven and, by doing so, are purified before they enter heaven." Clearly, purgatory is not a "second chance" but a state or place of purification for souls before they enter into the presence of God in heaven. The Church has based this practice, in part, upon references to expiatory sacrifices for the dead found in the Second Book of Maccabees (12:39). This book was deleted from the Old Testament by the Protestant Reformers because it contradicted their position on both purgatory and prayers for the dead.

Beyond the scriptural data, one finds an impressive array of practices which demonstrate how basic and fundamental is a belief in purgatory and prayers for the dead. In the account of the passion of the North African martyrs Perpetua and Felicity in A.D. 203, one reads of how one of the martyrs saw in a dream or vision her dead brother in torment, causing her to pray for his deliverance. The result of her prayer was that she saw him again — cleansed now — and "realized he had been released from his punishment." In A.D. 211, Tertullian advised Christians to pray for their beloved dead on the anniversaries of their passing from this world. St. Augustine, in his famous *Confessions*, records this remark of his dying mother, Monica, in A.D. 387: "All I ask you is this, that wherever you may be you will remember me at the altar of the Lord."

Catacomb inscriptions dating from the very origins of Christianity reveal similar themes; take, for example, in one burial ground, the following: "Sweet Faustina, may you live in God." "Peter and Paul, pray for Victor!" "Peter and Paul, remember Sozomen and whoever reads this."

This evidently indicates that what we are considering is not a medieval belief but something that is at the very heart of Christianity: the need to pray for the dead.

Prayers for the dead, in turn, presuppose that the dead need to be helped and can be helped. Since both heaven and hell are eternal states, the only option is an intermediate state from which release is possible; Catholic theology calls this state "purgatory."

Yet another historical fact is rather convincing. We know that Jesus was a devout Jew who attended the synagogue and went up to the Temple at Jerusalem for all the prescribed feasts. At the time of Christ (and to the present in Orthodox Judaism), prayers for the dead were offered. Three times a year (during the feasts of Booths, Passover, and Weeks) special remembrances for the dead were made. Jews still utter the "Mourner's Kaddish" after the death of a loved one for eleven months — the time Jewish Tradition assigns to the period of purification after death. Since this formed an essential part of Temple worship at the time of our Lord and since we nowhere read of His contradicting this practice, one must assume that Jesus accepted it.

Common sense and human experience demonstrate that most people (even most Christians) are not good enough at death for the experience of eternal bliss, nor bad enough for the fires of hell. Purgatory corresponds to this intuition and confirms our belief in a merciful Father who wants all His children to be saved. Far from causing laxity or presumption, this realization should inspire the mature believer to sentiments of true gratitude and the willingness to lead a yet holier life.

The doctrines of the Communion of Saints and the resurrection of the dead are among the most consoling, for they tell us we are not alone in our struggle here on earth, in our time of purification, or in our hour of glory. These teachings urge us on to a sense of Christian solidarity, as the members of the Church in time and eternity find that they are not separated from one another by the chasm of death, but in truth are united to one another by a bridge of prayers.

Afterlife

Q. *Somewhere in the Old Testament it says that "the dead know nothing." How does that square with our belief in the Communion of Saints?*

A. Many Fundamentalists are very fond of quoting this line from Psalm 6:5 in order to prove wrong the Catholic teaching on prayers to and for the dead. If they are to use this verse properly, what it demonstrates is that the psalmist did not believe in the resurrection of the dead, which was not commonly held in Judaism until only a century or two before our Lord's time. As a matter of fact, even in Jesus' day the doctrine of an afterlife was a sticking point between Pharisees and Sadducees. This is a classic example of what can happen to people who are bent on a literal interpretation of Scripture, especially of isolated texts. Christians always read the Old Testament in the light of the New Testament, and the Church has always interpreted vague or confusing passages in the light of more certain ones. Some people, however, are more intent on proving their debate partner wrong than in discovering the truth; proof-texting is a handy tool to disarm someone, but it does nothing for genuine dialogue or understanding.

Reincarnation

Q. *Please give me the Church's stand on reincarnation, about which we hear so much today. Is there anything to it?*

A. The belief in reincarnation seems to date back to India in the sixth century before Christ. The doctrine holds that all living creatures, gods included, are involved in a continuous process of rebirth; these beings ascend or descend the ladder of life according to the works they perform in a given life experience. Good deeds are rewarded in a new life by the attainment of a higher form of life (from a dog to a man, for instance), while an evil way of life is punished by movement down the ladder of perfection. This cycle is endless, and the only thing one could ever be sure of in this understanding of existence is constant insecurity and frustration.

The Incarnation of the Son of God, on the other hand, puts an end to the cyclical view of reality and history. In and through Christ, all existence is headed toward finality and completion at the end of time. All the Christian mysteries (from Jesus' conception and birth to His death and resurrection) are grounded in history and are unrepeatable events; when God acts, He acts with decisiveness and absoluteness — no need to try again. Because humanity participates in divinity through creation and, most especially, through the redemptive sacrifice of Jesus Christ, our lives are likewise unrepeatable events, laden with significance and dignity.

Aside from Jesus' own resurrection, we know that Mary shares in that glory, body and soul, through the privilege of her Assumption. As the first member of redeemed humanity, she stands forth as the pledge and promise of our own final resting in the Lord for all eternity, with no endless round of comings and goings as plants, animals, or anything else.

As God sees

Q. How can a soul in heaven be happy if a loved one is in hell?

A. Mortal sin consists in being possessed by something other than the one true God; that can be either a person or a thing — idolatry, in other words. The state of holiness in this life and heaven in the next is being possessed by and possessing Love itself. To the extent that one chooses things or persons over God, one is not holy and thus not ready to behold the face of God. When one is in the presence of Eternal Love, nothing and no one else will matter. As St. Paul puts it, "God will be all in all."

Humanly speaking, that may sound harsh or unfeeling, but it is important to recall that holiness is not the experience to which we humans are accustomed; our judgments are tainted by sin, and hence we judge by human (and, therefore, sinful) standards. What seems hard to imagine now will make infinitely good sense when our judgment is rectified in the Beatific Vision because in that moment we will finally see things as God sees them.

What I am saying, then, is that if we look at your question simply from a human standpoint, one can see your concern. What is necessary to bear in mind, however, is that in the glory of heaven, we will view reality from the perspective of God Himself, and we shall experience no sorrow, but rather understand this situation in the light of the holiness, the truth, and the justice of God.

Good works

Q. Last Sunday, while visiting a church on vacation, I heard a priest say during the sermon, I think, that salvation may be gained through good works. Is this what the Church teaches?

A. I hope you misunderstood the priest. The Church teaches that one is saved by God's free gift or offer of salvation received in faith. Nothing else can ever be added to Christ's saving death.

What, then, is the place of good works?

Having become a Christian, the believer must live like one, and that is where good works find their place. It has been said that one is not reborn *by* good works but *to* good works, and that is very true. Because one has received the gift of new life in Christ, he must give evidence of a lively faith by a godly life, especially by attending to the needs of the poor and the oppressed (cf. Mt 25:31-46). This style of life is not an attempt to curry favor with God, but is a response of love and a powerful witness to the grace of election. For a devout Christian, there can never be any position between faith and works, for the first necessarily leads to the second. The Epistle of James has given classical expression to this insight: "What good is it to profess faith without practicing it? Such faith has no power to save one, has it? . . . faith without works is as dead as a body without breath" (2:14, 26).

Despising oneself

Q. *I have been troubled by certain passages in Thomas à Kempis's* Imitation of Christ *in which he says we are to despise ourselves. Doesn't this conflict with Christ's words that we should love our neighbor as ourselves?*

A. In high-school literature courses we learned to interpret passages by seeking to understand the author and the culture in which he lived; that same principle works for biblical and theological works as well. The first point to stress in regard to Thomas à Kempis is that, while he may have been a holy man, he has never been canonized and never had an official teaching function in the Church. Therefore, his judgments on the living of the Christian life are as valid as his arguments are convincing.

Thomas à Kempis belonged to a school of thought which tended to depreciate certain aspects of life, especially the physical, for fear that human beings would lose control of themselves. We do not condemn him for this since it would be grossly unfair to evaluate him by twentieth-century standards of theology, sociology, and psychology. However, his limitations must be acknowledged, as must ours.

What does Thomas à Kempis mean by "despising" oneself? Does he mean it in the biblical sense? For instance, in several spots in the Gospels, believers are urged to "hate" themselves and their parents, so as to be better able to love God. Such expressions are hyperbolic in the Scriptures and were normal ways of speaking in the Hebrew or Aramaic of our Lord's day. It merely indicated the necessity of putting everyone and everything else in second place to God. If that is what Thomas à Kempis had in mind, fine; if not, I agree with you that it flies in the face of the Gospel injunction to love oneself. When spiritual writers conflict with Scripture, their opinion must cede to the Word of God.

Death before baptism

Q. My neighbors' baby died without baptism, and they are terribly upset. Is there anything I can say to help them?

A. This question comes up frequently in parish situations. The simplest answer might be that the desire of the parents that this infant become a child of God is a type of baptism in itself.

Furthermore, it is important to note that we (or even the Church) cannot limit God's love, mercy, and compassion to human (and even ecclesiastical) formulations, for God's ways are not our ways (Is 55:8).

St. Thomas Aquinas felt compelled to remind his readers that *Deus non alligatur sacramentis* ("God is not bound to the sacraments"). That is, although the sacraments are surely the ordinary means of grace, they are not the only means by which God can effect our salvation. And so, we commend such a child to God's fatherly care.

The power to forgive

Q. Born-again Christians often ask me why Catholics must confess their sins to a priest instead of directly to the Lord. How should I answer them?

A. It has become popular in some circles to speak about whether or not a person is "saved." In truth, however, salvation is an ongoing process in a person's life in which he or she attempts to grow ever closer to God. It is with the goals of growth and reconciliation in mind that the Church provides the Sacrament of Penance for its members. As defined by the Council of Trent, the Sacrament of Penance was instituted by Christ for the purpose of reconciling the faithful to God as often as they fall into sin after baptism.

According to the Church, there are three distinct facets of the sacrament. First and foremost is the need for contrition on the part of the sinner; that is, that the sinner feel sorrow for having sinned. Forgiveness is contingent upon a desire to be forgiven and a resolve to avoid that sin in the future. This sacrament is an encounter between the sinful self and the forgiving Christ. Nothing less than a true desire to turn from sin, to change one's life, to go through a conversion experience is required.

Secondly, the sinner must confess his sins and admit to having fallen in the eyes of God. We are told in the Epistle of James to "declare [our] sins to one another" (5:16), In admitting that we have sinned, we also acknowledge our need for the healing power of Jesus Christ in our lives.

The final component of the Sacrament of Penance is satisfaction. In addition to seeking the removal of the guilt of sin, the penitent should attempt to make some type of reparation for the wrongs committed.

The Sacrament of Penance, while criticized by many outside the Church as unbiblical, has definite scriptural foundations. At root, it is grounded in Christ's power to forgive sins. The Church maintains, on the basis of scriptural and historical data, that Christ passed on His authority to forgive sins to His disciples, for it is obvious from the Gospels that Jesus did indeed confer power and authority upon His apostles. Luke states that "Jesus now called the twelve together and gave them power and authority to overcome all demons and to cure diseases" (9:1). Priests do not claim to forgive sins on their own authority; they act as representatives of Christ and forgive sins in His name, just as the apostles were given the authority to overcome demons in His name.

In like manner, Jesus granted His apostles the power to forgive sins. Thus do we read: "I assure you, whatever you declare bound on earth shall be bound in heaven, and whatever you declare loosed on earth shall be loosed in heaven" (Mt 18:18). In rabbinic terms, this constitutes the authority to declare what is allowed or forbidden under the law. In John's Gospel we find an even more specific delegation of the Risen Christ to His apostles: "As the Father has sent me, so I send you" (20:21). The immediate follow-up then comes: "If you forgive men's sins, they are forgiven them; if you hold them bound, they are held bound" (20:23).

It is in fidelity to the Lord, then, that the priests of Christ's Church call all members of the Body of Christ to repentance, reconciliation, and a more perfect union with the Savior.

Mass and absolution

Q. I always get conflicting answers to this question: Does the Penitential Rite of the Mass absolve from sin? Must the absolution formula be used?

A. Yes, the Penitential Rite absolves from venial sin, but not mortal sin. And yes, the prayer of absolution must be recited in every Mass.

A great deal of confusion seems to exist on this score, but it is really quite simple. Mortal sin requires sacramental confession and absolution, while less serious sins do not.

'Born-again' people

Q. What did Jesus mean when He said everyone must be "born again"? Can "born-again" people sin and lose out on heaven?

A. John 3:3 is the verse in question. Jesus was indicating that due to our fallen nature, it is necessary to be "born again" of water and the Holy Spirit — a reference to baptism which incorporates a believer into Christ and His Church (cf. Rom 5 and 6; 1 Cor 12).

While baptism removes original sin, it does not remove the human inclination to sin. So, the logical question: "How do I know I am saved?" No absolute assurance is available; one must have recourse to the virtue of hope, which is a firm trust in God's goodness and mercy. Some

Fundamentalists hold that someone who is saved "knows" for sure, but St. Paul had some different ideas on the subject. He said the Philippians needed to "work with anxious concern to achieve [their] salvation" (2:12). Paul likewise warned against presumption in this matter: "Let anyone who thinks he is standing upright watch out lest he falls" (1 Cor 10:12). Certainly this was also the mind of Christ, who counseled constant vigilance as the best preparation for His coming (e.g., Mt 25).

Grace of conversion

Q. Billy Graham has preached the Word of God for many years and has brought many people to God. Why is he not given the necessary graces to become a Catholic?

A. The British journalist Malcolm Muggeridge went to Calcutta as a dispassionate person to do a job: to interview the phenomenon known as Mother Teresa. As he came to know this remarkable woman, he realized he had to discover what made her "tick" spiritually. Little by little, he came to ever deeper appreciations of the Catholic Faith. Eventually, Muggeridge wrote glowingly not only of Mother Teresa but of the Church which provided her with the impetus and support to "do something beautiful for God."

Asked by another reporter one day why, with his positive attitude toward Catholicism, Muggeridge had not himself become a Catholic, the wise old man responded: "No grace!" Some years later, Muggeridge did come into the Church. On that occasion, someone inquired: "Why did you finally become a Catholic?" His answer: "Grace."

The most critical things in life — beginning with life itself — are graces, or God's free gifts. Faith is the greatest grace and, therefore, the greatest mystery. St. Paul was the first Christian theologian to try to come to an understanding of the grace of election: Why had so many of the Chosen People rejected Jesus and so many pagans accepted Him? It is worthwhile to read his Epistle to the Romans on that score, particularly chapters 9-11.

Perhaps the more basic question is not why Billy Graham has apparently not received the grace to be visibly united with Christ's Church, but why you and I were — and, more important, what we are doing with that grace.

Jewish Jesus

Q. Christ was a Jew. What happened to cause the break from Judaism? How do we know that Catholicism is right, after all?

A. Yes, Jesus did have a Jewish mother and was thus legally a Jew. However, one must never forget that He was the divine Son of God. Therefore, the positions taken by Jesus during His earthly life cannot be dismissed as simply coming from just any first-century Palestinian Jew.

We learn in Matthew's Gospel that Jesus came not to abolish the law but to fulfill it (cf. Mt 5:17). We also know that in spite of the many disagreements Jesus had with the Pharisees, He agreed with them doctrinally (e.g., on the resurrection of the dead and the existence of angels). The critical issue was His claim to be God's Son. Remember: the ultimate charge brought against our Lord was that of blasphemy. The final break between Judaism and Christianity apparently took place at the Jewish Council of Jamnia in the last third of the first century when the followers of Jesus were excommunicated from the synagogue.

Many people then and since could accept Jesus' social teachings, but the question of His divinity still divides Christians from any other people who would regard Jesus as someone other than the Second Person of the Blessed Trinity. Our faith and certitude, then, rest on the sure foundation of the God who "can neither deceive nor be deceived," as we pray in the Act of Faith.

The Chosen People

Q. It really bothers me that the Jewish people have rejected our Lord as the true Savior. Why have they not been blessed with the gift of faith as they are God's Chosen People? Is this why Israel has so many problems?

A. This work of evangelization must be done with sincerity and love and never in a manner which is obnoxious and offensive. Any Christian intending to embark on a conscious plan to share the Gospel message with Jews needs to have a clear understanding of Paul's insights in chapters 9-11 of his Epistle to the Romans, wherein he describes — in an extremely nuanced way — the current status of Jews who do not accept Jesus as Lord. It is humbling to read that, in Paul's view of the situation, their present rejection of Jesus is a divine grace for Gentiles.

Whatever the relationship of Jews to Almighty God, however, it is clear that they are beloved of God as His special portion. Therefore, it is improper to hold that any of their historical difficulties are a punishment for non-belief.

The best and most effective invitation to Christian Faith is offered by the witness of committed Christians, who act as though they truly possess "good news," in which is found eternal life.

Jews and salvation

Q. In Romans 9:10-11, St. Paul seems to say that eventually all Jews will be saved. Can anyone be "grafted back" into Jesus after his time of testing on earth? Will all human beings, then, eventually be saved and allowed to enter the Kingdom of God?

A. Romans 9 is a very carefully woven argument, which needs careful examination. I do not think that Paul suggests that Jews will be "grafted back" into Christ after their lives are finished; after all, what we do or do not do in life has eternal consequences. Rather, when Paul speaks about the Jews' being reintegrated into Jesus, it seems that he is talking about the Chosen People as a whole; in other words, that at some future moment, the whole Jewish race will be given the grace to recognize Jesus as their long-awaited Lord and Messiah. This is a very important concept to understand because it involves the nature of God's making of covenants with man. Having entered into such an agreement with Israel, He will not (and cannot) back out of it, precisely because His nature as God requires Him to be Fidelity personified.

The question of the salvation of the Jews is unique because it is the only race of people to whom God ever pledged Himself in this unique manner. I fear that I cannot do justice to the issue in so short an answer as this column demands; therefore, the solution may be to commission an article on this topic in the near future. Several Jewish converts deal with this matter, including Edith Stein (recently beatified by Pope John Paul II), Cardinal Jean-Marie Lustiger of Paris, and Msgr. John Oesterreicher of Seton Hall University.

How God handles the Jews in this regard does not automatically indicate how others who fail to accept the lordship of Jesus Christ will be dealt with. Besides, if Jews as a race are saved, it will be in virtue of Jesus Christ's merits and their participation in them because that is the only way for anyone to be saved. How God works that out is His business, best left to His wisdom and providence. In the first and final analysis, salvation is a free gift of God to Jew and Gentile alike.

Original sin

Q. The nun who is responsible for the religious education program in this diocese recently ran a series of classes, the last one being on infant baptism. She told us that original sin is an invention of St. Augustine and that in the early Church children were baptized only as a consequence of a "dominant male" decision to have his whole household baptized. She urged us to wait until a child is old enough to make a conscious decision and then receive the sacraments of initiation as an adult. What does Rome teach on these topics?

A. The person in question should study a bit more theology before declaring St. Augustine as the "father of original sin." As a matter of fact, St. Paul discusses it at great length, especially in his Epistle to the Romans (cf. chapter 5) and in such a famous line as: "For just as in Adam all die, so too in Christ shall all be brought to life. . ." (1 Cor 15:22).

As regards the second reference, I suppose she means the baptism of Cornelius and his household, as recorded in Acts 10. Apparently your teacher has no inhibitions about projecting a personal agenda onto scriptural texts; in biblical scholarship this is generally termed "eisegesis" (which forces an interpretation onto a passage), in distinction to "exegesis" (which draws out a meaning which is there).

The question of infant baptism is an issue only for those who fail to understand either God's omnipotent reign over human hearts, His power and will to save all, and parental love which desires the very best for the children received from the Lord. This last point might be underscored a bit here: If parents truly love their children, they do not leave them to make critical decisions on their own but make them for their children for many years and only gradually give them a freedom which corresponds to their knowledge and maturity. No decent parent allows a child to determine whether or not he will go to school, or how often he will or will not eat. Surely, decisions of faith cannot be made in a vacuum either.

The Evil One

***Q.** Our priest recently said that there is no such thing as a devil or Satan, that these are simply metaphors used in Scripture to describe a presence of evil in the world. Is he right?*

A. When I was in grammar school, the sisters used to tell us that the Devil is never more powerful than when he is ignored or denied. And that is surely the case today. The Scriptures are shot through with mentions of the Devil, Satan, the Evil One; hardly a page of the New Testament can be found without references to a real, personal Devil. The existence of such an individual is official Catholic doctrine, and both Popes Paul VI and John Paul II have restated this on several occasions, reminding people of the Devil's reality, identity, and power. Or, as we used to say in the Leonine prayers after Low Mass, the Devil "goes about the world like a roaring lion, seeking the ruin of souls." Forewarned is forearmed. At the same time, Christians should not be unduly frightened by the Evil One, because "the one who is in you [Christ] is greater than the one who is in the world [the Devil]" (1 Jn 4:4).

Willing women

***Q.** With the severe shortage of priests around the world, why does the Church stubbornly refuse to ordain all the willing women?*

A. First of all, the so-called vocations crisis is not worldwide, but limited to Western Europe and North America — places sorely demoralized by materialism and secularization.

Second, the Church's refusal to ordain women is not a matter of obstinacy but necessity — if she is to be faithful to what she has received. What do I mean?

A detailed explanation of the "male-only priesthood" does not exist, and with good reason: it has never before been a point of contention. The Church rarely works out a full-blown theology until it is called for by the circumstances of the times. Thus the Church always believed in and taught the doctrine of the two natures of Christ; however, until the doctrine was attacked, definitive formulations were not brought forth. The clear statement of the hypostatic union was achieved at the Council of Chalcedon as a response to the Monophysite heresy.

In the current debate, we should realize that the burden of proof rests on those seeking to change Tradition. This is standard debate procedure, and one not adhered to by many of the partisans of women's ordination. The best argument against the ordination of women is really the simplest, but also the most easily caricatured: *it has never been done*. No other change resulting from the Second Vatican Council so clearly flies in the face of Tradition; a vernacular liturgy, permanent deacons, and even married priests all find precedent in Tradition.

The Holy Father has consistently said that the Church cannot ordain women; not that she also does not want to do it, just that she does not have the power to do so. The reason is that Jesus Christ, Lord of the Church, chose only men. "But Christ was limited by His own culture which had a low opinion of women," comes the retort. That might be true, at least in the sense that our Lord had to preach the Gospel to a people who were limited by their own cultural conditioning. However, Jesus never hesitated to break with other cultural patterns of His day (e.g., dining with sinners). How do we explain this apparent inconsistency, except to say that the all-male apostolic ministry is an expression of divine will?

Second, it's important to recognize that in the Christian Faith sexuality is not a matter of indifference, for Christianity is an incarnational religion which takes the flesh seriously. In the early Church the Gnostic sects tried to say that sexual differences did not matter; the reader will recall that the Gnostics had problems accepting the humanity of Christ. The Church responded by asserting the symbolic value of the flesh, as well as its real meaning as part of God's Creation. In the Christian scheme of things, neither sex is better than the other, just different.

Third, the reasons for a male priesthood are enhanced by Byzantine theology. When God chose to reveal Himself, He did so through the taking on of human flesh by the Second Person of the Blessed Trinity as God's Son. Anyone called to the priesthood since is called as a member of the one and unique priesthood of Jesus Christ. Just as Jesus was the icon (image) of the Father, so is the priest to be an icon of Jesus. This is also tied in with the so-called "scandal of particularity" which reminds us that God's ways are not our ways. For example, why did God call the Jews and not the Romans or the Greeks, who were certainly better educated and far more cultured? We do not know; nor do we know why men are chosen as instruments of sacramental grace, especially since the qualities they are expected to show forth in their lives are often looked upon as "feminine" virtues (like patience, humility, kindness). Perhaps the paradox itself contains the answer: God chooses whomever He wills to confound our human expectation and to show what an incredible new order of reality is being established. We must be comfortable in living with mystery.

Fourth, we are not dealing with a question of rights here, for no one (male or female) has a "right" to ordination. If persons had such a right, the

Church would not be able to set any prerequisites for holy rrders in regard to health or intelligence or moral living; all that would be necessary would be the assertion of a self-perceived inner call by the individual. No, a call to priesthood is one that comes from the Church and not from the individual. The biggest problem of all, however, is the strange idea that somehow sacramental ordination increases one's holiness or chances at salvation. Neither logic nor experience bears this out. Far from a question of rights, then, it is really a question of a diversity of roles and ministries in the Church — all of which are needed for the building up of the Body of Christ. In the natural order a man should not feel inferior to a woman simply because he is incapable of bearing children; his role is different and so it is in the Church.

Finally, we must remember that the role of a priest in the liturgy is to stand in the person of Christ (the icon of the Father), not as part of the people but as their head. In the liturgy we witness a union between the bride (the Church) and the groom (Christ). That spousal union is made visible and sacramental through a male priesthood — and only through a male priesthood.

Homosexuality

Q. If a homosexual is ordained a priest, is his ordination valid?

A. First of all, I think it important to refer to such a person as a man "with a homosexual orientation," rather than as a homosexual. Why? Because to use the latter expression suggests that his whole identity is summed up by his sexual "preference," and that would be very sad for anyone, homosexual or heterosexual. While sexuality is certainly an important part of one's identity, it should never be more than one part of the total personality; otherwise, one is being mastered by his or her sexual orientation and has thus obviously failed to integrate that aspect of oneself into one's complete personhood.

That distinction having been made, we can then move on to the question at hand. Men presenting themselves for the priesthood in the Roman Rite are expected to live a celibate (that is, unmarried) life, which necessarily implies a willingness to live without the genital expression of love. This expectation applies to anyone, regardless of sexual orientation, which has no effect on the validity of a man's ordination.

Are there priests, then, with a homosexual orientation? Just as certainly as there are those with a heterosexual orientation. Studies have shown, by the way, that such individuals in the Catholic Church are represented in about the same proportion as they are in Protestant denominations which have a married clergy.

The bottom line in all this, then, is that a priest of the Roman Rite is called upon to identify with the sufferings of Christ in many ways, including the voluntary and loving sacrifice of sexual activity, for the sake of the Kingdom. That task falls equally on a man with either a heterosexual or homosexual orientation.

Anglican priesthood

Q. Is the Anglican priesthood valid? Are their bishops in unbroken succession?

A. This question is very complicated, with no simple answer possible.

When King Henry VIII split from the Church of Rome, the Church of England had as bishops men who were all validly ordained and consecrated. Hence, they could validly pass on their orders to others — even if illicitly and in schism. In the time of Henry's son, Edward VI, the rite of ordination was changed, leaving out references to the power of offering sacrifice and thus raising questions about whether or not the Anglican Church still believed in a sacrificing priesthood and the eucharistic sacrifice of the Mass itself. Of course, if they did not, such ordinations were invalid. Reviewing the historical evidence available to him in the nineteenth century, Pope Leo XIII declared Anglican orders to be null and void because of the defect of intention noted above.

In the United States, however, the problem is even more confusing. After the American Revolution, the Anglicans in this new nation had to obtain orders from a source other than the mother country; many sought and received ordination from Eastern Orthodox bishops, who do have valid orders. This involvement with the Orthodox also occurred as a result of the Oxford Movement, when Anglicans became very conscious of their Catholic roots and very sensitive to the charge of an invalid priesthood. If an Anglican clergyman believes what the Church believes about the Eucharist and the priesthood and was ordained by a validly ordained bishop, he too is validly ordained. As is obvious, this is far more subjective than usual for questions of sacramental validity. However, this is the very procedure being used by the Holy See for the many Anglican clergy coming into full communion with us and also desirous of exercising a priestly ministry in the Church.

This topic of apostolic succession among the Anglicans is also a regular agenda item in the Anglican-Roman Catholic dialogue at both the national and international levels.

Saints

Q. Why is it that saints always come from a Catholic background? Are there no saints who hailed from other Christian sects?

A. The Church can only canonize individuals who have lived in full communion with her. Objectively speaking, other Christians are living in either schism or heresy; subjectively, of course, we cannot judge the spiritual state of others. Surely, however, the Church would never hold up for public emulation one who did not share in the visible unity of the Church.

Intercessory prayer

Q. Why do Catholics pray to the saints when Jesus is the sole mediator between God and Man?

A. Catholics agree that Jesus is the sole mediator between God and man, but that in no way makes prayer to the saints useless or wrong.

Many times one finds the New Testament recommending intercessory prayer (cf. Col 1:9; 2 Thes 1:11; 2 Thes 3:1; Jas 5:16), and very few Christians seem to have a problem with seeking the prayers of a fellow believer. A difficulty appears to emerge only when that believer has left this earth. But what difference should that make to one who affirms the resurrection of the dead? After all, we read that all are alive in Christ (cf. 1 Cor 15:22).

To recap, then, Jesus Christ is the sole mediator between God and man. No other person in heaven or on earth can take His place. The role of Mary or any other saint is to lead the believer to Christ. This subordinate form of mediation derives its meaning and efficacy from the Lord Himself and is not something the saints possess on their own.

Intercessory prayer is a powerful expression of the beautiful doctrine of the Communion of Saints whereby the saints in heaven, the souls in purgatory, and the faithful on earth are involved and concerned with one another's eternal salvation. Intercessory prayer declares our love for one another in the Church, as well as our faith that the bonds to Christ and His Church forged in baptism cannot be dissolved by death.

Sole mediator

Q. How can I convince my Fundamentalist friends that Catholics do worship Jesus? They are turned off by our saints and statues, which they think we idolize.

A. As pointed out above, the teaching of the Church is clear: Jesus Christ is the sole mediator between God and man. No other person in heaven or on earth can take His place. The role of Mary or any other saint is to lead the believer to Christ. This subordinate form of mediation derives its meaning and effectiveness from the Lord Himself and is not something the saints possess on their own. Therefore, it is important to distinguish between the adoration owed to the Persons of the Blessed Trinity and the veneration given to the saints.

Similarly, Catholics use medals and statues, but not as talismans or as objects of worship in violation of the First Commandment. Rather, these things are intended to be reminders or aids to devotion which focus one's attention on prayer and the practice of virtue. It would be a rare husband who did not carry in his wallet a photo of his wife and children, not because he worships the photo or his family, but because he loves his family and wishes to have a visual representation of them on his person. Nor have I ever heard a Fundamentalist take offense at the presence of statues of our country's heroes at national monuments. If the heroes of the nation can be so honored, why not the heroes of the Church? Catholics use sacred art in just this way, never fashioning "idols" for false worship.

Prayer to Mary (or to any of the other saints) is not an end in itself but is intended to be a means by which one is led to a deeper union with her Son. Classical spirituality even had a Latin maxim to illustrate the point: *Ad Jesum per Mariam* ("To Jesus through Mary"). True devotion to Mary never obscures the uniqueness of Christ because Catholics know that the only command of Mary recorded in the Scriptures is one that must be scrupulously obeyed: "Do whatever he [Jesus] tells you" (Jn 2:5).

In the final analysis, devotion to the saints can best be appreciated when one sees the saints in glory as the friends of God and fellow members of the household of faith. If our Fundamentalist friends are to understand this aspect of Catholic spirituality, that is probably the grounds which will make the most sense to them.

Assumption of Mary

Q. How can a teaching like the Assumption of Mary be required for belief when it is nowhere mentioned in Scripture?

A. Simply because a teaching is not explicitly taught in the Bible does not mean it is untrue or that it is not there implicitly — waiting to be uncovered by the Church's reflection on God's Word. It is necessary to recall also that the Church does not feel bound to the dictum of "*sola Scriptura*" (Scripture alone) because we believe that God has revealed Himself to us through both Scripture and Tradition. Some examples might be helpful.

Nowhere in the New Testament can one find the word "Trinity," yet no one espousing a Bible-based form of Christianity would hesitate to speak of the Godhead as a Trinity of persons. Why? Because the doctrine of the Trinity is implicitly taught in a variety of passages, even if not explicitly so.

What has often happened is that some non-Catholic Christians have had problems with various tenets of the Catholic Faith and then concluded to the nonexistence of scriptural support. At the same time, the Church has always believed that the silence of Scripture on certain matters opens the door to freedom.

This is certainly so in regard to the Marian doctrines of the Immaculate Conception and the Assumption of Mary. Taught in seminal form in the New Testament (cf. Lk 1 and Rv 12), constantly believed by the Church from earliest times, and nowhere denied in Scripture, the Church's meditation on these mysteries led to clearly defined dogmas.

It should also be noted that dogmatic definition is not an everyday occurrence in the Church, contrary to the opinion held by many outside the Church.

Perpetual virginity

Q. Why does the Catholic Church teach that Mary was a virgin all her life? After all, Matthew 13:55-56 speaks of the Lord's "brothers and sisters." As a high-school teacher, I would be interested in how the virgin-birth tradition began.

A. No Christian who takes the Scriptures seriously can doubt Mary's virginity up to the birth of Jesus since the Gospels are so clear on this point (cf. Mt 1:18; Lk 1:34). However, the Church teaches that Mary was a virgin not only when she conceived the Lord in her womb but for the remainder of her life.

Fundamentalists often contest this point, however, claiming a variety of biblical passages for support, including the one you cite. Another favorite is Matthew 1:24-25, which states that Joseph did not know Mary until she bore Jesus, coming to the conclusion that he did "know" her afterwards. Webster's Dictionary defines "until" as "up to the time that," which is the understanding opponents of Mary's perpetual virginity would need to have, but Webster indicates "until" can also mean "when or before." Thus, "until" implies no subsequent action in either standard English or biblical usage.

Regarding the so-called "brothers and sisters," it is crucial to realize that a deficiency in Hebrew and Aramaic makes it difficult to discern whether the expression carries the connotation of blood brothers and sisters, cousins, or some other relations between the two. One cannot prove that Mary had other children from the Gospel accounts for this reason.

However, why does the Church make such an issue over Mary's perpetual virginity? First of all, because it is a matter of preserving the truth. The Church has always taught that Mary was a perpetual virgin. This information can be gleaned from many sources, but especially from the earliest liturgical prayers in which reference is made to "the Virgin."

If Mary had not remained a virgin until death, why speak of her after the birth of Christ as such? If one has an uncle who is a bachelor, he is rightly referred to as one's "bachelor uncle." If he marries and thus ceases to be a bachelor, calling him a "bachelor uncle" would be senseless. In the same way, the early Church spoke of Mary as "the Virgin" precisely because of the belief that she lived and died a virgin. When this teaching was questioned in later centuries, we find the addition of the adverb "ever." Thus do the Creed of Epiphanius (circa A.D. 374), the Second Council of Constantinople (A.D. 553), and the Lateran Council (A.D. 649) all speak of the "ever-Virgin Mary." St. Augustine, St. Jerome, and St. Cyril of Alexandria followed the same usage, as did the Protestant reformers Luther, Calvin, and Zwingli.

The doctrine of Mary's perpetual virginity is not a statement that sex is bad, but it is an important statement regarding Mary's single-heartedness and the uniqueness of her vocation. She was called to be the mother of the Messiah; no other work could surpass it, and hence it was fitting that no other fruit should come forth from the womb which had carried the Redeemer of humanity. With no proof for other children born to Mary, and the weight of twenty centuries of tradition to the contrary, the burden rests on those who would deny Mary's perpetual virginity.

Veneration of Mary

Q. I don't believe in the worship of Mary or that she appeared at Fátima. Does that mean that I am excommunicated?

A. No Catholic can "believe in the worship of Mary"; we worship God alone! Veneration of Mary and the other saints and prayer to them are another matter; while no Catholic is forced to pray to saints, he or she cannot deny the doctrine that the saints can be approached in prayer and with efficacy — that is defined dogma, and failure to accept that teaching is tantamount to maintaining a heretical position.

Accepting or rejecting apparitions is a purely personal decision, and the Church never does any more than say that a particular apparition is "worthy of belief" but never that anyone must hold to such an event.

God's mother?

Q. Why and how can the Church teach that Mary is the mother of God? To be the mother of God, she would have to be before God and thus the Creator of all things. The Bible and the Church, however, teach that God is the Creator of all.

A. When the Blessed Virgin Mary is referred to as the "mother of God," the primary focus is on Jesus, not on her. The fifth-century Council of Ephesus insisted on according Mary the title of "Theotokos" (God-bearer), rather than "Christotokos" (Christ-bearer) to emphasize Jesus' divinity.

In other words, early heretics had argued that Jesus was not coeternal with the Father, and they attempted to demonstrate this by pointing to Jesus' origin in time from a human mother. The Church responded by distinguishing the Son's existence as the Second Person of the Blessed Trinity from all eternity and His assumption of a human nature from Our Lady in the Incarnation. To stress the continuity between the Lord's divine preexistence and His existence in time, and His uninterrupted state of divinity (not lost in the Incarnation), the council saw the appropriateness of regarding Mary as the Mother of God, that is, the Mother of the Second Person of the Blessed Trinity in His earthly life.

"Mother of God," then, is Christological and not Mariological in its emphasis.

Intercommunion

Q. Since the Pope and the head of the Anglican Church have celebrated Communion together, why can't Catholics and Episcopalians in this country do the same?

A. To set the record straight, the Pope and the archbishop of Canterbury never received Holy Communion from each other or with each other. When the Pope visited England, he went to Canterbury and there met with the archbishop. At the Cathedral of Canterbury, they joined in an ecumenical prayer service for unity, but that was not the Eucharist.

On many occasions, non-Catholic Christian leaders have expressed their desire for intercommunion with the Catholic Church, but each time Pope John Paul has given the answer of the Second Vatican Council: such intercommunion is not possible until the basic problems of faith are handled. In other words, the Eucharist can only be shared among those who share a common faith. Unfortunately, that is not yet the case between ourselves and the Church of England.

Intercommunion again

Q. There is one Catholic stance which has bothered me for years: We acknowledge the Real Presence of Christ in the Eucharist of the Episcopalians, but we do not permit intercommunion with them. Does this make any sense?

A. First, a correction: We do not formally acknowledge the validity of the Eucharist of Episcopalians. When Pope Leo XIII declared Anglican orders null and void, that eliminated any possibility of a valid Eucharist for them. However, some historians have suggested that Anglican orders in the United States might be valid because of Eastern Orthodox bishops being used as co-consecrators here for many decades. Be that as it may, valid orders and a valid Eucharist do not automatically bring about intercommunion.

Eastern Orthodox and Roman Catholics recognize the validity of each other's orders and, in fact, all the sacraments. However, we do not have intercommunion. Reception of Holy Communion from one another implies ecclesial communion which, regrettably, does not yet exist. Until such time as that visible unity does take place, no intercommunion is possible. Surely this should be a daily intention of ours in our celebration of the Eucharist.

Are religions equal?

Q. Recently a visiting priest said that all religions are equal in God's sight, and that all people who live good moral lives have the same chance at salvation. Is this possible?

A. I hope he did not say that, particularly if he happened to be a missionary. Surely all religions have elements of truth within them, and to the extent that they can lead human beings to God, we rejoice. However, the Second

Vatican Council (especially in its Decree on Missionary Activity and Decree on Ecumenism) and Pope Paul VI in his apostolic exhortation *Evangelii Nuntiandi* were most careful to observe that while all religions must be respected, not all are equal. Indeed, Christians have a serious obligation to share the truth of the Catholic Faith, which alone represents the full message of God to man.

Jesus was embarrassingly clear on this point. He said, "I am the way and the truth and the life" (Jn 14:6). Note, He did not say, "I am A way, A form of truth, A way of life." No, He was absolute, and this was what caused both Jews and Gentiles to bristle. Jews had no difficulty in viewing Jesus as one teacher among many; most of them could not accept Him as the definitive voice of God. Romans, who had hundreds of gods, were not bothered by the early believers' assertions that Jesus was a god; after all, what was one more? What upset the Romans was the claim that taking Jesus for God required one to abandon all others. Every time I write along these lines, I get letters from irate readers who call this approach to the Catholic Faith arrogance. I regret that, but the teaching does not come from me: It comes from Christ Himself, and as St. Paul put it, "I am not ashamed of the gospel. It is the power of God for the salvation of everyone who believes: for Jew first, and then Greek" (Rom 1:16).

Ecumenism

Q. *Pope John Paul II has conducted services with the archbishop of Canterbury, as well as at the Lutheran church and Jewish synagogue in Rome, and last October with all kinds of pagans and others in Assisi. Is it possible that these acts could be scandalous, in that they promote religious indifference?*

A. The Second Vatican Council urged Catholics to join with other Christians to pray for the complete unity of the Church, and to turn to the one God with Jews and other non-Christian believers, when possible, to seek His blessings of peace and harmony in the troubled world we inhabit.

No one could ever accuse Pope John Paul of religious indifferentism or of causing it; on the contrary, he has been a staunch and vocal advocate of total orthodoxy in presenting the Catholic Faith — never watering it down for any reason. Thus he did not hesitate to inform the archbishop of Canterbury that an Anglican decision to ordain women would be a source of further division. In his meeting with world religious leaders at Assisi, he was demonstrating the power of religion for the good of humanity and presenting it as a viable and powerful alternative to atheism, particularly in its political expression as Marxism.

When ecumenism is correctly practiced, no religious indifference is possible. Jesus said that only the truth could make us free; therefore, a unity founded on something less than the full truth would be a very weak unity — and not permanent. Healthy ecumenical (between Christians) and interreligious (between Christians and non-Christians, for example) dialogue occurs when we acknowledge genuine differences and then endeavor at least to understand them and perhaps even to bridge those gaps — all the while doing so in ways that respect the dignity of the individual and the integrity of the faiths in question.

Democratization

Q. Did Vatican II decree the democratization of the Church? I think the process has been a disaster.

A. The Dogmatic Constitution on the Church (*Lumen Gentium*) makes it clear that Christ established His Church with a certain order or hierarchy. Thus do we read that, "By divine institution bishops have succeeded to the place of the apostles as shepherds of the Church" (*Lumen Gentium*, no. 20). That means that democracy (understood as "counting noses" to determine the content of the Faith) and Catholicism are mutually exclusive. In other words, the Faith we profess is one that is revealed and handed down, not voted on by each new generation as one might decide to amend the Constitution.

At the same time, Vatican II officially recognized what any sensitive and intelligent pastor or bishop always knew, namely, that one should consult people (laity, clergy, or Religious) when they are affected by decisions, especially as to the best way to implement certain policies. The council also recognized that the laity often have expertise in areas which the clergy lack; therefore, good leaders will seek out the advice and counsel of those who are uniquely qualified in a particular field (e.g., finances or education).

As a result of this realization, certain structures of a consultative nature have come into existence. At the universal level, the popes have convoked synods (gatherings of representative bishops from around the world) to provide them with input on such diverse matters as the priesthood, the family, penance and reconciliation, catechesis, and then the laity, in the fall of 1987. In dioceses, bishops rely on their priests' councils to apprise them of diocesan needs and to suggest possible courses of action. Both synods and priests' councils are examples of what is called collegiality — the collaboration between the pope as the head of the college of bishops with his brother bishops or between the local bishop and his body of priests.

Canon law now requires pastors to have finance committees. Many pastors also find great value in parish councils, although universal Church law does not mandate these.

It is important to note that these bodies are not legislative but consultative in nature, and when they are properly used they can offer the pope, a bishop, or a pastor invaluable assistance in coming to a decision, which always rests with him.

Problems have surfaced with these structures when they have been misused in a variety of ways. Thus, some pastors have abdicated their lawful authority to a committee, while others have merely sought to manipulate these groups by "packing" them with "yes-men." Sometimes lay people have usurped the prerogatives of the pastor and have reduced him to a functionary or hired hand. When clergy and laity understand and accept their unique roles and respect each other, tensions and conflicts do not result. Finally, one should recall that St. Paul often spoke of the Church as a body, a reminder that a Church without a head is lifeless.

Descent into hell

Q. What do we mean in the Apostles' Creed by saying that Jesus "descended into hell"?

A. This is a reference to the verse in the First Epistle of Peter which tells us that between His death and resurrection, our Lord "went to preach to the spirits in prison" (3:19). The traditional explanation of this passage is that Jesus went to the just souls (in hades, the underworld, sheol, limbo, or the hell of the just — all synonyms) who had lived under the Old Covenant and had died without hearing the Gospel preached. Jesus then shared with them the good news of salvation and thus offered them the opportunity to avail themselves of this salvation.

Degree of ambiguity

Q. On Easter morning, Jesus told Mary Magdalene not to touch Him. A week later He told Thomas to touch Him. Why the contrast and inconsistency?

A. Both passages you identify are post-resurrectional appearances of Jesus, recorded in the Gospel of John. Some Fathers of the Church thought Jesus was asking Mary Magdalene to have greater respect for His risen and glorified Body than to try to relate to Him in a purely physical manner. However, that brings us to the Lord's encouragement for Thomas to do just the opposite. Why the difference? Only conjecture is possible.

One explanation might be that the invitation to Thomas to touch was an invitation to believe, with the physical act merely a way to bring about the deeper spiritual reality. Or again, some authors suggest that Jesus was telling Magdalene not to sully Him with mundane contact in His new mode of existence.

No absolute answers exist for many dilemmas posed in Scripture, especially those connected with the awesome mystery of the Resurrection. Hence, some degree of ambiguity should not only be tolerated but even accepted willingly, lest we attempt to box God into our own neat categories, making Him our creature rather than the other way around.

The Creeds

Q. How do we reconcile the fact there is no mention of the Eucharist in the Apostles' or Nicene Creed?

A. The Creeds are statements of basic beliefs, the cardinal tenets of the Christian Faith, from which flow other doctrines. Belief in the Eucharist follows from two statements in the creeds, namely, belief in Jesus Christ and an acceptance of His Church. Belief in the Incarnation and in the propitiatory sacrifice of Christ to His Father leads to the Eucharist, which continues those two mysteries in the life of the Church. Similarly, to say that one believes in the Church implies a belief in what she teaches and in what is necessary for her ongoing life in the Spirit; certainly, the Eucharist falls into that category as well.

For all or many?

Q. *Some people argue that the Latin text of the Consecration says Christ's Blood would be shed "pro multis" (for many), not "for all"? Please explain.*

A. *Multis* is a Latin translation of the Greek *hoi polloi*, which is best rendered in English as "*the* many" (not "many") because it means "the crowd" or mass of humanity; in other words, "all." Therefore, our present translation is quite on target when it declares that Christ's Blood would be shed "for all" (*pro multis*). As readers know, I am not a great fan of the International Commission on English in the Liturgy because of their rather poor translations, but in this instance they are certainly right. At the theological level, would anyone be willing to hold that Christ did not, in fact, die for *all* people and not simply for *many*? The former is Catholic doctrine, while the second is heresy. In point of fact, not all will be saved, but that is not Christ's fault or the Father's will.

Union with Christ

Q. *What does it mean to "have a personal relationship with Jesus Christ"?*

A. The expression can mean a great deal, very little, or nothing at all. Some people speak of having a personal relationship with the Lord in such a way as to suggest that Jesus could be one's "buddy"; blasphemy or presumption are involved when one reduces the sovereign Lord to the level of the manipulable.

On the other hand, St. Paul indicates that through baptism a believer is incorporated into Christ, with a real union resulting. That initial relationship is then nourished through prayer, the Scriptures, and the sacraments, especially the Eucharist.

A relationship with Christ, then, is essential for every Christian. The only caution is that the transcendence of God (His absolute otherness) be kept in view as one enjoys the benefits of his immanence (his nearness revealed in Christ).

Questions to test for balance are: Do I feel as though I am known and loved by Christ as an individual? Do I hear His challenge to grow into His image more and more, leaving sin behind?

Did Jesus do enough?

Q. What are we to make of that passage in St. Paul which says that we are to make up in our own lives what is still lacking in the sufferings of Christ? Isn't it blasphemous to assume that Jesus didn't do enough?

A. The passage you refer to comes from Paul's Epistle to the Colossians: "Now I rejoice in my sufferings for your sake, and in my flesh I am filling up what is lacking in the afflictions of Christ on behalf of his body, which is the Church. . ." (1:24). Many people have the same initial reaction to this verse as you, until they understand the profound insight which was St. Paul's.

This passage reflects a very highly developed ecclesiology, whereby Christ continues His work of redemption in and through His Church. What Paul is saying is that Jesus did not simply suffer and die in our stead (although He surely did that), but that each of us — precisely as members of His Body, the Church — must continue His paschal mystery through our own participation in it. Thus it is that we "fill up what is lacking." Not that Jesus did not do enough, but that we must do more: We cannot be mere spectators, in order to benefit from the salvation He wrought on Calvary; we must be active participants. Jesus as Head of the Body suffered for the whole Body, but each and every member of the Body must likewise suffer in union with the Head.

And so, Head and members share a common fate: Having suffered with Christ, we can merit the glory of the Resurrection.

The Passion

Q. As I read the Passion narratives again this Holy Week, Jesus' cry of abandonment (Mt 27:46) hit me again. Did Jesus despair on the cross?

A. You refer, of course, to our Lord's words from the cross: "My God, my God, why have you abandoned me?" Many people question this as you do. The only logical explanation, it seems to me, is to take the most obvious. This quotation is the opening line of Psalm 22, and it does indeed sound like despair. However, I think it is necessary to read on to the conclusion of the psalm as one then discovers the progress of the tormented soul from seeming abandonment by God to the realization that he is most surely in God's hands. Thus does the hymn end on a note of confident and absolute trust in the Lord.

St. Matthew would have been using "shorthand" here. We have all heard people say, for example, "Kate Smith sang 'God Bless America.' " Do they mean the artist sang only the words "God Bless America" and then sat down? Or do they mean that she sang the song, the first words of which are "God Bless America"? Similarly, the evangelist was saying that Jesus prayed the psalm, which began with those words and obviously went on to its conclusion.

The psalm reads at its conclusion:

"And to him my soul shall live; my descendants shall serve him. Let the coming generation be told of the Lord that they may proclaim to a people yet to be born the justice he has shown" (Ps 22).

God as Mother

Q. Is it theologically sound to refer to God as our Mother?

A. We all know that God is neither male nor female; however, when God in Christ chose to reveal the inner life of the Trinity, He specifically spoke of God as Father. Some people point to scriptural passages in which feminine qualities are ascribed to God; they then extrapolate on that to legitimize the use of the title "Mother" for God. It is important to realize that never once does Scripture call God "Mother" directly; some passages say that God behaves in a maternal manner toward His children, and our Lord spoke of His desire to gather all of Jerusalem around Him, as a mother hen does her chicks. However, these are similes and not overt equations. On the other hand, many Scriptures quite clearly refer to God as Father.

It seems to me that we must be very careful in tampering with the revealed Word of God, particularly when people often have decidedly political agendas in pushing for such changes. Certainly, it is not incorrect to see in the Godhead the fullness of all characteristics, which in us are most often seen in only one sex or the other. It is something entirely different to move from that to talk about a feminine God or even a hermaphroditic God.

Evolution

Q. Can a Catholic believe in evolution?

A. Evolution is not a doctrine, hence one does not "believe in" it. Evolution is a scientific theory which has significant support in the scientific community but has never been proven. That having been said, Catholic theology provides believers with a way to safeguard the biblical doctrine of creation and to accept the theory of evolution at the same time.

The first two chapters of Genesis offer two stories of creation, which are considerably different at the literal level, the most obvious difference being that Genesis 1 presents man created last while Genesis 2 shows man created first. However, we are here dealing with Hebrew poetry, which is not intended to be taken literally. At the level of meaning, Genesis 1 and 2 are not mutually exclusive but complementary. The theological point in both stories is that man is the crown of creation.

Two principal doctrines taught in Genesis are the following: God is the source of the entire created order: God "breathed into" man His own divine life.

A Catholic can accept the theory of evolution if also willing to admit that God began the evolutionary process and then personally intervened when a creature had reached that perfection which was fit to receive an immortal soul. This approach takes seriously the biblical data (using Scripture as its sacred authors intended it to be understood) while simultaneously maintaining an openness to scientific inquiry. Of course, faith and science can never contradict each other because, when engaged in properly, both seek to lead people to truth and, ultimately, the Truth who reveals Himself in the Scriptures and in the world of nature.

Pursuit of truth

Q. Why do Catholics seem more interested in philosophers, such as St. Thomas Aquinas, than in the direct message of the Bible itself?

A. Catholics are not more interested in Aquinas than in the Bible. They are interested in the pursuit of truth, which comes about when people investigate reality from a variety of angles.

Rational beings have always held that all truth is one; therefore, it is not correct to separate sacred truth from secular truth. In fact, the acquisition of what may appear to be merely secular knowledge can be extremely beneficial in increasing one's appreciation of the Word of God. That is why Catholic biblical scholars are trained in many fields: linguistics, anthropology, archaeology, and history.

The study of philosophy reveals what man, unaided by grace and revelation, can comprehend of the mystery of life and even of God. The Church then adds the dimension of faith to that and evolves the science of theology, enabling us to grow in our understanding of both divine and human realities.

The biblical authors themselves had a wide range of human knowledge; this is especially evident when one turns to the Wisdom literature or the writings of St. Paul — rather heavily influenced by Greek (pagan) philosophy.

The magisterium

Q. So often your magazine mentions the magisterium. What is it? Is it the final authority in the Church?

A. Very simply put, the magisterium is made up of the Pope and the bishops teaching in union with him. Catholic doctrine is taught by them, individually or collectively, in an ordinary fashion or in a solemn manner (e.g., ecumenical council or a papal *ex-cathedra* statement) and is binding upon the faithful when they teach what the Church has always taught and believed. The teaching authority of the Church can never propose new doctrines for acceptance, as Congress might legislate or the Supreme Court might adjudicate brand new positions; rather, the function of the magisterium is to safeguard the Deposit of Faith and to present it anew to each succeeding generation.

At times, the official teachers in the Church will "define" dogma at a given point in history (e.g., Vatican I on the infallibility of the Church or

Pope Pius XII on Mary's Assumption). But that does not mean a new teaching is being invented; rather, what has always been believed is being proposed for belief in a formal manner.

More generally, however, there will be no extraordinary exercise of the Church's teaching authority; the teachers will simply teach through addresses, documents, and the like, all of which reinforce the ongoing Tradition. Therefore, one can readily see the magisterium is indeed the final arbiter of Catholic doctrine for the whole Church.

Infallibility

Q. I often hear about the Pope being infallible, but I want to know under what circumstances he is infallible. Is it always, or must certain conditions be met?

A. The charism of infallibility is that gift whereby the Holy Spirit preserves the Church in the truth of the apostolic faith. The Fathers of the First Vatican Council saw infallibility as the means by which "the whole flock of Christ might be kept away from the poison of error and be nourished by the food of heavenly doctrine." To speak of "papal infallibility," then, is to identify only one aspect of infallibility, which is a gift to the whole Church for the sake of the whole Church. The charism of infallibility comes into play when the Pope, as head of the college of bishops, or the entire body of bishops (in union with the Pope) speak the Faith of the Church. The Second Vatican Council expressed it thus:

"The Roman Pontiff, head of the college of bishops, enjoys this infallibility in virtue of his office, when, as supreme pastor and teacher of all the faithful — who confirms his brethren in the Faith (cf. Lk 22:32) — he proclaims in an absolute decision a doctrine pertaining to faith or morals. . . . The infallibility promised to the Church is also present in the body of bishops when, together with Peter's successor, they exercise the supreme teaching office" (*Lumen Gentium*, no. 25).

What does this mean concretely? The Church teaches that the Pope is infallible when teaching on matters of faith and morals and authoritatively speaking *ex cathedra* (from the chair of Peter), as the vicar of Christ on earth. This is a very specific and limited power. People outside the Church sometimes have the impression that the Pope can pronounce infallibly on any topic he chooses. As is obvious from reading the official ecclesiastical documents cited above, this is not the case; infallible teaching is limited to faith and morals. Furthermore, neither the Pope nor an ecumenical council can "create" or "invent" new doctrines and propose them for belief. An infallible dogmatic definition means that the particular doctrine at issue has always been taught and believed, but that this is now being said formally and solemnly.

A female Church

Q. I've noticed that you frequently refer to the Church as "she." How come, especially since the whole hierarchy is male?

A. You are quite observant! The simplest answer is that I speak of the Church in feminine terms because the Sacred Scriptures do. St. Paul consistently used feminine images to describe the Church as either the bride of Christ (e.g., Eph 5:22) or our mother (cf. Gal 4:26). Hence the pronoun "she."

Paul very deliberately spoke of the Church in personalistic language because the Church is not an amorphous, anonymous multinational corporation. On the contrary, the Church is the bride of Christ redeemed by her Bridegroom; the Church is the mother who brings us to birth through her sacraments, especially baptism.

It seems to me no accident that so many unfortunate attitudes toward the Church have surfaced just when people began to "depersonalize" the Church. After all, it's so much easier to be overly critical of an institution than of one's mother.

To suggest that the Church should not be referred to in feminine terms because of the male hierarchy is to mistake the hierarchy for the whole Church.

3. MORALITY

Praying to die

Q. My aged mother suffers excruciating back pains, relieved only with drugs. She is in gradually deteriorating condition and wants to die (she prays to do so). Is this wrong?

A. When I was a child, the sisters always taught us to "offer up" our little pains and aches. We don't hear that too often anymore, and a lot of human suffering is "wasted." By that, I mean this: Every human person must undergo a certain amount of pain in this life, some more than others. It seems to me that our choices are only two: To become bitter, asking, "Why me?" Or to accept the suffering, growing in and through it, and uniting it to the sufferings of our Divine Savior on the Cross. Assist your mother in doing the latter.

Wanting to die and be with the Lord is not sinful, in and of itself. What should be prayed for, however, is that God's will be done in one's life. If that means suffering, so be it. If that means release from suffering through death, so be it. If that means release from suffering through a cure, so be it. Stake out the options to your mother in this manner. Most importantly, though, give your mother a cause for which to suffer in a good sense, perhaps for the intentions of the Holy Father or for an increase in vocations to the priesthood and religious life. This will help her make some sense out of her suffering and likewise reinsert her into the life of the whole Church.

Nuclear weapons

Q. Can a U.S. serviceman be excommunicated for guarding nuclear weapons as part of his duties? My son has been told this, and I think he has been given incorrect information.

A. I think he has, too.

First of all, the Holy Father has indicated that a policy of deterrence (which is what maintaining nuclear weapons is) is a morally acceptable option, as long as efforts at a just and lasting peace are underway. In light of the ongoing dialogue between Washington and Moscow, I think that condition is verified. I would view your son's activity as peacekeeping, rather than war-making. The moral dilemma for a believer would occur if he or she were ordered to use destructive nuclear weapons on civilian population centers or in an unprovoked first strike, since both of these scenarios would violate the traditional just-war theory held in Catholic moral theology from the time of St. Augustine to the present.

At any rate, no penalty of excommunication is leveled against a serviceman even in those circumstances. Personal responsibility is a legitimate question, pushing him to choose between an order and an informed Catholic conscience.

The Lord's name

Q. It has become common practice for many Catholics constantly to use the names of Jesus and God in anger, frustration, or disgust. Doesn't the Second Commandment apply any longer?

A. Most priests would probably agree that one of the most frequent sins heard in confession is the breaking of the Commandment which says: "Thou shalt not take the name of the Lord thy God in vain."

Such violations range from blasphemy (any thought, word, or action that expresses contempt for God), to perjury (the deliberate swearing to falsehood), to cursing (the deliberate calling down of evil or spiritual harm on another person). Children and even some adults confess to "cussing" when they really mean the use of vulgar language, which is not a sin against this Commandment but more properly related to the Sixth or Ninth Commandments. However, blasphemy, perjury, and cursing (in the precise sense) are rather infrequent occurrences for the average Christian.

Most often, however, sins against the Second Commandment come about through the irreverent use of God's name — and this is usually a bad habit more than an example of hardcore sin. Not that these lapses are excusable, but it's necessary to put them into perspective.

Ten years ago a simple "Oh, God" would have been "bleeped" off television. Today, much stronger fare is routine on radio and television, as well as in film. A desensitization has thereby taken place, and now to correct even a child on this matter can bring condescending smiles which suggest that the Christian adult is just a bit out of step with modern life.

This phenomenon means that the general acceptability of misusing God's name is increased while at the same time one's culpability for the offense is decreased. Simply because something is accepted does not make it right, however. Christians need to be pacesetters rather than passive receivers of cultural conditioning. Remember that St. Paul urged his readers to *transform* the world and not conform to it (cf. Rom 12:2). A common adage makes the same point more bluntly by reminding us that dead fish go with the flow downstream; only the live ones go against the flow. How can believers help to reverse society's cavalier attitude toward the Lord's name? By developing for themselves, first of all, what we might call a "spirituality of the holy name."

A spirituality of the holy name will be demonstrated by what we say and do, as well as by what we do not say. Negatively, it will involve a personal commitment never to misuse the name of God. Positively, it will mean the development of an attitude of praise and gratitude upon hearing the name of the Lord. Further, it will cause us to begin a personal campaign to encourage others to respect the sacred name, whether among family, friends, or the media. Finally, such a spirituality will have a very practical effect on the way we live our lives, so that others will know by our actions that we are people who worship a God who is the source of all life and whose Son has saved mankind from sin.

Observing the Second Commandment with love and devotion enables us to sing the greatest of all hymns with genuine conviction:

Holy God, we praise Thy name!
Lord of all, we bow before Thee!
All on earth Thy scepter claim,
All in heaven above adore Thee.
Infinite Thy vast domain,
Everlasting is Thy reign!

Gambling

Q. I love to play bingo and lotto, but I hear so many people say that all this gambling is wrong and the Church shouldn't be involved with it. Would you please give some straight answers on the morality of gambling in general and the Church's association with it in particular?

A. Gambling is no more inherently evil than is drinking. Circumstances dictate whether the behavior is problematic or not. For example, if you like an evening out with other people, enjoy the excitement of chance, and use money which is not needed for any other purpose, I see nothing wrong with bingo or other games of chance. When gambling becomes compulsive or causes a person to fail to live up to genuine commitments (financial and otherwise), then a moral difficulty exists.

Ear-piercing

Q. I was told in high school that it is wrong to get one's ears pierced because it is a mutilation. However, a priest friend told me otherwise. What is the Church's position?

A. Mutilation is a technical expression in moral theology, meaning the removal of a part of the body, such that a body function cannot be performed (e.g., sterilization). It also implies an unnecessary surgical procedure (e.g., amputation when an alternative would be just as effective). Removal of a foot which is gangrenous is not mutilation since the loss of the part enables the whole to function properly.

That having been said, it should be clear that ear-piercing is not mutilation. Perhaps your high-school teacher just wanted to discourage the practice, but it's certainly not a sin — however annoying it can be for teachers or parents to see large earrings dangling from their girls' (or boys'!) ears.

Divine Office

Q. Are priests under obligation to recite the Divine Office?

A. Yes, they are. Upon ordination to the diaconate (permanent deacons are normally dispensed from this because of prior business and family obligations), a man solemnly promises to pray for the Church each day by reciting the Divine Office or Liturgy of the Hours. The obligation is of the same nature as the faithful's duty to attend Mass on Sundays and holy days of obligation, binding under pain of serious sin, if a priest has omitted one of the major "hours" (e.g., Lauds or Vespers) without just cause.

In this way, the Church is highlighting the fact that those who stand at the altar to minister publicly must be men of prayer in private, too. They are, in fact, the official "prayers" of the community.

Capital punishment

Q. Governor Casey of Pennsylvania was petitioned by the bishops of the state to stay the execution of a convicted murderer. Although the governor is anti-abortion, he refused their request, saying there was a difference between the innocent human life in the womb and that of a guilty murderer. I tend to agree with him and wonder why the bishops don't.

A. I am sure the bishops of Pennsylvania accept the governor's distinction (a most necessary one) regarding the difference between an innocent baby in its mother's womb and a convicted murderer. That is why they asked the governor for "clemency," that is, mercy. That having been said, they obviously have difficulty with the state's exercise of capital punishment.

Traditionally, Catholic morality has acknowledged the right of the state to engage in capital punishment, with certain conditions being fulfilled. Increasingly, however, that has moved toward toleration more than a full-throated approval. Pope John Paul II has been most reluctant to cede this right to the state in any kind of unqualified way; in fact, he has intervened on many occasions on behalf of people on death row, in much the same way as the bishops of Pennsylvania. The Church's hesitancy in this regard today seems to be rooted in a concern about the cavalier way in which human life is viewed in contemporary society; the hierarchy tend to see capital punishment as contributing to that devaluing of human life and so caution against its use.

Aside from the moral considerations, studies show that capital punishment is not very effective as a deterrent and that the affluent can escape the full force of this penalty through clever lawyers and greater financial resources than those available to the poor. For all these reasons, there seems to be an emerging consensus in the Church today away from an endorsement of capital punishment and toward a hesitancy in regard to the practice, if not outright opposition.

Movies

Q. Is it a sin to view a movie which the bishops have rated as morally objectionable?

A. I suppose you are referring to the rating system used by the United States Catholic Conference. While this is not an infallible guide to the cinema, it is a good guide. If someone were to choose consciously to see a film he knew to be morally objectionable, he would have to have extremely strong reasons for the action, if he intended it to be a moral action. For example; someone may realize that a movie glorifies violence or sexual promiscuity and vividly portrays these things; however, he might see the film for certain compelling motives (a course requirement, for example). A person must know himself very well in order to depart from general viewing standards, lest he become infected with the disease himself: as computerese puts it, "Garbage in, garbage out." Furthermore, no committed Christian should patronize films which offend against public morality; otherwise, the peddlers of indecency are receiving their support from those who should instead be doing everything possible to put them out of business.

Pornographic viewing

Q. What is the position of the Church on a married man enjoying pornographic material?

A. The Church's attitude toward pornography is the same for everyone, married and single alike: Pornographic viewing (whether films or photos) is sinful, whether done alone or with others (even one's spouse). Why? Jesus put it most succinctly: "Everyone who looks at a woman with lust has already committed adultery with her in his heart" (Mt 5:28). Needless to say, that works the other way around as well. Pornography demeans the human person, both the one depicted and the one viewing the material, reducing a human being to little more than an animal in heat. Psychologists also now know the connection between this (which seems like a harmless, private activity) and subsequent acts of violence. Sometimes people note that they get involved in pornography "to improve their marriage." If this kind of smut is needed to improve a marriage, one or both partners should be seeking professional help from a physician, priest, or psychologist, or all three.

Sins of impurity

Q. If a girl was molested at the age of three or four until the age of fourteen, when she finally left home, would she be responsible for sins of impurity? The girl in question actually forgot everything until she was an older woman and now wants to know if she has to confess those sins.

A. Children under the age of reason (usually given at seven) are incapable of sin of any kind. What you describe does not sound as though the girl (even at the older ages) was anything but a victim; therefore, there is nothing to confess, in my judgment.

Permitted sex

Q. What is the Church's teaching on oral sex between married persons during regular intercourse?

A. Traditional moral theology distinguishes between oral sex as an end in itself and as a means to the end of a completed act of intercourse. The first instance would always be viewed as immoral, while the second could be morally justified, provided it did indeed lead to a normal act of intercourse and was engaged in willingly by both parties.

I decided to respond to this question because it is coming in with greater frequency. I suspect the reason for this is that more and more couples are foregoing artificial contraception and are practicing natural family planning. In those training sessions, couples are often told to find alternate modes of expressing affection during periods when they do not perform the marital act. Therefore, it is necessary to repeat that oral sex can never be regarded as a legitimate substitute for normal intercourse.

I would conclude with a practical thought on this subject by Dr. John Kippley of the Couple to Couple League International: "The fact that moral theologians do not condemn cunnilingus and fellatio as foreplay for complete marital genital intercourse says nothing about the advisability of their use in any given marriage. . . . Even when both [spouses] are willing, there are additional questions about the frequency and the extent to which couples should pursue the maximization of carnal pleasure, at least habitually, but such questions are best discussed with a good spiritual advisor." This remark is part of a pamphlet entitled "Marital Sexuality: Moral Considerations." It is available to readers of TCA through the generosity of Dr. Kippley, free of charge. Simply send a stamped, self-addressed envelope to the organization at: P.O. Box 111184, Cincinnati, OH 45211.

Occasions of sin

Q. Our daughter is a senior in high school. She says that the priest who teaches her religion told the class that kissing and embracing were not sinful as long as they did not go as far as orgasm. I told her that was incorrect, and she argued with me. Who is right?

A. Whether or not kissing and embracing are sinful (mortally or venially) might not be the best question to raise with young people. As a former high-school teacher and now a college professor, my concern would be how prudent it is to encourage teens and young adults to engage in activity which may well lead them to "the point of no return." Theologically speaking, your daughter's priest teacher is correct, as long as the kissing is not prolonged and of such a nature that it will precipitate sexual intercourse. My own advice in those situations has always been to urge youngsters not to put themselves into situations of potential difficulty — what we used to call near occasions of sin.

Living together

Q. Is it a sin for a boy and girl to live together before being married, even if they don't sleep with each other?

A. Without being cute, one can say that sleeping together is not a problem, but what goes on before and after sleeping is.

It seems to me that an intelligent and realistic understanding of human nature would keep a young couple living in separate homes until after marriage. The sexual drive is one of the most powerful; in our society, premarital chastity is hard enough to live without placing oneself under additional strain and temptation.

What you describe is imprudent at best and an occasion of sin at worst. Furthermore, this kind of an arrangement would also be a source of scandal since the average person would presume, naturally and legitimately in my opinion, that the couple were indeed engaging in marital relations.

Premarital sex

Q. Where in the Bible is the subject of premarital sex discussed?

A. Part of the Christian inheritance from Judaism is the Decalogue, which has always been seen as condemning sexual acts outside marriage. Therefore, the New Testament simply picked up on that where the Old Testament left off. Some passages which condemn premarital or extramarital sex are the following: 1 Corinthians 6:9ff; 1 Corinthians 7:12-20; 1 Corinthians 10:8; 2 Corinthians 12:21: Colossians 3:5; Revelation 22:27.

Days of rest

Q. I have read that holy days of obligation are to be days of rest, like Sundays. Does that mean that Catholics should try to take these days off from work?

A. Of the six holy days of obligation observed in the United States, only two correspond to civil holidays, and so, their full observance is complicated and impeded. If at all possible, abstinence from work on these days would be praiseworthy, but if one's job would not permit that, it suffices to attend Mass on these occasions.

From tlme to time, people question the advisability of maintaining so many holy days of obligation, given our American cultural situation. My own feeling is that, precisely because of our cultural situation, we need these special days of observance, if for no other reason than to enable our people to shine forth as witnesses to a different and higher standard of religious practice. Keeping the holy days is a wonderful way of proclaiming that we Catholics march to the beat of a different drummer, observing God's calendar rather than that of secular society.

Sunday obligation

Q. Many years ago, I was told that if one could not attend Sunday Mass because none was available, then one could not vacation in that area. Is that still the Church's position?

A. No, I am unaware of that ever having been officially taught by moral theologians; perhaps an overzealous pastor might have presented that position as Church teaching. As a matter of fact, prior to modern transportation, impediments to Sunday Mass were quite real, even for people who lived within normal parish boundaries in rural areas, let alone for travelers.

The Catholic Church exhibits genuine pastoral concern for her sons and daughters, not wanting to make the Sunday Mass obligation odious; at the same time, she stresses the absolute centrality of Sunday Mass in the life of a believer, who would never excuse himself lightly from this obligation.

Sunday observance

Q. What is your opinion about eating out on Sunday? It seems to me that we are thus forcing people to work as cooks, waiters, etc.

A. Your question certainly reveals a great deal of sensitivity to both the Sabbath observance and the dignity of others; however, I would not have qualms of conscience about this. Eating out on a Sunday is an act of enjoyment for many people and, presumably, some of the people working to make that possible will get their own opportunity to eat out on other Sundays.

Sunday shopping

Q. When inquiring about the morality of Sunday shopping, I have received conflicting opinions from priests. Is it sinful or not? If so, is it gravely sinful?

A. No unnecessary work should be done on Sunday, and that includes shopping. It is good to recall that although an individual may find shopping a pleasant diversion or even a convenient way for a lonely person to meet others, Sunday shopping likewise requires Sunday working for some people on that very account.

Sunday work not only destroys the Sabbath rest for those directly affected but also contributes to the breakdown of the family since, in most homes, there is now no single day when the whole family will be present for even a meal.

How seriously sinful the activity is depends upon the motivation and the frequency with which one engages in the practice.

Devotion at Mass

Q. I am approaching my eighty-eighth birthday. Going out becomes more difficult with each passing day, so I rely on a local priest to bring me Holy

Communion and to hear my confession. However, I am still upset about missing Mass and wonder if I am committing sin. Can you help me with this problem of conscience?
A. First of all, let me congratulate you on your ripe old age, and secondly for your obvious and great devotion to the Mass. So many people make a career out of finding excuses why they cannot or should not participate in Sunday Mass; your dedication is a breath of fresh air, and I hope it serves as a positive example for others.

That having been said, let us recall that God never demands the impossible. If you are truly incapable of getting around or of doing so only with the greatest discomfort, our Lord understands and loves you for the effort and desire. I am sure that your priest has told you the same thing. Watch the television Mass in your area and unite your prayers to those of the rest of the Church gathered in churches throughout the world. As a special intention on Sunday, I would urge you to pray for those who take their Sunday Mass obligation less than seriously, that they would experience a true change of heart.

Missing Mass

Q. When did it cease to be a mortal sin to miss Mass on a Sunday or holy day of obligation without good cause?
A. It didn't. Unfortunately, some people act as though it did. The Sunday Mass obligation is critically important to the living in a fully Christian life. Even someone like Hans Küng, never known to be a "hard-liner," has remarked that "you can't belong to the club if you don't go to the meetings."

An interesting ecumenical sideline to this: I am told that in certain branches of the Eastern Orthodox Church, failure to attend Sunday liturgy for three consecutive weeks results in an automatic excommunication.

Suicide

Q. Can people who have committed suicide now be buried with a Mass? This recently happened in my parish, and I was quite taken aback.
A. The Church generally denied Christian burial to suicides on the presumption that such a person had succumbed to an act of final despair, thus denying the infinite mercy of God.

With the advent of modern psychology, we now understand that most people who commit suicide are not emotionally stable and are thus incapable of giving either the full reflection or the full consent necessary to commit a mortal sin. As a result, the Church does provide such individuals with Christian burial, both to console their families and to pray that they may experience in death the peace they so lacked in life.

More on suicide

Q. I recently read an article in which the author tried to console the family of a suicide victim. She said prayers should be offered that the poor person had received the grace of final repentance in his last moments. How is it possible to die in mortal sin and still be saved?

A. When the Church comes to moral conclusions, she always does so after taking into account the data which science can give on the nature of the human person. Therefore, biology, psychology, and sociology are all helpful tools in telling us essential facts about the person who performs a particular action. One of the most important determinants of personal guilt is whether or not full consent was given to an action (the other two are objectively grave matter and full knowledge of the evil).

It is hard to imagine anyone in full possession of his or her mental faculties committing suicide. Thus the Church gives that person the benefit of the doubt by providing Christian burial, praying that the deceased will experience a merciful judgment.

It should be noted, by the way, that Christian burial (which includes the Funeral Mass and interment in consecrated ground) is by no means a statement of the Church's approval of a person's life, except in the most minimal manner. Hence, the Church only excludes from its rites "notorious public sinners" in order to avoid scandal. One must also remember that funerals have a twofold function: prayers for the salvation of the deceased and prayers for the consolation of the survivors. The Church, then, does what she does best — prays — leaving judgment to Almighty God.

Procreation

Q. Is it right for a young couple who do not want any children to enter into Holy Matrimony and, at the altar, promise to raise their children in the Catholic Faith when deep down they really don't want any children?

A. An openness to children is an essential element of Christian marriage. Love and life are the primary goals of the married state: love manifests itself in new life; life is the fruit of love. Spouses must see themselves as co-creators with Almighty God. God's love was so great that one could say His love could not be contained within the "confines" of the Trinity but "had" to spill over into the work of creation. Similarly, the love between a husband and wife must take on flesh in procreation; anything less than a willingness to see that happen is a defective form of love.

Christian spouses need not always positively desire children, but they cannot morally act to prevent new life. Furthermore, a firm and absolute resolve at the outset permanently to exclude children renders a marriage null and void.

Homosexuality

Q. My "son" told me he is "gay." How do we handle this with God and with the AIDS scare?

A. I wonder why you put the word "son" in quotation marks in your question. I hope it is not an act of rejection or sarcasm since this would be a fundamental betrayal of your vocation as a Christian parent. The fact that your son broached this topic with you is a tribute to his confidence in your ability to understand him and love him; don't let him down.

Not knowing any of the particulars (like his age and lifestyle), I can only offer some general advice. Assuming that he is an adult and confirmed in his homosexual orientation, remind him equally of God's love for him and God's law for all people (that is, that sexual intercourse is reserved for the married state). Let him know that you accept him and want to help him live a happy, well-adjusted life, not denying his orientation but integrating it into his total way of life, which necessarily includes his Christian commitment. Suggest that he find a good confessor or spiritual director who can help him do just that. Tell him that you expect him to rise to this challenge and that you are praying for God to give him an abundance of grace to do so.

If he fails from time to time (and you know it because he has told you or you have strong reasons to suspect this is the case), urge him to set himself right with the Lord through the Sacrament of Penance. Offer him positive encouragement, and do not allow him to become preoccupied with his sexual orientation, so that it becomes a major focus of attention for him or others, because that is when things usually get out of hand. If all of the above is in place, I don't think you'll have to worry about your son and AIDS.

Homosexuality again

Q. Your recent answer on homosexuality was, in my opinion, an example of waffling on Church teaching. You seem to give a great deal of consolation to those who have a deviant lifestyle.

Q. I have followed your writings for some time, especially your statements on homosexuality since I am a homosexual man. Your last piece on this matter was completely in line with your usual procedure of "fag-bashing."

A. It's not often that a writer can get letters from both ends of the spectrum to declare that he is certainly in the opposite camp!

To the first person, let me respond by simply noting that I most clearly enunciated Catholic teaching on homosexual activity, that is, that it constitutes an objective moral disorder. Presumably, that is why the second reader is angry with me; however, to state that a particular action is morally problematic is not to engage in "bashing" of any kind. Having given the first part of the Church's teaching, I then moved on to ask the father to behave in a loving and compassionate manner toward his son; this is equally a goal the Church sets before all people. It is nothing more and nothing less than hating the sin but loving the sinner. If anyone has a problem with either part of the presentation, his difficulty is not with me but with Christ. Sorry.

Divorced Catholics

Q. I am a divorced and remarried Catholic in the process of petitioning for an annulment. While I understand why I cannot receive Holy Communion, I cannot understand why I cannot go to confession and be absolved of sins other than my adulterous second marriage. Please explain.

A. Repentance and conversion are complete acts, not partial. One cannot be sorry for all one's sins except one. When we say that Jesus is Lord, we mean He is the Lord of the totality of our lives, thus not permitting us to carve out little areas which are kept under our own lordship. I trust you can see the rationale, then, for the Church's position.

Forgiveness

Q. Why is the Church ready to forgive a woman who has had an abortion but will not forgive someone who remarries after a bad first marriage and is now very happy?

A. The Church is willing to forgive anyone who repents of sin (because God is). Presumably, the woman who comes to confession after an abortion is sorry for that sin and is prepared to promise never to commit it again. Someone involved in an invalid marriage (which constitutes an ongoing state of adultery) is not sorry for that sin and, from what you describe, is intent on maintaining the relationship. No forgiveness is possible because no repentance is present.

I trust you see that the Church's attitude of openness is the same for all sinners; it is the attitude of the individual sinner which usually makes the difference.

Sacramental life

Q. I am divorced and remarried. May I receive Holy Communion?

A. Divorce, in and of itself, does not constitute an impediment to a full sacramental life in the Church. The problem comes with a remarriage. Let me explain.

Remarriage presumably involves sexual intercourse. However, since God and the Church do not recognize divorce, each and every sexual encounter in the second, invalid union is to be viewed in a literal sense as an act of adultery. Can one go to confession and receive absolution? Only if one is truly sorry for offenses committed and sincerely intends to avoid such sins in the future. Therein lies the difficulty with a remarriage. Unless one is willing to live as "brother and sister," a sacramental life is ruled out, but one should still attend Sunday Mass and engage in prayer, seeking

God's assistance to deal with the present situation in such a way that God's will can be done. This is particularly important when children are involved and no separation is really possible.

In this day when "everyone" rushes up to Communion — often in an unthinking and unprepared manner — it might be well to heed the advice of Cardinal Joseph Ratzinger, Prefect of the Congregation for the Doctrine of the Faith. He suggests that Catholics, from time to time, may wish to abstain from Holy Communion to stand in solidarity with those who cannot receive the sacraments, doing penance with them and for them; this act of sensitivity would go a long way to make them feel less noticed or even ostracized.

It should be mentioned, however, that under no circumstances should anyone make a sacrilegious Communion out of human respect.

Welcome home

Q. I was married for six years and then divorced. I remarried and was divorced again. I am single and have been for the past five years. I want to return to the sacraments. Can I be helped?

A. Your situation is very easy to handle since you are presently living as a single woman. All you need to do is go to the Sacrament of Penance, confessing all the sins since your last confession. Be sure to tell the priest that the second relationship is finished and that you intend to live by our Lord's commandment which forbids divorce and remarriage.

Thank God He has given you the grace to return. And welcome home!

Scandal

Q. I am a divorced, remarried Catholic. My former spouse and I are in the midst of an annulment proceeding. I know that I cannot receive the sacraments at the present time. If the decision is negative, I will still be unable to receive the sacraments, but what about other rites, like the blessing of throats, stations of the cross, or going to confession (for consolation or counsel), even without obtaining absolution? Would any participation in these other ceremonies be a cause of scandal?

A. Your letter gives evidence of a great deal of sensitivity and spiritual maturity. You are correct in noting your inability to receive the sacraments; however, I think you are carrying the problem further than the Church does.

The Church encourages people in invalid marriages to keep as close to Christ and the Church as their situation permits; practically speaking, that means everything but the reception of Holy Communion and the Sacrament of Penance. For attendance at Mass and devotions or sacramentals, there should be no concern about scandal since these are completely open to you. My only reservation would be in regard to going to confession at regularly scheduled hours because that could give the impression to others that you are receiving the Sacrament of Penance. What I would suggest is to arrange with a priest to become your spiritual director and seek his advice and counsel by special appointment.

Invalid marriage

Q. May I call your attention to a question with the heading of "Reconciliation"? I am sure you will want to correct your answer in a later edition. Certainly we would not encourage anyone to go to confession while still in an invalid marriage. Confession should wait until immediately before convalidation.

A. The writer is referring to my advice for someone in an invalid marriage (which can be quickly validated because of no previous valid union) to go to confession and get the situation straightened out forthwith. My understanding of the original question was that a validation could take place immediately. Beyond that point, however, a person could conceivably go to the Sacrament of Penance while still in an invalid marriage if he/she promised not to live as husband and wife until such time as a validation could take place.

Unreasonable

Q. I am seeing a devout Catholic gentleman, with a view to marriage. I am awaiting an annulment, which is rather certain by all evaluations. Our relationship is very healthy; we enjoy each other's company, whether going out for an evening or saying the Rosary together. The problem is his mother, who insists that we break off the relationship unless and until my annulment comes through. Is she being unreasonable?

A. If everything is as you suggest, then I do think your would-be mother-in-law is acting in an unreasonable manner.

However, I would not be too sure about a decree of nullity until I had a document in hand.

Annulments

Q. My husband was divorced, and we are in the process of seeking an annulment so that we can be married in the Church. Can I now receive the sacraments, or is that still forbidden?

A. Applying for a decree of nullity does not guarantee the obtaining of such a decree. Most dioceses review potential cases and "weed out" cases with no chance of success. Of the cases then accepted, an even more thorough review is required.

The priest who heads one marriage tribunal informs me that he accepts about sixty percent of the cases presented, and that of that number about eighty percent are resolved in a manner permitting the parties involved to enter into a sacramental union.

The proper procedure while you wait, then, is to abstain from sexual relations until the case is completed. That failing, both you and your intended husband must refrain from receiving Holy Communion since he is presumed to be still validly married.

Annulment rights

Q. My marriage of twenty-three years was annulled seven years ago. I was never notified that an annulment had been applied for, nor on what grounds it was granted. Did I not have a right to this information?

A. At the very outset of every procedure for a decree of nullity, the second party must be contacted, or at least every effort must be made to do so. The reason I couch the response somewhat carefully is that there are times when the respondent's whereabouts are unknown; however, contact must be attempted to give that person an opportunity to offer important information bearing on the validity of the marriage.

If this was not done, your rights were violated, and you can seek canonical redress.

'Validation of marriage'

Q. My husband and I were married by a minister. We now have children baptized in the Catholic Church and want to get our marital situation rectified. What do we have to do?

A. All you need to do is go visit your parish priest and ask him to begin the process of having your marriage validated. It only involves filling out some forms and then going through a ceremony of vow renewal. Welcome home!

Annulment again

Q. A friend has begun annulment proceedings and was told by his parish priest that he can receive Holy Communion right now. Is this correct?

A. I presume that the person in question has remarried civilly. If that is the case, the second union is adulterous and he is ineligible to receive the sacraments until he has repented of the sin, which, in this instance, would require him to refrain from sexual intercourse with the woman of the second union until such time as a decree of nullity were obtained and the marriage could be witnessed in the Church.

If a priest did indeed tell him he could return to the sacraments immediately, he was acting in a totally irresponsible manner, for it does not acknowledge the existing moral problem and also presumes a judgment in favor of the person petitioning for the annulment — an unwarranted presumption. After all, suppose the marriage tribunal ruled that the man's first marriage had been a valid marriage, in what position would he be then? As the Scripture says, the man's second state would be worse than his first!

Annulments continued

Q. I have been asked many questions about annulments of Catholic marriages and also of Protestant and civil marriages when it concerns marriages with a Catholic party. I have also been asked if children of annulled marriages are illegitimate.

A. In the young life of this magazine, questions about annulments have already come up several times; however, let's try to explain the basic principle again.

By Christ's teaching and the law of the Church, a valid, consummated marriage is indissoluble. A decree of nullity states that some ingredient necessary for a valid union was lacking and, therefore, no real marriage ever existed.

Catholics must observe the Catholic "form" of marriage (that is, a ceremony before a priest or deacon and two witnesses); failure to do so renders a marriage null. Non-Catholics, on the other hand, are not held to this law; hence, their unions witnessed by ministers or civil magistrates are valid. If a Catholic and a non-Catholic attempt marriage without observing the Catholic form of marriage, that marriage is invalid. This last point often becomes important if the marriage fails and the Catholic partner seeks an annulment in order to marry in the Church at some future moment. Frequently enough, too, a couple in such a situation will subsequently want their marriage "blessed" in the Church; this is a simple procedure whereby the man and woman renew their vows before a priest and two witnesses.

Children of an annulled marriage are legitimate because, according to both civil and canon law, such a union was presumably entered into in good faith and is considered a "putative" (alleged or supposed) marriage.

Annulment questions are too complex and individualized to answer adequately in a place like this. For particular instances, one's parish priest or diocesan marriage tribunal should be consulted.

Annulments once more

Q. I can't understand what the Church is doing with annulments nowadays. I know a woman who was married for fifteen years and had four children, and even she got one. Of course, a friend of mine says if you have money or connections, you'll definitely get one.

A. Although the tone of your letter is rather accusatory (and unfairly so, in my opinion), I still want to give it a detailed response because easily a fourth of the questions to *The Catholic Answer* deal with marital problems, and especially with annulments. I hope that giving a broader background treatment will help people understand "what the Church is doing."

When the Church uses its judicial system to examine the validity of a marriage bond, it is engaging in a work of justice and not a work of mercy. Both supporters and detractors of the revised annulment process seem to be confused in this regard. Therefore, some background information might be helpful.

A decree of nullity (commonly but inaccurately referred to as an "annulment") is the Church's declaration that, after proper consideration, a determination has been made that the necessary qualities were lacking to one or both parties of the marriage, so that the *consortium totius vitae* ("total sharing of a common life") envisioned by Vatican II was impossible.

In other words, what was taken to be a marriage was lacking in some essential characteristics; simply put, no marriage really existed. This is quite different from a divorce, which is the declaration that a real marriage is now broken by some authority. Catholic theology, taking at face value the words of Christ in the Scriptures (cf. Mk 10:9), refuses to grant power to any human authority (civil or ecclesiastical) over a valid, consummated, sacramental marriage.

More than a decade ago the Holy See gave marriage tribunals in the United States permission to use special norms to handle annulment cases. This experimental process was apparently viewed quite favorably by Rome because, with a few exceptions, the process was incorporated into the revised Code of Canon Law and thus extended to the universal Church. Although critics can sometimes cite particular abuses, by and large the new norms have achieved justice in a way the old system could not.

It's important to note that having the Church's tribunal open to a Catholic is not a privilege but a right, flowing from one's membership in the Church. Therefore, every parish priest can be approached with confidence regarding an annulment and, if need be, the judicial vicar of the diocese, who is the chief judge of the local tribunal.

The length of time and fees involved in annulment cases vary significantly from diocese to diocese. Usually these differences are the result of whether a particular tribunal has sufficient staff (both priestly and secretarial). Although the media frequently try to show that an annulment is related to a petitioner's wealth or prestige, one must realize that the modest fees (sometimes as low as two hundred dollars) do not begin to cover the costs involved. Furthermore, it is extremely unlikely that any case has ever been denied because of the inability to pay. Incidentally, it's ironic how normally charitable Catholics can turn harsh when the rich or the famous obtain the same consideration as anyone else. Should justice be denied simply *because* these people are rich and famous?

The biggest difference between earlier annulment procedures and the present norms is the admissibility of psychological evidence. This was a direct response to Vatican II's call for the Church to be open to valid insights coming from the social sciences. Pope John Paul II has enthusiastically supported this approach and reminded the judges of the Roman Rota (the marriage court of the universal Church) of their obligation to take seriously such testimony.

As the process begins, one must recall that the Church believes that marriage has the benefit of law, which is to say that the burden of proving invalidity is on the person requesting the decree of nullity. What are the grounds for such a decree? The first and easiest is "lack of form," which means the marriage ceremony did not take place according to the Church's requirements; the second most common grounds is "lack of due discretion" or lack of consent. Here is where the psychology of persons and marriage itself comes into play.

"Lack of discretion" refers to insufficient knowledge or reflection on the part of one or both spouses, such that the marital consent given on the day of the ceremony was defective. Full knowledge includes knowledge of the self, the other, the demands of marriage; adolescent fantasies do not produce Christian marriages.

If one party or both parties proved unable to fulfill the obligations of marriage from the very beginning, no marriage ever took place. True, spouses receive a special sacramental grace through matrimony, but theology also tells us that grace builds on nature. In other words, if the necessary prerequisites are not possessed by the spouses, no growth will ever occur. Immaturity, instability, dependency on drugs and alcohol, promiscuity — all are warning signals of potential marital problems. In reviewing a failed marriage, a petitioner should look for the presence of these indicators before the marriage ceremony took place. Information about one's early life, personal relationships, and life in the Church are critical, as are the details about the courtship, the honeymoon, and the marriage itself.

Finally, some clarifications are in order. According to Church law, neither divorce nor remarriage brings about an excommunication. However, someone who is divorced and remarried (civilly), cannot receive the Eucharist because the present relationship is considered one of adultery. The solution to the problem is to investigate possibilities for an annulment and to refrain from conduct proper to marriage until such time as a decree of nullity would permit a Christian remarriage.

The correct conclusion to come to is that marriage should be carefully prepared for. This is a responsibility of the couple but also of the Church. It is to be hoped that extra care at this end of the marital spectrum will obviate the necessity of a judicial process at the other end.

Decree of nullity

Q. What is the view of the Church on a second marriage blessed by the parish priest but not annulled?

A. Your question has me confused. I suspect you mean that someone was previously married and that marriage still stands. Now that person is living in an invalid second marriage.

If my reconstruction is correct, then no priest can touch that union. His "blessing" would be a sacrilege, inasmuch as he cannot bless what is an adulterous relationship in the eyes of God.

The only way an invalid second marriage can be "blessed" is if a decree of nullity is obtained for the first marriage. Then the priest would ask the couple to renew their consent in a private ceremony, and that marriage would be fully recognized by the Church.

Contraception

Q. Can a man who has had a vasectomy receive Holy Communion?

A. Assuming the man has repented of his sin and has gone to confession, he can resume a normal sacramental life since any sin can be forgiven, given the proper disposition. The same is true, of course, of a woman who would have a hysterectomy for contraceptive purposes.

Undoubtedly, some people will point out what they consider to be an inconsistency, namely, couples who practice artificial contraception habitually are unable to receive the sacraments. The difference is that one act is ongoing, while the other is finished. I should note, however, that someone who is purposely sterilized as an act of birth control must truly repent of that sin; failure to do so makes each and every subsequent act of intercourse a sin of contraception, just as though he or she were using the pill or an IUD.

I cannot stress sufficiently how important honesty is in one's dealings with God. A priest in confession can be fooled. A penitent can even deceive himself, but God knows the heart and judges accordingly.

Vasectomies

Q. Your recent answer about vasectomies prompts this question: Is there any way for subsequent acts of intercourse not to be considered contraceptive?

A. I have received many questions on this.

Let me summarize what I said originally: If someone submits to a sterilization procedure (whether male or female) for the purposes of excluding the possibility of future children, all subsequent acts of intercourse must be regarded as contraceptive. This is just a matter of logic and fairness of evaluation. Otherwise, a person could easily be sterilized, run off to confession, and then engage in sexual intercourse with "impunity" for the rest of his or her life. On the other hand, the person who might possibly be open to future children but took "the pill" would be involved in a sin of contraception for each performance of the sexual act while on the pill.

It seems to me that if one has truly repented of a sin of sterilization, has gone to confession and received absolution, the only proper way to deal with the problem thereafter is to relate sexually as though one were not sterilized by practicing natural family planning. That is the only way I can see a person performing the marital act in honesty and integrity after a vasectomy or tubal ligation.

Sterilizations

Q. In regard to sterilizations and the reception of the sacraments, what about the following? Couldn't a person be sorry for the act of sterilization and then hope God would grant a child, in spite of the procedure? Would natural family planning still be required as a sign of goodwill? Would it be wrong to try to reverse the process?

A. I have received dozens of letters in response to my statement about observing natural family planning after a sterilization as a sign of repentance, which tells me that I certainly hit a raw nerve. I stand by that statement as reflecting good moral theology and good pastoral theology.

Surely one can hope for God to do anything, but to make God's action almost impossible and then pretend to be open to His will is just a bit hypocritical. Perhaps an example would clarify my point. Why not remove my brain and then say that I am still open to the prospect that God will keep me alive? That absurdity is rather apparent, isn't it?

Finally, yes, I neglected in my original answer to note the possibility of seeking a reversal of the sterilization procedure. Several physicians wrote to remind me that this is becoming more feasible as time goes on. It goes without saying that this would be the best sign of true repentance.

Valid marriage

Q. Is a marriage performed outside the Church ever valid?

A. Yes, in two situations.

The first involves two non-Catholics. If they contract a marriage, it is a valid marriage in the eyes of the Church. This is usually of interest to Catholics only when such a marriage has broken up and one of those persons is considering remarriage to a Catholic. In other words, if a non-Catholic has been in what the Church deems to be a valid marriage, that person is not free to marry in the Catholic Church unless a decree of nullity can be obtained from the Church.

The second concerns a Catholic. If a Catholic intends to marry a non-Catholic and a marriage in the presence of a priest or in a Catholic church would cause serious family problems, for example, due to anti-Catholic bigotry, the local bishop can grant the couple a dispensation to marry before a non-Catholic minister or justice of the peace. I should emphasize that this kind of permission is not given casually and the need for it, in my judgment, signals rather serious problems for the relationship in the future. All other obligations for a Catholic marriage remain: attendance at prenuptial instructions, signing of promises to raise the children Catholic, and maintenance of the Catholic Faith for the Catholic party, of course.

Hysterectomy

Q. Do you need a priest's permission to have a hysterectomy if it is necessary?

A. When you say "necessary," I presume you mean for medical reasons and not for contraceptive purposes. If that is the case, no permission is needed since the intent of the surgical procedure is to bring about wholeness and healing to the person. Removal of the organs for contraceptive purposes, however, constitutes a mutilation of the body and brings about a situation such that all successive acts of intercourse are contraceptive and, therefore, sinful.

Of course, in those instances one cannot obtain "permission" of a priest as though one were seeking a dispensation from some man-made law.

Fetal testing

Q. What is the Church's position on prenatal screening such as amniocentesis for genetic studies and fetal alpha protein levels?

A. The Church has no objection to such testing, provided the motivation is correct. Your own hesitancy indicates that you know that not infrequently these tests are used to inform parents of genetic defects in unborn children, so as to urge them to opt for an abortion. This is certainly an immoral use of what could be a wonderful tool.

How could these tests be properly utilized? Physicians tell us that the discovery of certain defects in the womb can actually head off the problem before birth. Fetal surgery is a whole new and developing phase of medicine; it emphasizes the important aspect of the unborn child as a patient, worthy of all care and attention, underscoring the child as full humanity.

Parents who are told about potentially deformed children are offered a special grace to accept these children as gifts from Almighty God. It is never compassionate to snuff out life, on the pretext that death in the womb would be better for the child than a less than perfect existence after birth. Using that criterion, who among us would have ever been born? God's ways are not our ways, and thank God for that. As a loving Creator, He does know better than we, and we need to trust Him.

Casting your vote

Q. Can a Catholic in good conscience vote for pro-abortion candidates? Some friends say you have to look at the whole picture, while others say certain positions (like favoring the killing of the unborn) are automatic disqualifiers from consideration by civilized people, let alone Christians. I am confused.

A. In a society like ours, in which so much is interpreted politically, it is risky to answer a question which can appear to some like a political endorsement (or condemnation) of individual candidates. Not to tackle this issue, however, would be a serious breach of duty on my part.

I have consulted widely on this and am giving over the space for this question to a theologian who has grappled with this matter in great depth for several years now. Our guest respondent is Father Robert Barry, O.P., who holds graduate degrees in theology, political science, and philosophy from the Aquinas School of Theology in Dubuque and the University of Wisconsin, as well as a doctorate in moral theology from the Catholic University of America. He is currently serving as Visiting Professor of Religious Studies at the University of Illinois, Champaign-Urbana:

"When the Congregation for the Doctrine of the Faith issued its *Declaration on Abortion*, it said that laws which would 'admit in principle the licitness of abortion,' could not be supported and that Catholics could not 'take part in a campaign in favor of such a law, nor vote for it.'

"While some might interpret this to mean that Catholics were only prohibited from voting for pro-abortion laws, it would seem that the aim of this magisterial teaching was to prohibit Catholic support for abortion candidates as well. This seems to be the case because they are prohibited from participating in a 'campaign' to promote abortion, which would imply giving political support by voting for pro-abortion candidates.

"Catholics have a moral obligation not to vote for pro-abortion candidates. All persons have a common moral obligation to take ordinary, non-risky and non-burdensome actions to protect innocent human life. By refusing to vote for pro-abortion candidates, Catholics can partly fulfill this obligation, but by voting for these candidates, Catholics would be violating this duty.

"Determining if political candidates are pro-abortion or not can be difficult to practice, however, because candidates often camouflage their true beliefs about abortion. Abortion advocates hold that abortion is fully moral, legal, and unobjectionable. Others hold that they are 'personally opposed to abortion, but they do not want to impose their views on others.'

"The first category of abortion advocates simply cannot be supported by Catholics because they publicly and explicitly espouse the killing of the innocent. Good laws require that equal protection be given to the weak and the strong alike. This is one reason why absolute prohibitions of murder, rape, and torture are good laws. Absolute prohibitions of abortion are also good laws because they protect the weak and vulnerable unborn from those who could exploit them for their own interests.

"These abortion supporters cannot be endorsed for public office because a legitimate candidate for public office must support the principle that all are to be equally protected by the law. But these kinds of abortion supporters exclude the unborn from these protections and allow them to be exploited by the powerful, and this disqualifies them as legitimate representatives of the community. To vote for these pro-abortionists is to vote for those who unjustly disqualify others from the protections of the law, and that is an unjust vote.

"The second class is more difficult to judge because they, too, are abortion supporters, but of a much more subtle kind. To see that they do support abortion, ask yourself the following question: If a candidate for public office sought the support of pro-life voters by claiming that he or she was 'personally in favor of abortion, but did not want to impose those views on others,' would you consider such a candidate to be truly pro-life or something of a wolf in sheep's clothing?' This example shows that one who uses this 'personally opposed, but' argument is a milder form of pro-abortionist, but a supporter of abortion nonetheless. I do not believe that such candidates could be supported: they are probably more dangerous than explicit pro-abortionists because they are more cunning.

"Furthermore, candidates who invoke the 'personally opposed, but' argument should not be supported because they violate some of the basic tenets of our pluralist democracy. It has been a common principle of our public life that any serious individual should be free to express opinions on matters concerning the public good. However, those who use the 'personally opposed, but' argument do not believe that personal opinions on some issues can be freely expressed in the public forum. Whatever the reason for this attitude is, this attitude is dangerous because it is a subtle form of self-imposed censorship that is harmful to freedom of speech. If a person in America supports pro-abortion legislation, he or she should be free to speak about it because it is an issue of such importance.

"All public officials in our democracy are obliged by the Constitution to protect life, liberty, and the pursuit of happiness. To espouse abortion is to violate that obligation in a most serious manner, and whoever should espouse abortion would either explicitly or implicitly violate that Constitutional obligation. Thus, I believe that a vote for a pro-abortion candidate cannot be morally permitted."

Father Barry's points are very well taken. But perhaps, in conclusion, we might add a thought from the distinguished Catholic ethicist Germain Grisez. Commenting on the argument against "single-issue" voting based on candidates' views on abortion alone, Grisez agreed that "single-issue voting is irrational." But, he added, "The proper standards for evaluating candidates for public office are competence and character, [and] any individual seeking public office who supports the legality — much less the public funding — of abortion, manifests character which makes him or her unfit for public office. I will vote for such an individual only if the alternative is someone of equally bad character and in some other respect less suited for the office."

Moral dilemma

Q. As a pharmacist, I am called upon to dispense prescriptions written for birth-control pills and also to sell condoms as part of my duties. What is the Church's teaching on what my response should be on these matters?

A. The dilemma you describe is one shared by many committed Catholic professionals. For example, does a Catholic lawyer agree to take divorce cases? Does a Catholic doctor or nurse participate in abortions? Or does a Catholic politician vote in favor of abortion? As Archbishop McCarrick wrote in these pages some months back, sometimes a conflict between one's Catholic value system and one's career will occur, and the only way out may be to forego the career, in fidelity to one's Christian vocation.

In your situation, perhaps the problem can be worked out simply by asking the boss to have someone else deal with the areas which are problematic for you. I am presuming, of course, that you are only an employee. If you were the owner, you would presumably not be having the crisis because you wouldn't be allowing these items to be sold in your store to begin with.

Abortionists

Q. Why doesn't the Church excommunicate Catholics who make their livelihood by performing abortions (like doctors) or those who work for Planned Parenthood, or who promote abortion publicly?

A. The Church does not have to do this because they are already excommunicated, *ipso facto*, that is, the performance of the act automatically incurs the penalty. That presumes that such people know that the law of the Church threatens that sanction and yet they continue in that behavior. Occasionally, the Church does issue a formal decree of excommunication or make public an excommunication. A case in point was the instance in Rhode Island a few years back when a Catholic woman persisted in heading the state office of Planned Parenthood. Because of her obduracy and the grave scandal she caused, her state of excommunication was publicly noted by diocesan officials.

It should be remembered that the ultimate purpose of excommunication is to bring the erring person to his or her senses, so that a repudiation of the offense occurs, repentance takes place, and then reconciliation.

Excommunication

Q. Why is abortion a matter for excommunication, while killing a two-week-old baby is not?

A. All mortal sin effectively excommunicates someone, in that such a person cannot receive Holy Communion until he or she has confessed the sin and has resolved to avoid the sin in the future.

Certain actions, however, are so heinous that the Church shows her revulsion by making formal the excommunication. Abortion is one of those crimes. An excommunication for abortion can only take place, however, if the person knows of the penalty in advance and still goes through with the act.

Excommunication can be found in the New Testament in passages like Matthew 18:17 and 1 Corinthians 5:5. The Church regards the procedure as a deterrent to the performance of a particular action. Once the penalty is inflicted, the Church hopes the sinner will see the error of his ways, repent, and be reconciled with Christ and His Church.

Many laws protect a baby already born (at least at present), but no legal protection exists for the unborn for all nine months of his or her vulnerable life. The penalty of excommunication for abortion extends to the mother, all medical personnel, anyone who offers the mother moral or financial support to abort, as well as those who publicly campaign for legalized abortion. Incidentally, no formal notification of such excommunication is necessary, as it takes effect as soon as the action is performed.

Excommunications

Q. In discussing automatic excommunications in the 1983 Code of Canon Law, you mentioned violations of the seal of confession, absolution of an accomplice, and participation in or procurement of an abortion. Could you explain those in greater depth?

A. The first two deal with a priest and the Sacrament of Penance. A priest may never, under any circumstances, divulge anything to anyone of what he has learned about a penitent in the administration of the Sacrament of Penance; that restriction would also apply to a layperson, for example, if that individual had been used as a translator for the sacrament. The second matter is concerned with a priest's granting absolution to someone with whom the priest himself has committed a sin. As you can see, the sacrament would be reduced to a charade if this second situation could prevail. Regarding the abortion excommunications, since I have discussed these before, I shall only touch on them briefly now. Those who encourage someone to have an abortion, help pay for one, or participate in the procedure in any way (nurse, surgeon, anesthetist) — all are excommunicated. That presumes, of course, that they know the penalty in advance and still go through with their cooperation. The fourth involves the sins of apostasy, heresy, or schism.

Excommunication again

Q. I recently saw you on the "Larry King Show" with an ex-priest. You said he was excommunicated; he said he was not. The issue never seemed to get resolved. What is his actual status in the Church?

A. A television talk show is not the ideal forum in which to handle complex theological matters. In a sense, both of us were correct.

The 1983 Code of Canon Law limits automatic excommunication to four offenses: desecration of the Eucharist; laying violent hands on the pope; violation of the seal of confession or absolving an accomplice; participation in or procurement of an abortion. So to that degree the other party was speaking accurately.

However, when a man leaves the priesthood, fails to obtain a dispensation from celibacy, and subsequently attempts marriage, he is suspended from the priesthood and cannot receive the sacraments because of the objective state of sin in which he is living. This is similar to the case of the divorced and remarried and is, *in effect*, excommunication. That was my point. But technically, it is not *actual* excommunication.

His situation could be regularized in one of two ways. First, he could leave the woman with whom he is living and petition for reinstatement in the active ministry. Second, he could petition the Holy See for a decree of laicization which would return him officially to the lay state (all the while remaining a priest but barred from functioning as such, except in an emergency) and permit his marital union to be validated in a church ceremony. In addition, such a man would agree never to teach religion, administer a Catholic school, or exercise any liturgical role whatsoever (even that of lector or extraordinary minister of the Eucharist). These restrictions are not placed on the laicized priest to be vindictive but to safeguard the integrity of the Faith and the Sacrament of Holy Orders, for the good of the whole Church.

Papal confession

Q. Does the Pope go to confession and to whom?

A. Yes, he does — every week. The Pope has a regular confessor of his own choosing. Your question seems to suggest that simply because the Holy Father can exercise the charism of infallibility on certain occasions, he is also personally sinless; obviously, this is not so. He needs the Sacrament of Penance just as much as any other member of the Church, perhaps even more so due to the tremendous responsibilities he is required to bear.

Worthy reception

Q. I recently went to confession and was told by the priest that it was perfectly permissible to receive Holy Communion without having gone to the Sacrament of Penance. I was under the impression that one could not receive in the state of sin.

A. One must be in the state of grace before receiving Holy Communion, which means the absence of mortal sin, to put it negatively. Your priest was obviously referring to this when he said it is not necessary to go to confession before each reception of the Eucharist, and he was right. If, however, one is conscious of serious sin, then one must use the Sacrament of Penance.

Catholic guilt

Q. What do I tell my non-Catholic wife who criticizes the Church for being so guilt-oriented?

A. I'm not so sure what your wife means. On the surface, it sounds rather anti-Catholic.

Psychologists inform us that guilt is a rather neutral feeling; it can be good or bad, depending on the situation. For example, if a man kills his neighbor, he may feel guilty afterwards — and that is an appropriate reaction, especially if it leads him to repentance, along with a change of heart and behavior. On the other hand, some people see fault or sin under every rock, even when it isn't there at all. Such individuals are unhealthy psychologically and spiritually, requiring, in all likelihood, the assistance of both a psychologist and a priest.

The Church, who understood and practiced psychology long before Freud came on the scene, has always encouraged people to evaluate themselves and their actions in accord with the truth; that is, to face reality. If that picture is negative, guilt is the correct and necessary first step. If the picture is positive, the Church never fosters guilt. In fact, she calls such a negative evaluation by the pejorative name of scrupulosity, which is regarded as a vice and not a virtue.

Scrupulosity

Q. I write to express my strong disapproval of your disparaging remarks about scrupulosity in a recent issue of TCA. You don't seem to be sensitive to the tremendous problem people have with this. In fact, there is even an organization for such people, on which I am enclosing information.

A. I certainly did not intend to slight anyone who suffers from scrupulosity. My point was merely to note that overattention to the potential sinfulness of any and every human act is not an indication of holiness (as some presume) but rather an aberration. I still stand by that evaluation, without in any way condemning individuals who suffer from the affliction or attributing moral guilt to them.

I have read the literature you enclosed and would recommend the organization to those who think they might benefit; it is sponsored by the Redemptorist Fathers: Scrupulous Anonymous, Liguori, MO 63057.

Common sins

Q. What are the most common sins of our time?

A. Without sounding flippant, I would say the most serious sin of our day is the failure to recognize sin. So true is this that the psychologist Karl Menninger could write a book entitled *Whatever Became of Sin?*

Your question implies that each age has its own "favorite" sins, and I am inclined to agree with you. Modern man seems to have special problems related to the preservation of human dignity. Materialism and sexual excesses are clear examples of assaults on the human person. These often occur because of the prior modern difficulty of an inability or refusal to acknowledge one's creaturehood before God. If I truly saw myself as a finite creature, I would not be so prone to act like a lord in my acquisition of things and in my domination of other people.

However bad individual sins (or sinners) might be, when evil is regarded as evil, the remedy is near at hand. When one refuses even to admit the existence of a moral problem, the evil simply spreads.

Why this contemporary difficulty? I would venture to guess that it is due to a doctrinal position which wonders (or denies) if God can indeed forgive all sins of all people or, the flip side of the same coin, if God could ever punish anyone. The Catholic Faith responds affirmatively to both queries, which brings real balance in one's living of the Christian life.

The human race began in the state of original holiness and then experienced original sin, with innumerable personal sins following in its wake. A return to holiness is effected through the Sacraments of Baptism and Penance, which do not seek to catalogue sins, but to eliminate them.

The sinful self

Q. How often should I go to confession? As a convert, I find confession very difficult and unpleasant. Besides, I find myself committing the same sins over and over again.

A. Certain aspects of confession are unpleasant for anyone (convert or not), and they probably should be. An honest confrontation with the sinful self is difficult but necessary if genuine reform or conversion is to occur.

The frequency of confession is a personal need and decision. The law of the Church requires one to seek out sacramental forgiveness only if conscious of mortal sin; that is the minimum standard only. A devout person, however, will endeavor to grow in holiness, and this effort is assisted by the grace offered in the Sacrament of Penance and by the guidance of a spiritual Father.

Sacramental grace and good spiritual direction provide invaluable helps for a penitent to understand his or her behavior patterns and thus avoid situations which lead to temptation and sin. Most importantly, a believer must also be possessed of a spirit of confidence in the struggle against evil because he or she realizes that the power of Christ is equal and superior to any worldly allurement, "for there is One greater in you than there is in the world" (1 Jn 4:4).

Mortal and venial sin

Q. Does the Bible distinguish between mortal and venial sins?

A. Yes, it does. One clear example comes from the First Epistle of John: "If anyone sees his brother sinning, if the sin is not deadly [mortal], he should pray to God and he will give him life. This is only for those whose sin is not deadly. There is such a thing as deadly sin, about which I do not say that you should pray. All wrongdoing is sin, but there is sin that is not deadly" (5:16f). Because of passages like this one, the Church has traditionally distinguished between mortal and venial sins although certain Fundamentalist sects are rather loath to do so. The Church uses the distinction to help people see the degrees of seriousness to their actions and to assist them in living the Christian life, so that they will not be unduly burdened by sins that are not mortal and, at the same time, will not be insensitive to the detrimental effects of all sin — mortal and venial alike. Of course, mortal sin calls for sacramental confession and absolution, while venial sin can be forgiven in a variety of ways.

Does sin hurt God?

Q. I believe that we need to make reparation to God for our offenses. When I try to tell others that, I am countered with, "God is in heaven; He can't be hurt by our sins!" I am always at a loss for a good response.

A. Of course, God cannot be hurt by our offenses, in terms of His absolute state of perfection, which theologians speak of as God's intrinsic glory. However, His extrinsic glory is affected by our failures to lead lives worthy of our Christian calling. When people outside the Church see us sinning, they question not only our holiness and/or sincerity but also the whole meaning of life in the Church and, ultimately, the power of Christ to transform human lives.

At a more personal level, it is worthwhile to reflect on how a God of love can be wounded by our refusals to love. The most powerful lesson of God's vulnerability is found by gazing at a crucifix as we behold God, in Christ, literally loving us to death. Many spiritual writers down the centuries have noted that the psychological torment our Lord suffered on the cross (from the hatred of His persecutors and from what He knew would be man's consistently ungrateful response to His love revealed in His saving death) brought Him far greater pain than the physical agony.

4. SACRAMENTS

Disagreement

Q. I have just finished reading "Disputed Questions in the Liturgy Today" by John Huels. He seems to contradict almost every position you have ever taken in TCA. Who's right?

A. To summarize the author's positions briefly: (1) He argues for a return to the original order of the sacraments of initiation, such that they are celebrated as baptism, confirmation, Eucharist. (2) He holds that canon law does not really forbid lay preaching during the celebration of Mass. (3) He maintains that the ban on altar girls is not in force. (4) He takes a rather negative posture toward concelebration, particularly because it creates "male dominated liturgy." (5) He opposes Mass intentions because it gives "undue emphasis" to the particularity of that eucharistic celebration. (6) He calls for the elimination of "unnecessary Masses," that is, poorly attended ones. (7) He states that First Penance need not always precede First Holy Communion. (8) While acknowledging that canon law places the greatest restrictions on the use of general absolution, he still indicates that it may be employed in wider circumstances than normally considered valid. (9) Regarding the anointing of the sick, he thinks that since so many pastoral ministers encourage people to be anointed who are technically ineligible, the law should be changed. (10) He suggests that Mass not be celebrated for a mixed marriage, given the ban on intercommunion. (11) He does not imagine that the Holy See's letter on concerts in church was intended to inhibit sacred concerts, which sounds rather plausible.

I take the time to outline these positions because I have received a number of questions on this book from clergy and others who work with the liturgy. On the matters of lay preaching, female altar servers, First Confession, and general absolution, his positions are completely at variance with canon law and liturgical law. Having dealt with all of those topics in TCA over the past two years, I shall not repeat myself here.

On the age for confirmation and the correct order, I think the author espouses a reasonable proposal, namely, to return to the ancient usage, still in effect in the Churches of the East.

His negative attitude toward concelebration seems more dictated by radical feminist concerns than others. I have problems with the way concelebration usually occurs: lack of matching vestments for priests; poor placement of concelebrants, so that the congregation's view is obstructed; inability of priests to communicate at the proper time. It seems to me that having priests present in cassock and surplice and receiving Holy Communion if they wish offers a greater possibility for a dignified celebration of the eucharistic sacrifice. Certainly nothing in theology or law mandates that a priest concelebrate every time he participates in Mass and to suggest that he should is indeed excessively clericalistic.

The author's bias against Mass intentions appears to stem from lack of comfort with a strong emphasis on the sacrificial dimension of the Eucharist. His desire to eliminate poorly attended Masses only seems to reflect good common sense, unless such a Mass is genuinely needed for particular individuals (e.g., hospital workers at 6:30 A.M. on a Sunday).

To declare that abuses in pastoral practice should cause a change in those to be anointed is like saying that since many people cheat on their income taxes, the IRS should exempt everyone from payment.

I heartily agree that the older practice of not permitting a mixed marriage to take place during a Nuptial Mass is eminently sensible. Why start off a marriage with visible divisions, right at the altar?

As you can see, Father Huels and I disagree on some substantive issues, but not entirely. On some matters, we reach the same conclusions but for different reasons. In all honesty, however, I could not recommend the book for parish liturgical committees or the like because of the overriding tone which creates disrespect for liturgical norms, in my opinion.

Sacrament of the Sick

Q. Last week two priests were here at our nursing home for a Mass of anointing. The first said that only baptized Catholics could be anointed while the other said that even a Jew could receive the Sacrament of the Sick and pray for healing. Who was right?

A. Way back in grammar school, we were all taught that baptism is important not only because it takes away original sin but also because it provides us with access to the other sacraments. In other words, an unbaptized person cannot receive the Sacrament of the Sick. While a priest might surely pray for the physical well-being of any human being and might confer a blessing on that person, he cannot anoint such a person since he or she is incapable of receiving the sacrament.

What about non-Catholic Christians who express a desire to be anointed? While it is true that they are baptized and hence incorporated into the Body of Christ — even if imperfectly — still they are not in full communion with the Church and should not be treated as though they are. In emergency situations or in times of persecution, that norm can be mitigated. For example, if an Eastern Orthodox Christian were in danger of death and did not have access to one of his own priests, I would not hesitate to hear that person's confession, anoint him for death. That, however, does not appear to be the situation you have described.

Deacons

Q. We have a lay deacon in our parish who, for some time, has distributed Holy Communion. Now he gives the Sunday homily while the priest just sits there. Someone said the deacon also officiated at a wedding recently. Is all this permissible? Many people find this hard to take. My husband says if this man can do all this legitimately, he wants "equal time."

A. First of all, there is no such thing as a "lay deacon." All deacons are members of the clergy; some are "transitional" deacons who will become priests, while others are "permanent" deacons. The latter may be married men who study for a prescribed period of time and, upon ordination, generally maintain their secular occupations and so serve the Church in a part-time capacity.

Deacons — whether transitional or permanent — may proclaim the Gospel at Mass, distribute Holy Communion, officiate at baptisms and weddings, as well as at Benediction of the Blessed Sacrament. Transitional deacons may also preach; permanent deacons usually require a special mandate or certification from the bishop since their theological education is not equivalent to that of men preparing for the priesthood, and their grasp of theology must be carefully determined before allowing them to preach.

If your pastor "just sits there" week in and week out — never preaching himself — I would question that; after all, preaching is a serious pastoral responsibility. Strictly speaking, however, nothing you describe is illicit. To get "equal time," your husband would have to go through a diaconal formation program and be ordained.

The basic problem in so much of this, however, is that in recent years there has been a confusion of roles and ministries in the Church, what Pope John Paul II has referred to as "the laicization of the clergy and clericalization of the laity." A healthy spirituality of the layperson's vocation is needed, emphasizing the place of the layperson as a witness to Christ and His Church in the world, with the focus of priests on the preaching of the Word and the administration of the sacraments. This "division of labor" would go a long way toward fostering a sense of unity and complementarity, and likewise eliminate attitudes of competition and divisiveness.

Sacramental administration

Q. *Which sacraments are deacons permitted to administer?*

A. Deacons serve as ordinary ministers of the Holy Eucharist and baptism. They may also witness marriages and preach in a liturgical setting. They may not grant absolution or anoint the sick — nor, of course, celebrate Mass.

It is worth noting that, liturgically and sacramentally speaking, any baptized Catholic can perform most of the same functions with appropriate episcopal delegation. This highlights the "bridge" aspect of the diaconal ministry but also raises other questions about the specificity of the diaconate.

Reconciliation

Q. When my daughter married outside the Church two years ago, neither my wife nor I attended the ceremony. I explained to her our reasons and her own status. What I said then was that her action excommunicated her, made her ineligible to receive the sacraments, rendered her incapable of standing in as a sponsor for baptism or confirmation, and required absolution from a bishop for her reconciliation. We have established some contact with her and her husband, and perhaps now is the time to try to bring her back to the Church. Any suggestions? Did I accurately describe her situation?

A. Your standing on principle is surely admirable, as is your desire to have your daughter fully reconciled with the Church. However, you did make two errors. First, marriage outside the Church does not constitute a formal excommunication. In many ways the practical effects are the very same, but the penalty as such is not invoked. Second, to be reconciled, she need only go to confession to any priest, who will undoubtedly launch her on the road to have her marriage recognized by the Church.

As you can see, the process is really quite simple.

Absolution formulas

Q. Is it permissible for a priest to ad-lib the words of absolution at the end of confession, instead of using the usual formula?

A. When you say the priest uses something other than the "usual formula," I must question the validity of the action. Surely the words, "I absolve you from your sins, in the name of the Father, and of the Son, and of the Holy Spirit" must be used. If he says words in addition to the formula, that would be a different story.

It never ceases to amaze me how so many priests arrogate to themselves the right to change the prayers which belong to the whole Church, usually under the guise of making the rites more "meaningful" to the people. I always like to remind these men that Richard Burton became recognized as a great actor not by changing the words of Shakespeare's plays but by bringing a life and dynamism to them which made them come alive. That is the function of a celebrant, too. Tampering with sacramental formulas is foolish, prideful, and dangerous.

First Confession

Q. Please explain why children are receiving First Holy Communion before their First Confession.

A. In the late 1960s and early 1970s, some catechists argued that children were not ready for their First Confession at the age of seven; some went so far as to say that confession traumatized children. Neither contention was ever supported by scientific data. However, the Holy See allowed experimentation along these lines to go on for several years and then mandated a return to the traditional order of the sacraments.

Having prepared hundreds of children for the sacraments, I can say with certainty that children who are properly catechized do indeed know the meaning of sin and forgiveness, including the personal experience of these. Frankly, if they cannot understand the very natural and human reality of sin, how can they understand the supernatural reality of the Eucharist? Nor have I ever come upon a child "traumatized" by confession at any early age. I have, however, seen teenagers quite disturbed by making their First Confessions when they had just committed extremely serious (even mortal) sins. Psychologically speaking, it is far better to introduce children to the Sacrament of Penance when they have no significant personal sins, thus giving them the necessary confidence and feeling of "comfortableness" in approaching the merciful Lord, as well as developing in them the habit of using the sacrament frequently for personal direction and the increase of grace.

General absolution

Q. I'm so confused. One parish near me has offered general absolution at least twice a year; my own pastor says it's forbidden. Who is right?

A. Your pastor is, but let me explain in some detail. General absolution arose out of a misunderstanding or misapplication of the norms for communal penance services. Some assumed that simply because a large crowd appeared for the Sacrament of Penance and an insufficient number of priests were available, the conditions prevailed for the granting of general absolution without private confession of sins (as has always been done in combat situations).

This view was wrong on two scores. First, if general absolution is granted, the congregation must be told that the absolution is valid only if all mortal sins are confessed within the year, and further that another general absolution may not be sought out until private confession has taken place. Second, general absolution was never envisioned as a normal alternative to private confession and, in fact, was intended to be most exceptional, involving extreme circumstances wherein penitents would have grave spiritual need without access to the sacrament for a prolonged period of time. Such a situation is barely imaginable in the United States. Canon 961 of the Code of Canon Law and recent statements by Cardinal Joseph Ratzinger of the Sacred Congregation for the Doctrine of the Faith lend their weight to the position I have just outlined.

Why did general absolution become so prevalent in some places? The desire to eliminate auricular confession by various liturgists and theologians, and the inclination of some people to take the easiest way out, all combined to make this option so popular. For centuries Protestants have accused Catholics of seeking "cheap grace"; the swiftness with which some Catholics responded to this deformation of penance gave an ironic credibility to the Protestant charge.

A friend of mine, whose parish had advertised general absolution services for years, tells me that they used to attract upward of a thousand people. This year it was announced that the penance service would have no general absolution but only private confession. Thirty-five people showed up. What does that say about the parish's maturity in faith and about what the clergy there allowed or encouraged to happen?

It's strange that in an era when the cult of the individual is so strong, the Church should do away with one of its strongest signs of commitment of personalism and replace it with the anonymity of the crowd. Throughout Lent, Pope John Paul II stressed repeatedly that *the availability of private confession is a sign of Christ's love for each one of us as individuals,* sacramentalized in the one-to-one encounter between priest and penitent. This revolutionary good news, so desperately needed today, is only obscured and confused by contraindications such as the improper use of general absolution.

Confession

Q. I used to go to confession once a month, but now with having to go face-to-face, I am embarrassed. My priest says I shouldn't be. Will we ever return to the old rite?

A. Your question has me puzzled because you seem to indicate that in your parish church the penitent has no option to receive the Sacrament of Penance anonymously. If that is so, this is in complete violation of canon law: It is the right of every Catholic — not the priest — to decide on confession anonymously. If your parish does not have provision for this possibility, your pastor should be approached and apprised of the problem and your desire (legitimate) to have the situation changed. Refusal to do so should be reported to diocesan officials, as this is a most serious matter, affecting people's rights and spiritual welfare in no small way.

By the way, the differences between the old and new rites for the Sacrament of Penance have nothing to do with confessing face-to-face or behind the screen; those options have always existed.

Public baptism

Q. We just had a public baptism in our church. Everyone involved was in some kind of irregular situation, as far as the Church is concerned. Is this proper? I'm not trying to be judgmental; I'm just confused.

A. Church law indicates that baptizing an infant presumes the child will be brought up in the practice of the Faith. From what you describe (in some detail in your original letter), this was all rather lacking in the present case. While I think we need to be compassionate and certainly never give the impression of "punishing the baby" for the sins of the adults, pastoral prudence and a reverence for the sacraments requires a priest to address such situations very carefully. Minimally, the ceremony should not have been public, especially since you say "everyone" knew of all the difficulties. Furthermore, the event should have been used (and maybe was, but unbeknownst to the congregation) as a "teachable moment," in which the principal parties were invited to regularize their relationships with the Church.

Infant baptism

Q. Catholic priests refuse to baptize infants unless the parents make solemn promises they are not sure they can keep. Why should innocent babies be thus penalized and remain "guilty" of original sin?

A. Priests do not refuse to baptize babies; they may, for good pastoral reasons, delay baptism until the proper conditions are in place. To administer any sacrament, faith is required — either the faith of the individual recipient or, as in the case of infant baptism, a "borrowed faith" (that of the parents). In the baptismal liturgy, the parents are asked if they intend to raise the child as a Catholic; they promise to do that. If they "are not sure," they have no right to promise to do so. If they are reasonably certain they will not (based on their own pattern of Catholic practice), they commit sacrilege to make their pledge.

Logically, why would any parents present their child for incorporation into the Church if they find that life burdensome themselves? Removal of original sin is indeed an important aspect of this sacrament, but the idea of membership in the Church is equally important and inseparable from the first: One is freed from the clutches of the Devil only to be embraced by Christ's Church. A lack of interest in that dimension bespeaks a lack of understanding of the full meaning of baptism. What is needed, then, is for the parents to obtain better information or to engage in the necessary conversion process, so that their lives may be models for their infant's growth in faith.

One final note: Who is penalizing the child — the Church or the parents? A calm and reasoned analysis should uncover the correct answer.

RCIA

Q. My husband is a Lutheran and wishes to become a Catholic. Our parish priest says he must go through the RCIA program, but my husband's work schedule does not allow him to participate in the classes. The pastor says he should wait until his schedule changes. What do you say?

A. RCIA stands for "Rite for the Christian Initiation of Adults," a restored series of ceremonies to bring converts into the Church. The whole process is really quite beautiful and has the wonderful effect of introducing candidates to the entire parish community and thus involving everyone in a person's entrance into the Church, at least to some degree.

I am somewhat surprised, however, that your husband is being put off because his work schedule does not allow him to attend the RCIA classes.

Surprised for two reasons: first, the RCIA is mandatory only for those who are not baptized and is entirely optional for those who are coming into full communion with the Catholic Church from some denomination which has valid baptism (which the Lutherans do); second, I would suppose that any priest would be so delighted at the prospect of a new Catholic, that he would go out of his way to facilitate the process.

My advice is to seek out another priest. If nothing positive results, contact the diocesan office. I cannot imagine that your bishop would place participation in an optional rite above a person's salvation.

Original baptism

Q. If a baby is in danger of death, I know that any doctor or nurse can baptize. If the baby gets well, can he be baptized in church by the parish priest, or is the original baptism good enough?

A. You are correct that anyone may baptize in danger of death, but "rebaptism" is not only unnecessary but sacrilegious. You will recall from your study of the catechism that three sacraments (baptism, confirmation, holy orders) imprint what is referred to as an indelible mark; that is, they confer a permanent character on the recipient, marking him or her for life.

When the child leaves the hospital, God willing, the parents may arrange with their parish priest for what is called "supplying of ceremonies." It is a public celebration in which all the rites not performed in the emergency baptism are now done (e.g., the anointings, the clothing with the white garment, etc.). This gives family and friends, as well as the parish community, an opportunity to share in the joy of this new life brought into Christ's Church.

Godparents

Q. Can a non-Catholic be a godparent for a Catholic?

A. No, for obvious reasons, namely, that someone who does not share our Faith cannot promise to provide the candidate with an example to follow. For social reasons, a non-Catholic may serve as a Christian witness to a baptism, but his name is not entered into the baptismal register, or onto the certificate; nor should the impression be created that he is indeed a godparent. In that instance, at least one Catholic party (of either sex) must serve as a sponsor.

Lay people

Q. Under what circumstances is it permissible for lay people to lead eucharistic prayer services, held in lieu of Mass?

A. The Holy See has just released a document on this very topic, with mission lands in mind, for the most part.

The format would be the regular Liturgy of the Word, followed by the Lord's Prayer, the rest of the Communion Rite and a Post-Communion

Prayer. The person presiding could be a deacon or extraordinary minister of the Eucharist. This option should not be used hastily since genuine spiritual need should exist. Furthermore, the document notes that this service cannot be used in a place where Sunday Mass is celebrated at least once. In other words, it must truly be a "priestless" place.

While it is certainly true that being deprived of the Eucharist is undesirable, it is equally true that Catholics should never become accustomed to the reception of the Eucharist apart from the priestly ministry or apart from the celebration of the Mass. Otherwise, we are moving toward an ecclesiology and sacramentology which fails to link Eucharist and priesthood, which is, of course, precisely what our Lord did on Holy Thursday night by instituting both sacraments together.

Female ministers

Q. How does our Holy Father feel about female eucharistic ministers? It makes me very uncomfortable to approach one, even though I am a woman myself.

A. All too often people's complaints about extraordinary ministers of Holy Communion sound as though the issue is the sex of the individual, and that is not the point in terms of theology or church law. The Holy Father is most concerned that this permission is improperly used in the United States, indeed that it is grossly abused. This is such a major crisis that Cardinal Martinez-Somalo, prefect of the Congregations for the Sacraments and Divine Worship, made specific reference to this in his address to the American archbishops in Rome for the synod between the Holy Father and his Curia and the representatives of the American hierarchy. Pope John Paul also alluded to this problem in his apostolic exhortation *Christifideles Laici.*

We have all witnessed situations in which priests sit in the rectory having coffee on Sunday mornings while lay people distribute Holy Communion or where the option of both species is employed specifically to justify the use of laity as extraordinary ministers of Holy Communion. The adjective "extraordinary" sets the tone — they are to be used in extraordinary circumstances and having them every week or even every day hardly sounds extraordinary.

My judgment against the practice has nothing to do with the sex of the person and everything to do with what ordination means and what the Eucharist demands.

Lay ministers

Q. Since your magazine began publication, you have addressed several questions regarding lay ministers of the Eucharist. I am bothered by the fact that you constantly refer to them as "extraordinary ministers." This term is no longer appropriate. In August 1978, it was reported that the Congregation for Divine Worship approved a provisional translation of a

"Rite of Commissioning Special Ministers of Holy Communion." Note was made of the fact that such ministers should be called "special" instead of extraordinary. This change in terminology underscores an important point: "Extraordinary" seems to indicate what is beyond the usual or ordinary. On the contrary, it appears that the Roman Congregation does permit such special ministers to function under ordinary conditions, and thus it is perfectly licit for such special ministers to distribute Holy Communion on a regular basis in many parishes throughout the United States.

***Q.** Your answers to questions on extraordinary ministers of the Eucharist are always so negative. Wouldn't a positive response be better? These people are just trying to do their job and help the priest; they don't want to replace him and would be delighted if enough ordinary ministers existed to serve the parish.*

A. The proper translation of "*minister extraordinarius*" is, obviously, "extraordinary minister." Some American liturgists did not like the sound of that because, as I have argued repeatedly, "extraordinary" sounds so extraordinary. Therefore, they sought to change the adjective to "special," but that switch was never approved. As a matter of fact, should any doubt exist, the official English translation of the revised Code of Canon Law says plainly: "The extraordinary minister of Holy Communion is an acolyte or other member of the Christian faithful deputed in accord with Can. 230.3" (Canon 911.2).

Furthermore, in all the documents from Rome, in all the papal addresses and in the speech of Cardinal Martinez-Somalo (prefect of the Congregations for the Sacraments and Divine Worship) to the American archbishops last fall (1989), the word consistently and exclusively used is "extraordinary." Words do have meaning, and that is why that word is retained. The Holy See views the use of extraordinary ministers as an unusual occurrence, resulting from emergency situations; thus it regards the present American scene as anomalous at best and aberrant at worst. I could not state the case any stronger. Until we get our act together on this one, we will continue to witness confusion on the uniqueness and sacredness of both the priestly and lay vocations, as well as the meaning of the Eucharist.

As far as being "negative" toward this phenomenon, I don't know how it is possible to applaud something so blatantly wrong and in violation of all liturgical norms, and done on so grand a scale in our country. In general, I do not think most extraordinary ministers are to blame personally; rather, they have been sold a bill of goods by their priests who, for a variety of reasons, wish to pass off this unique aspect of their ministry to the unordained. Frankly, I suspect we have dealt with this topic enough over the past two years, and I would prefer to declare a moratorium on it. What I have said to this point faithfully reflects Church teaching and discipline. Any person of good will can readily perceive that; those of bad will shall not accept it, regardless of how often the case is argued.

Eucharistic ministers

Q. Last year we received a wonderful newly ordained priest. He asked to leave, however, because he could not tolerate all the lay eucharistic ministers (he was forbidden to distribute Communion, except at the Masses he celebrated). He said if his next parish is the same, he may just as well leave the priesthood. I feel so bad for this young man. What is happening to cause such problems?

A. So many people have asked about extraordinary ministers of the Eucharist that I want to devote more space than usual to a topic which is apparently of great concern to a broad cross-section of our readers.

When may a non-ordained person distribute Holy Communion? According to *Immensae Caritatis* (Pope Paul VI's decree permitting this practice) and the revised Code of Canon Law, only under the following clearly defined circumstances: the lack of an ordinary minister of the Eucharist (priest, deacon, or acolyte); the inability of an ordinary minister to function because of ill health or advanced age; an unwieldy number of communicants with an insufficient number of ordinary ministers.

It is clear that *Immensae Caritatis* had behind it good intentions, but the lived reality in the United States has had negative consequences. This is one of the most serious problems to emerge in the postconciliar Church in America, since it touches on the very heart of Catholic Faith and practice ("the source and summit of the Christian life," as Vatican II refers to the liturgy) in a most visible way, affecting every Catholic.

How? First, several items in brief — some sad, others merely strange. For example, in some parishes, the sick now receive the ministrations of a priest (especially the Sacrament of Penance) only irregularly, if at all, forcing them to feel abandoned and marginalized from the mainstream of Church life.

Another example: Although the number of communicants probably peaked around 1968, no complaints were heard about "long" Communion lines. Yet some liturgists argue the necessity of having lay people as ministers of Holy Communion by suggesting that the distribution of Communion should not exceed seven minutes. The height of irony is reached, however, when some celebrants sit for a meditation period of roughly that length *after* Communion.

In some parishes it has become routine to have lay people assist with Communion, regardless of the number of communicants or available clergy, even for small daily Mass congregations. Because of the extensive use of extraordinary ministers, many parishioners see their priests only when they are celebrants at Mass. This means that priests are absent from their people at the peak moments of parish life. On the other hand, in not a few parishes priests are available to greet the people before and after Sunday liturgy — but are not available for Communion.

The improper use of extraordinary ministers of the Eucharist is, of course, a violation of correct liturgical procedure. However, two other serious problems also present themselves: a lost sense of the sacred and a distorted view of the lay apostolate.

We must have a deep sense of the sacred. The making of distinctions contributes to that sense: What we wear to the beach is inappropriate for church; the rock music of the radio is out of place in a worship service. Were we not to distinguish in this way, all of life would be a plateau, with no mountains and no valleys.

By permitting nearly anyone at all to distribute the Eucharist, we are communicating a message at the symbolic level that this action is really not all that special. What is anyone's responsibility is no one's responsibility. Surely that is what young boys mean when they say they are not interested in the priesthood because "anybody can do what you guys do."

The usual reason given for the use of extraordinary ministers of the Eucharist (namely, time constraints) fosters the American "in and out" mentality of Sunday Mass. The effect is to blur distinctions of any kind in the Church, forgetting that such distinctions are natural to the human person. This approach, though almost always innocent, nonetheless culminates in a desacralization of the Church, the Eucharist, and the priesthood. We have already seen strong indications of this development, and that is why Pope John Paul II criticized the abuse of the permission for extraordinary ministers as "reprehensible." Interestingly enough, the desacralization of religion does not increase our appreciation of life in general; rather, it vulgarizes both.

One final area of concern revolves around the significance of the lay apostolate. It never ceases to amaze me as a priest that when I invite people to become active in the work of the Church, almost invariably they volunteer for liturgical ministries. This demonstrates that Vatican II is still not fully understood. The whole point of the council's theology of the laity was that the laity had their own unique role to play in bringing the Gospel to contemporary humanity — *in the world, not in the sanctuary.*

The Church operates, at the sociological level, on the principle of a "division of labor." Theologically, this is referred to as a "diversity of roles and ministries." St. Paul expressed this in his analogy to the human body (1 Cor 12:12-22). Of course, all members are equal, but not all have the same function. Equality is not sameness. To reduce the living out of one's baptismal commitment to a sacramental ministry is to mistake the part for the whole. It also involves serious role confusion. The role of the priest is to preach and administer the sacraments, so that the laity can be faithful witnesses in the world, thus inviting people there to follow Christ.

In terms of lay participation in the liturgy, a diversity of roles also exists. To suggest that full liturgical participation requires lay ministers of the Eucharist is to misunderstand this point. To be present and to take an active part in the singing and praying is full participation; anything else is a strange form of anticlericalism, which is really very clericalistic at root. In his bicentennial message to the United States, Pope Paul VI reminded us that the role of extraordinary ministers is not "the ordinary expression of lay participation."

Baptism makes us one — not the act of gaining access to a ciborium. In some dioceses, pastors have been forced to use these ministers as a sign of their acceptance of Vatican II or "the priesthood of the faithful." Yet, ironically, all the arguments brought forth to justify this practice actually diminish the noble calling of Christian laypersons, and suggest that the only real Catholics are priests, or at least people who do "priestly" things.

Please note that we are not concerned with heresy here but with an imprudent, unwise liturgical practice, reflective of bad sociology. Like other Americanisms in the Church, this one fails to take a holistic view of reality, neglects long-range implications, and does not take seriously the nonverbal, symbolic power of liturgical communication.

The only solution to this pastoral problem is for bishops and laity alike to insist that *Immensae Caritatis* be carefully followed. The decree itself reminds clergy of their important obligations here:

"Since these faculties are granted only for the spiritual good of the faithful and for cases of genuine necessity, priests are to remember that they are not thereby excused from the task of distributing the Eucharist to the faithful who legitimately request it."

The correct interpretation of this decree will result in an increased reverence for the Eucharist, as well as an increased reverence for the apostolate of the laity.

More on lay ministers

Q. Why does our parish send lay ministers to give Communion to the shut-ins, especially since we have three priests? Doesn't it dawn on them that these people might want to go to confession? Furthermore, why are they called "extraordinary" when they're there more than the priests?

A. I hate to belabor the point about extraordinary ministers of Holy Communion, but my mail (with easily one hundred questions about this matter every month) indicates this is a major liturgical problem in the U.S. Cardinal Martinez-Somalo of the Congregations for the Sacraments and Divine Worship said the same thing to the American archbishops when they went to Rome in the fall of 1989.

Surely priests cannot excuse themselves from bringing the Eucharist to the homebound, and if they do use extraordinary ministers, it must be done in such a way that these people do have the opportunity to receive the Sacrament of Penance on a regular basis. Unfortunately, my experience leads me to conclude that this is not the norm.

Eucharistic ministers again

Q. Who has the right to decide on who becomes a eucharistic minister? Let me offer some examples of why I am concerned: (1) One Sunday a eucharistic minister went to the tabernacle before Mass, brought the ciborium into the sacristy, and started filling up an empty ciborium to be used in the Offertory procession of the next Mass. When the pastor was told that she was using already consecrated hosts, he replied that the questioner was "too concerned about little things." (2) On another occasion a parishioner walked into the sacristy and found a eucharistic minister pouring the Precious Blood down the regular sink (we don't have a sacrarium). When confronted with this, the woman said, "Oh, it's just wine, and I don't like wine!" (3) I know of divorced/remarried who function as eucharistic ministers. Is this permissible?

A. First of all, we should get our language straight. The Church refers to the people who exercise the ministry you describe as *extraordinary* ministers of Holy Communion. They are so called because they are to function only in extraordinary circumstances; they distribute Holy Communion and are not ministers of the Eucharist (only priests are, in that they confect or bring about the Eucharistic Presence).

All that having been said, what you discuss are veritable horror stories. And we wonder why people lose their Faith in the Real Presence and even leave the Church!

Those chosen for this extraordinary ministry should be extraordinary people, in terms of their knowledge of the Catholic Faith, their acceptance of Catholic doctrine, and their living of the Catholic life. The first example you cite demonstrates abysmal ignorance; the second, a lack of faith; the third, a failure to live up to Catholic morality.

One final note: Whether or not a church has a sacrarium (that is, a special sink in the sacristy with a pipe going directly into the ground rather than the sewer system), the Precious Blood may not be poured down any sink, nor may It be reserved in the tabernacle (even from one Mass to the next on a Sunday, for example); It must be consumed immediately after Communion or at least right after the conclusion of the Mass.

Communion lines

Q. I have been away from the Church for a long period of time. When I last went regularly, fewer than twenty percent of the congregation received Holy Communion; now it seems that everyone does. What brought about this change?

A. At times one rejoices at the more frequent reception of Holy Communion; at other times, it is a cause for depression. Let me explain.

Prior to the time of Pope Pius XII, the Communion fast was from midnight, and that made it very difficult for many people to receive often, especially at the later Masses on a Sunday. The fast was mitigated by Pius

XII to three hours and then by Pope Paul VI to one hour. Following upon the leads of Pope Pius X and the other popes of this century, priests began to encourage frequent Communion, all well and good.

While all that was occurring, a reduced sense of sin was creeping in the back door, so that the long confession lines began to disappear, to be replaced by long Communion lines. As you note, it is not unusual now to find ninety-five percent of a congregation coming forward at Communion time, while an average parish priest will have heard five to ten confessions on Saturday night. Let one example serve. If the polls are correct, eighty percent of American Catholics of childbearing age practice artificial birth control, and only the smallest minority of them confess it as a sin; there is one huge category of people who are making unworthy Communions, objectively speaking. All kinds of other sins could be mentioned as well.

At any rate, I hope that we can reach a stage of equilibrium between the dozen or so communicants of former days and the "pew emptying" syndrome of the past fifteen years. Acknowledgment of sin, sorrow for it, a firm purpose of amendment, and reception of the Eucharist all go together; separated from one another, we have a defective sacramental theology and practice.

Receiving Communion

Q. Recently a visiting priest celebrated Sunday Mass. With the extraordinary ministers of Holy Communion standing around the altar, he distributed Communion to them before taking it himself. He then received only after the entire congregation.

Q. I have been asked to serve as an extraordinary minister of Holy Communion in my parish. I really don't understand why we need them since we have three full-time priests and an extra one on the weekends. Are all these people giving out Communion to get things over more quickly?

A. I have written on this issue on several occasions, but it keeps popping up, leading me to conclude that this is an area of major liturgical abuse in the United States. Certainly the Holy Father must think so since he specifically addressed this topic in one of the *ad limina* visit talks to the American bishops.

On the first matter, the General Instruction of the Roman Missal indicates that the hierarchical structure of the Church is to be visible in the reception of Holy Communion. That means that the celebrant (or concelebrants) communicates first; he then gives Communion to the deacon (the deacon does not take it but receives it, like any other communicant); next would come any others exercising a particular liturgical function; finally, the congregation.

The second example seems to reflect a desire to have extraordinary ministers of Holy Communion just for the sake of having them. This flies in the face of *Immensae Caritatis* (the document which first permitted this practice), the Code of Canon Law, and the clear statements of Pope Paul VI and Pope John Paul II. These individuals are called "extraordinary" for the very reason that they are to be used only in extraordinary circumstances. My mail suggests that this is not the usual procedure in most American parishes, which is why the Holy Father has asked bishops to tighten up their local norms, to make them coincide with universal law.

Proper Communion?

Q. At my brother's funeral recently, all nineteen of his children and grandchildren were present. Only one daughter and her children go to church regularly; however, at Communion everyone went up to receive. Is this permitted now?

A. No, it's not. Unfortunately, it is all too common an occurrence, so much so that the American bishops have directed that missalettes carry the notification that Holy Communion may be received only by Catholics *in the state of grace.*

It is understandable that family members would want to receive Holy Communion at a relative's funeral, but sacrilegious Communions do no one any good. A helpful pastoral practice employed by many priests is offering people the opportunity to go to confession at the funeral home the night before, as well as reminding them at that time about having the proper disposition for Holy Communion.

Communion in hand

Q. During the Pope's visit to the states this fall [1987], I noticed several people approach him for Communion with their hands held out. I had read that the Pope disapproves of Communion in the hand and won't engage in the practice. What is the rationale for it, anyway?

A. Pope John Paul II frowns on the practice of Communion in the hand for a variety of reasons, not least of which is that universal liturgical law forbids it. He has done it himself on occasion to avoid controversy at the altar, but has made clear to national hierarchies where he visits his desire for people receiving Holy Communion from him to receive on the tongue.

A little history would be helpful here. For the first few centuries, Holy Communion was received in the hand. As eucharistic doctrine developed and as eucharistic abuses increased (using the sacred host for magical or satanic rites, for example), the Church gradually withdrew the option, so that already in eighth-century Spain Communion on the tongue was mandated, and by the early Middle Ages that was the case for the whole Church — as is still the case in all the churches of the East, both Catholic and Orthodox.

During the Protestant Reformation, Communion in the hand came to the fore again as a way of asserting the priesthood of the laity and at the same time of denying the Real Presence of Christ in the Eucharist. For these reasons, the Church held firm in requiring Communion on the tongue.

In modern times, some countries (like Holland, France, and Canada) had begun to experiment with Communion in the hand. In the 1969 document *Memoriale Domini*, Pope Paul VI outlined all the reasons why Communion in the hand was inadvisable and why the traditional method was to be preferred and maintained. However, he did indicate that in countries where the contrary practice had begun illicitly, the hierarchy by a two-thirds vote could petition the Holy See for permission to have Communion in the hand.

The illicit practice of Communion in the hand had never been widespread in the United States, and the American bishops had consistently voted against the option. Therefore, it was quite surprising when a bare majority of bishops voted for it and subsequently received authorization to introduce the practice in this country in 1977. Most countries of the world do not permit Communion in the hand; a visitor, then, would have to follow local custom.

A priest must have moral certitude that a communicant will not profane the sacred species if he or she takes Communion in the hand. Furthermore, if a priest chooses to distribute Holy Communion by intinction (dipping the Host into the chalice), Communion in the hand is not permissible.

Altering Mass

Q. In our new parish we are constantly upset by liturgical problems. For example, often the priest just sits for Communion and allows lay people to distribute the Eucharist. Our daughter was told in school that genuflection is no longer practiced and that she had to receive Communion in the hand or else no one would give her Communion. Are we wrong to be so upset?

A. You are quite correct in being disturbed. Your rights as Catholics are being violated. The Code of Canon Law states that Christ's faithful have a right to be instructed in the Faith of the Church and to have the rites celebrated for them according to the mind of the Church. If you have accurately described everything, each is an instance of a serious abuse.

Pope John Paul II has repeatedly spoken out strongly against the practice of having lay people distribute Holy Communion unnecessarily. He has specifically said that priests who fail to minister the Eucharist themselves exhibit a "reprehensible attitude." The Pontifical Commission for the Authentic Interpretation of the Code of Canon Law recently reminded all that lay people are never to serve as extraordinary ministers of the Eucharist when sufficient priests and deacons are available; that does not mean simply as celebrants of the Mass, but just available.

On the second matter, the liturgical books are quite clear about the importance of a genuflection to express adoration of the eucharistic Christ. A bow does not fulfill those requirements, regardless of how devout or profound it is.

In the third case, your daughter has every right to decide to receive Holy Communion in the traditional manner, and no pressure should be exerted on her by anyone to do otherwise. The Holy Father has spoken emphatically on that score as well.

If I were you, I would have a serious talk with the priest(s) in question. If changes are not effected immediately, I would write to the bishop, asking him to vindicate your rights as members of Christ's Church. This kind of nonsense should not be endured for the sake of peace or under any other pretext. Furthermore, if you are confused and agitated, chances are that many other people are as well.

A disturbing silence

Q. What do you think about a priest who does not say "Body of Christ" or anything else when distributing Communion? Should I still say "Amen"?

A. A priest's regular omission of the Communion formula is baffling, to say the least, leaving people to speculate about the reasons behind what is obviously a rather deliberate act. Talk to him about it, indicating that his refusal to use his part of the formula inhibits you from making the profession of faith in Christ's Real Presence which is both your right and your obligation. Saying "Amen" to nothing seems pointless, except as a way of reminding the priest of what he should have said.

Kneel or stand?

Q. I have read that in certain places the bishop will not allow the faithful to kneel for Holy Communion. Don't the laity have the right to decide this for themselves?

A. In the first several centuries, Holy Communion was received by the faithful in the standing position, signifying the risen life of those who received the Risen Christ. As personal devotion increased, kneeling became much more common. The Church of the East has generally maintained the tradition of standing. Therefore, legitimate claims can be made for either posture. At the time of the liturgical movement in this century (just prior to and immediately following Vatican II), standing once again came into favor. Although liturgical law permits either posture, the General Instruction of the Roman Missal indicates that if the faithful stand to communicate, they must genuflect before receiving. I must say that I have seen this done in only two parishes in fifteen years.

The decision to stand or kneel for Holy Communion rests totally with the communicant, and no one can be forced to stand as a condition to receive the Blessed Sacrament. Pope John Paul II has specifically addressed this matter in *Inaestimabile Donum*, in which he spoke forcefully against several eucharistic abuses.

Frequent reception

Q. I recall that before the Second Vatican Council a priest could receive Holy Communion at one Mass each day and, when saying several Masses, he received only at the last Mass said. Do I remember correctly?

A. No, you don't.

The celebrant of a Mass must always receive Holy Communion; otherwise, the sacrifice is incomplete. What you are confused about is that in the preconciliar liturgy, a priest who was binating (the technical term for offering two Masses in one day) would not take the second ablution of water and wine after Communion. He did, however, always receive Holy Communion.

While on the subject of priests and multiple Masses, it should be noted that a priest should never celebrate more than one Mass a day, without good cause. On Sundays, he may binate with no permission. The Church discourages too casual a recourse to bination or trination because of the truth contained in the proverb which reminds us that "familiarity breeds contempt."

Precious Blood

Q. Quite often in our parish we have a considerable amount of consecrated wine left at the end of Communion. It is too much to be consumed by the ministers. One priest says we should simply pour it into the special sink in the sacristy; the other says that is forbidden and that it must be consumed. Who is right?

A. Under no circumstances is the Precious Blood to be poured down any sink, even the special one in the sacristy (which leads not to the sewer but directly to the ground). Nor is any of the consecrated wine to be kept in the tabernacle, even from one Mass to the next. All of the Precious Blood must be consumed at the end of the Communion Rite. If such excess amounts exist, it would seem that too much wine is being consecrated.

Intinction

Q. Is dipping the host in the chalice of wine allowed? I have seen it done in some churches and have been told it is not allowed in others.

A. First of all, let us recall that after the Consecration one is no longer dealing with bread or wine but with the Body and Blood of Christ. Therefore, our language must be precise and reflect that change in substance. Now, on to your question.

The procedure you refer to is called Communion by intinction and is a venerable tradition in the Church, both East and West. It had fallen into disuse in the West for centuries but was rediscovered in the liturgical renewal of Vatican II and is completely acceptable. In fact, I use it every day because it connects us of the Latin Rite with the other rites of the

Church and because it enables communicants to receive easily under both forms or species.

Two cautions, however. If the celebrant chooses this option (and the choice is his), those receiving may not take Communion in the hand, for obvious reasons. Second, communicants may never take the Sacred Host in their hand and then dip it in the Precious Blood themselves, since this would be the equivalent of self-communication, which is always forbidden.

Liturgists at the bishops' conference have also recommended this method of distributing Communion under both species because there are no health hazards which could at times be present in receiving from a common chalice. If, however, someone is taking medication or has alcohol-related problems, he or she should simply give the priest some sign before receiving that only one species is desired.

Self-Communion

Q. Is it incorrect for an extraordinary minister of Holy Communion to give the Eucharist to himself?

A. Again, I imagine you are speaking of Mass. No one, except for the celebrant or a concelebrant, may self-communicate — and that prohibition includes deacons, who must receive the Sacred Host from the priest. In fact, if a priest is not concelebrating but simply attending the Mass, he may not self-communicate, either.

The only instance in which an extraordinary minister of Holy Communion may give himself the Eucharist is during a Communion Service over which he presides; obviously, in such circumstances there is no priest to offer Communion and hence the necessity of self-communicating.

Self-intinction

Q. I am a seminarian who recently served as a minister of the chalice at a Sunday Mass. To my amazement, four communicants in a row approached the chalice and self-intincted. I didn't know what to do, and when I mentioned it to the pastor later, he said he never heard that the practice was forbidden and further, he added, "Anyway, I don't think God minds." I was stunned by his attitude and didn't know how to respond.

A. Self-intinction is strictly forbidden, since it is tantamount to self-communication. If the priest employs the legitimate option of intinction, it is he who must dip the Sacred Host into the chalice and then place It on the tongue of the communicant.

As far as the pastor's cavalier attitude toward liturgical law, I can only say that as the guardian of the Eucharist (which the ordination rite told him he would be) he should know about the proper way for the worship of God to be conducted — and he should care. After all, there is nothing which the

Church does which is more important and of more eternal significance than the sacred liturgy.

When people have told me that they don't think "God minds," I have always asked them when He told them so! This is not just an attempt at a cute retort but is designed to get people to think through their statements, by which they presume to bypass Christ's Church and speak directly on behalf of the Almighty. Rather arrogant when you really consider it in all its implications.

Whole Christ

Q. At daily Mass some time ago, a visiting priest discovered the key was not in the tabernacle. Quite embarrassed, he asked us to wait until after Mass, went over to the rectory, and eventually located the key. My question is: Could he have given us some of the consecrated wine, instead of making us wait?

A. I imagine the priest did not realize the key was missing until after his own Communion. Presumably, then, he had already consumed the Precious Blood. Had he not done so yet, he certainly could have shared the chalice with the congregation (which was small, I suppose, since you note that it was a weekday).

The principle involved is that the whole Christ is contained, offered, and received under either form — bread or wine. Sometimes priests bring the Precious Blood to sick people who cannot swallow solid food and so are unable to consume the Sacred Host.

Must Catholics receive under both species?

Q. I was taught "in the old days" that receiving Holy Communion under the form of bread alone brings with it all the graces necessary, and that one has truly received the whole Christ. Now I hear people say that it is crucial to receive under both forms. Isn't receiving under the form of wine just an option and not a necessity? And what about recovering alcoholics?

A. The clear teaching of the Council of Trent and of the contemporary liturgical documents is that the whole Christ is received under either form. To suggest that one receives Communion "better" when doing so under both species is tantamount to heresy. That having been said, the documents do refer to Communion under both kinds as a "fuller sign," and hence the availability of the option. When Communion is given under the form of wine, especially from the chalice, care must be taken that the Sacred Species will not be spilled. Of course, the priest may decide to dip the Host into the chalice (intinction), enabling all to receive under both forms with a minimum of difficulty; this is the manner of reception in all the Eastern Churches (both Catholic and Orthodox). As you correctly note, this procedure is an option, bringing with it no obligation to employ it nor any additional graces. Regarding recovering alcoholics, it would seem wise to consult one's physician, since some people can tolerate some alcohol with no adverse effects while others are disturbed by even a drop. By the way, not infrequently a priest will give Holy Communion under the form of wine alone to a sick person incapable of swallowing solid food.

Wine and AIDS

Q. I am concerned about not drinking the wine when receiving Communion. Although I know that Jesus said we should drink His Blood, I am wary of the AIDS epidemic. What should I do?

A. First of all, in receiving Holy Communion, we do not "drink *wine.*" Rather, we partake of the Lord's Body and Blood.

Second, receiving Holy Communion from a common chalice has raised some health questions recently. In the military, for example, the practice is actively discouraged. Therefore, no one should feel compelled to receive under both forms; after all, we know that the whole Christ is present under either form.

Third, one alternative is for the priest to distribute Holy Communion by intinction (dipping the Sacred Host into the Precious Blood and then placing it on the communicant's tongue). This is the venerable manner used in the Churches of the East. Please note, however, that when Communion is distributed in this fashion, the communicant may not receive in the hand, nor may the Host be dipped in the chalice by the communicant.

Wine and altar boys

Q. What is the Church's position on offering wine from the chalice to altar boys?

A. I have been careful to correct readers before on language in reference to the Eucharist: We do not receive wine in Holy Communion; we receive under the form of wine. There is a big difference.

Anyone who can receive Holy Communion is permitted to receive under both species. My own experience makes me hesitate to offer Communion under the form of wine to children for two reasons: fear of spilling the Precious Blood and concern over silly behavior when drinking from the chalice. I have witnessed both, as have many priests, and hence my caution. Doctrinally and liturgically speaking, however, age has nothing to do with a priest's decision to offer Holy Communion from the chalice, but other considerations (such as I have alluded to) do need to be a part of such a decision.

Both species

Q. We receive the Body of Christ in Holy Communion. Why can't we receive the Blood of Christ, too, as the Bible says we should?

A. A knowledge of biology informs us that when we have before us a living body, we obviously have an individual with blood in his veins.

Sacramentally speaking, the Church has always held that receiving under one species (whether in the form of bread or wine) brings us the whole Christ.

You mention that the Bible commands us to receive Holy Communion under both species. I am unaware of any such passage. I think it is presumed that this would be the case, but it is surely not necessary. As the Church grew from a tiny community of believers to the sometimes massive congregations we have today, Communion under both forms became unwieldy, giving an opening to undignified and unbecoming receptions from the chalice. Hence, the norm came to be reception of the Eucharist solely under the species of bread.

The Protestant reformers were so intent on the necessity of both species that they exaggerated their position to the point that they argued that failure to receive Holy Communion under both forms invalidated the sacrament. At the Council of Trent, the Church reacted strongly to this by completely forbidding lay reception from the chalice precisely to underscore the error of the reformers.

Since Vatican II, as no one seriously questions the validity of Communion under one form, the Church now feels comfortable again in permitting both species under certain conditions, namely, that there be a special occasion and a properly catechized congregation and sufficient ministers for the chalices. The dignity of the celebration must likewise be safeguarded.

Besides having the faithful drink directly from the chalice (which can present some health hazards), a venerable tradition of the Eastern Church is possible: intinction. In this procedure, the priest dips the Sacred Host into the Precious Blood and places it on the tongue of the communicant.

Communion under both species is a fuller sign of the presence of the Lord in the Eucharist. While it is very beautiful, it adds nothing to the sacrament itself; therefore, its use must be determined by liturgical norms and good pastoral practice.

Protestant Eucharist

Q. In a recent TCA, you said that "20 years ago the celebration of the Eucharist on Sundays was a rarity in most Protestant churches; today that is the norm for many." I found this statement both encouraging and somewhat unclear. Has any Protestant sect taught about transubstantiation, sacrificial character, and the Real Presence of Christ in Holy Communion as professed and taught in the Catholic Church?

A. My statement was not intended to be a declaration of the validity of non-Catholic Eucharists but simply an acknowledgment that the Eucharist had begun to resume its place at center stage of the worship life of many non-Catholic Christians.

Regarding Protestant eucharistic belief, certain positive developments have occurred. In the multilateral theological discussions which have gone on over the past twenty years, certain "agreed statements" have been produced. Within the Faith and Order Commission of the World Council of Churches, some surprising documents have seen light of day. Surely they do not reflect the totality of eucharistic doctrine of Roman Catholic or Eastern Orthodox believers, but they are steps in the right direction. Even more promising are the agreed statements on the Eucharist resulting from the Anglican-Roman Catholic dialogue and the Lutheran-Roman Catholic dialogue.

The more frequent celebration of eucharistic services in non-Catholic communities may be very helpful in returning the "person in the pew" to an appreciation of the Holy Eucharist at the "gut level," while the theological statements engage the professionals in a dialogue which brings about deeper understanding and a return to authentic doctrine.

Intercommunion

Q. Can anyone other than a Catholic ever receive Holy Communion in a Catholic church?

A. The National Conference of Catholic Bishops has recently announced the necessity of placing a notice in parish missalettes regarding this very matter.

The general law of the Church permits only Catholics in the state of grace to receive Holy Communion. Non-Catholics may do so under the most restricted conditions: the Christian in question must not have access to his or her own minister for a prolonged period of time and should be in a situation of grave spiritual need (e.g., a time of religious persecution); that same person must profess the same eucharistic faith as the Church; and he or she must request Communion on his or her own initiative. As should be obvious, those conditions would be rather hard to verify in the United States. Does the Church hold to this to be mean-spirited? Not at all, for something extremely fundamental is at stake here.

Indiscriminate intercommunion undermines both the Eucharist and the Church. Catholics see a deep relationship between eucharistic Communion and ecclesial communion. It is not an accident that the names of the bishop of Rome and the local bishop are mentioned in the eucharistic prayer, as this recalls the fact that any who would *receive* Communion must *be* in communion with those two successors of the apostles, for it is through union with them and under their authority that this particular Eucharist is effected. Thus, one must already be a member of the Body of Christ, the Church, in order to receive the Body of Christ.

Some argue that intercommunion will hasten the day of Christian unity, but this assertion does not correspond to reality. Denominations that practice intercommunion are no closer to one another today than when they started. Just ask the Episcopalians and Old Catholics. Not infrequently, they become sloppy in their efforts at dialogue, precisely because they have "jumped the gun." Four centuries of disunity cannot be undone in the twinkling of an eye.

Under similar conditions, can Catholics receive from non-Catholic clergy? That would only be possible if the minister was validly ordained; otherwise he would not be able to confect (consecrate) the Eucharist: no valid priesthood, no valid Eucharist. For the most part, that would mean that Catholic reception of Communion could only occur through the ministrations of Eastern Orthodox priests. However, it should be observed that, in general, the Orthodox hold to an even stricter discipline on this than we. Therefore, we would not be welcome to receive Holy Communion from them, even were our own law to permit it.

Not receiving Communion can, at times, be an excellent form of penance offered for the success of the ecumenical movement. For example, I always encourage non-Catholics present at Mass (especially for occasions like weddings and funerals) to use Communion time to pray for Christian unity, so that Christ's will that His Church be one will become a reality. Tolerating anything less than the full reality does a disservice to the cause of unity and the integrity of the Eucharist.

Eucharistic prayer

Q. Our pastor ad-libs (I presume) a eucharistic prayer; at least it's not a published one. Does the Church have a new eucharistic prayer? If it does not, can a priest make up one of his own? This makes me wonder if the Mass he celebrates is a true Mass, with a valid Consecration. I know the priest would become angry if I asked him about this.

A. In the United States, four eucharistic prayers are in general use, as well as two for reconciliation and three for children — all approved. No others can be used for any reason — even if they might be permissible in other countries. "Ad-libbing" is strictly forbidden at all times.

If the extemporizing affects the words of Consecration, the validity of that Eucharist should be questioned. For example, if the priest would alter the words of institution to say: "This is a SIGN of my Body," the celebration would be invalid.

Whether or not the priest would become angry when approached is immaterial. The Eucharist belongs to the whole Church, and no priest has the right to tamper with it. If a courteous and respectful conversation achieves nothing, the bishop needs to be brought in on the matter to correct this serious abuse.

Host recipe

Q. Our parish uses the following recipe for making hosts: flour, baking soda, salt, brown sugar, oil, and water. I thought only flour and water could

be used. When I mentioned this to our pastor, he said he got the recipe from the diocese and that the bishop approves of it. Is this correct?
A. According to Pope John Paul's *Inaestimabile Donum* and the Code of Canon Law, only flour and water may be used in making bread for the Eucharist. Other additives are certainly illicit. No priest or bishop has the authority to change the matter for the sacraments; this is a grave abuse which should be brought to the attention of diocesan authorities. I doubt they are aware of this, certainly could not approve of it, and would be required to stop the practice, so serious is this deviation.

Communion hosts

Q. Who makes the Communion hosts and where?
A. In general, the hosts are made by cloistered nuns. How this tradition came about I am not sure. However, it is a way for the nuns to support themselves. At the symbolic level, it is also an opportunity for these holy women to be involved in the prayer life of the Church in the world. This kind of activity is very appropriate for nuns whose whole life is one of prayer and sacrifice for the Church and the world, which is precisely the thrust of the eucharistic sacrifice of the Mass.

In point of fact, however, anyone is permitted to make the breads to be used in the Mass, provided the correct recipe is followed, namely, whole wheat flour and water, with no additives of any kind. The bread is to be unleavened in the Western Church, so that the continuity with the Passover Supper is apparent. Therefore, when the General Instruction of the Roman Missal says that the bread used for the Eucharist should look like bread, one must understand that it is unleavened bread that it should resemble, that is, a matzo, not the bread one normally finds on dinner tables.

Finally, some might find it interesting to learn the origin of the word "host" for the altar bread. It comes from the Latin "*hostia*," which means "victim," referring to what the bread will become at the Consecration.

Weak faith

Q. From some of our pastor's preaching, I have come to wonder if he really believes anything of the Catholic Faith any longer. If his faith and moral life are weak, can he still celebrate a valid Mass?
A. If the situation is truly as serious as you suggest, I certainly hope that you and other parishioners have contacted the appropriate ecclesiastical authorities.

The basic question you ask, however, is equally important. The Church confronted it head-on in the fourth century in the Donatist controversy. At that time, many priests and bishops had lapsed from the true Faith, and people wondered about the validity of the sacraments they had administered: "If a heretical priest baptized me, was I really baptized?"

St. Augustine and other Fathers of the Church put forth the position of the Church rather succinctly: the personal holiness or worthiness of the minister does not affect the validity of the sacraments. For valid celebrations, a minister need only intend to do what the Church intends, using the required matter (e.g., water, bread, wine) and form (that is, correct liturgical text).

This teaching should set your mind at rest because it is a powerful reminder that the principal celebrant in every sacramental encounter is not the individual priest, but Jesus Christ.

Latin Mass

Q. Is it proper for a Catholic to attend a pre-Vatican II Latin Mass? Is this a licit Mass? Can someone properly receive Communion at one of these services? What is the status of the old-line church set up by Archbishop Lefebvre? Is there a complete break with Rome or is there any dialogue and hope for reconciliation?

A. One must make several distinctions before endeavoring to offer some answers here.

First, Mass in Latin according to the revised rites of Pope Paul VI may be celebrated at any time.

Second, as a result of an indult of Pope John Paul II, the pre-Vatican II rite or, more properly, the Mass of Pope St. Pius V (also referred to as the "Tridentine Mass" because it was a product of the reforms of the Council of Trent) may be celebrated with the permission of the local bishop when certain conditions are satisfied: genuine spiritual need of the petitioners, along with their acceptance of the validity of the new Order of Mass and no attempt to "politicize" the liturgy or the Church by pitting one rite against the other.

Third, the Mass offered by certain schismatic groups, most notably those associated with Archbishop Marcel Lefebvre, is a real problem. If these priests are validly ordained (and most if not all of them are), their Masses are valid but illicit since they are not in communion with their local bishop or the Bishop of Rome. Their celebration of Mass and attendance at their Masses constitute acts of disobedience to legitimate ecclesiastical authority. To the extent that this disobedience is conscious, deliberate, and obstinate, it is sinful most especially because it breaks the bond of unity in Christ's Church. To the extent that it is of a more emotional nature, personal guilt is diminished.

Confessing to schismatic priests is another matter. According to the revised Code of Canon Law, a priest who has faculties in one diocese may presume to enjoy them universally unless he is explicitly barred elsewhere. Lefebvrites, however, do not have faculties to grant absolution from any bishop in union with Rome. Therefore, it would be hard to see the validity of their administration of the Sacrament of Penance and, similarly,

Matrimony. A genuine emergency would be a different story, for even a laicized priest can function in such a situation.

Archbishop Lefebvre was a brilliant theologian and a famous missionary bishop; his act of schism is, therefore, all the more unfortunate. Upon his election, Pope John Paul II tried to heal the breach by offering the archbishop and his followers the option of maintaining their liturgical practices *on condition* that they acknowledge the validity of the decrees of Vatican II and the Mass which followed. Archbishop Lefebvre declined, and so continues to live outside full ecclesiastical communion. Inasmuch as he was a very old man with no episcopal successor, the movement would necessarily have died if he had not consecrated a bishop — which action automatically excommunicated him. The best we can hope for is that the Holy Spirit will move the heart and mind of the archbishop to return to Catholic unity with all his followers.

Fasting

Q. Is there still a rule on fasting before Communion. I see so many people chewing gum and eating candy that I wonder.

A. I wonder, too, and have brought this to the attention of communicants on occasion.

The Eucharist fast is quite simple nowadays: abstinence from all solids and liquids for one full hour before receiving Holy Communion. A much mitigated fast applies to the sick. Water does not break the fast, nor does medicine.

The reason for the fast is to serve as part of one's preparation to encounter the Bread of Life. The experience of physical hunger reminds a person of that deeper hunger which can be satisfied by Christ alone.

Aside from breaking the eucharistic fast, activities such as you describe are gross violations of common courtesy, let alone indicators of irreverence for the Church and the One whose House it is.

Special privilege

Q. At Mass on Christmas morning, the priest announced that we could receive Holy Communion again even if we had done so the night before. Was he correct? I thought Communion could be received only once a day.

A. Yes, the priest was right.

The revised Code of Canon Law does permit the reception of Holy Communion twice in one day, with no special reason having to exist. However, no more than twice is possible, regardless of circumstances. That decision was made recently by the Roman Commission for the Authentic Interpretation of the Code.

I must say that I was somewhat concerned that in not a few letters writers have suggested that attendance at Mass is useless if one does not receive. What about divorced-remarrieds then? More than that, however, this often-repeated opinion reveals a mistaken understanding of the Mass: the central act of the Eucharist is Christ's self-oblation to the Father. This is Christ's action — not ours. And it is of value, no matter what we do. Certainly, the celebration of the Eucharist takes on added meaning when someone receives Holy Communion, but the objective merit of the eucharistic sacrifice is the completed, redemptive action of Jesus Christ, sacramentally re-presented upon the altar. To assert otherwise is to confuse divine initiative and human response.

5. DIVINE WORSHIP

Symbol of faith

Q. Our parish recently had a Jewish-Catholic wedding. At the time of the ceremony, the crucifix was taken out of the sanctuary, so as not to offend the Jewish side of the family. Is this correct?

A. The first point to make is that a Jewish-Catholic wedding is extremely offensive to the Jewish community, and the Jewish party is excommunicated as a result. Rabbis who perform these ceremonies have no standing in the Jewish community and are considered mavericks who make a good living on doing what no respectable rabbi would even consider.

But on to your specific question. It makes no sense to me to withdraw the symbol of the Christian Faith from our church simply because nonbelievers will be present. Indeed it appears to me to be akin to a denial of one's Faith.

However, I have an even more interesting question: Was the Blessed Sacrament removed from the church, too? After all, that is even more to the heart of the matter. For five years, my work required me to "rub elbows" every day with Jewish leaders; we had a wonderful working relationship, and I count many of them as personal friends to this day. That did not happen, however, because either partner in the dialogue denied or soft-pedaled his or her particular faith commitment.

Marian Year

Q. I heard so much about the Marian Year but never really knew what it was. Maybe I found out about all the activities only after it had been explained, which I probably missed. Can you explain it for me?

A. Prior to the Marian Year of 1987, one had been celebrated in 1954. Very simply put, it is a time set aside to reflect on the place of Mary in the mystery of redemption and in the life of the Church. The recent Marian Year did much to rekindle and reemphasize the centrality of our Lady in Catholic spirituality — something which may have been lost in some quarters due to misinterpretations of the Second Vatican Council.

Theotokos

Q. Why do Eastern Rite Catholics pray to the Theotokos during the liturgy, while Western Catholics do not?

A. Of course, we do. "*Theotokos*" is just the Greek word for "God-bearer" or "Mother of God." At the very beginning of the Mass, in the Confiteor, we pray to our Lady; in the heart of the eucharistic prayer, we note that we join our prayers to those of "the Virgin Mary, the Mother of God."

The Blessed Sacrament

Q. I attended Mass in a church where the Blessed Sacrament is exposed twenty-four hours a day. Even during Mass the Sacrament remains exposed. Is this permissible?

A. While I would be among the first to applaud making available such devotions as perpetual adoration, I would equally deplore the abuse you describe. By no means is Mass to be celebrated in the presence of the Blessed Sacrament exposed. The prohibition exists for reasons of logic, theology, and a proper sense of the dramatic. Even in the preconciliar era, during Forty Hours when the Blessed Sacrament was not reposed for the celebration of Mass, Mass could not be celebrated at the high altar but rather at a side altar.

Christ is not jealous

Q. Several months ago, you recommended having various devotions take place while the Blessed Sacrament is exposed, including the Rosary. I know a priest who says that this is improper, inasmuch as the Rosary is directed to our Lady, thereby ignoring the eucharistic Christ. Do you still stand by your original statement?

A. Although I have treated this topic once before in these pages, I now have before me a Roman response, which might give more credibility to my original statement. Jesus is not jealous of His Mother; prayers directed to her do not offend Him if He is present. After all, as God, Jesus is present everywhere and at all times; using that logic, one can never speak to any other being, let alone pray to the saints. A recent letter from the Congregation for Divine Worship, however, makes two important points: (1) Citing Pope Paul VI's *Marialis Cultus* (no. 46), it notes that the Rosary is certainly "Christocentric and renders praise to Our Lord Jesus Christ: (2) The matter is not one of conflict between two devotions but of the need for catechesis to throw into relief the specific characteristics of each devotion and thus enriching the devotional life of the people of God."

Benediction

Q. Is there a rule any longer about how often Benediction of the Blessed Sacrament should be celebrated? Most parishes I know of never have it. What about Forty Hours?

A. To the best of my knowledge, there has never been a rule regarding the frequency of Benediction. It seems to me that any pastor should be interested in providing his people with a balanced spiritual diet, which should include all the richness of the Catholic spiritual life. Naturally, this means that the Mass holds pride of place, being that it is, as Vatican II described it, "the source and summit of the Christian life." However, that also implies there are other prayer forms which should supplement the eucharistic sacrifice of the Mass. In that category I would place the Liturgy of the Hours (for example, Sunday Vespers during Advent and Lent), the Rosary for May and October, and Novenas which have special significance to a particular community.

For each of these, I would begin with Exposition of the Blessed Sacrament, engage in the specific devotion, and end with Benediction. This has the effect of centering our entire devotional life on the eucharistic Christ. It should be noted that the Blessed Sacrament cannot be exposed simply to give Benediction; rather, Benediction is the culmination of prayers, readings, and hymns.

The revised liturgy has reemphasized the communal nature of Christian worship, and that is good. However, the individual and personal element (which is also necessary) has been lost in certain cases. In my experience, eucharistic adoration helps to recapture that dimension.

The traditional Forty Hours Devotion has been replaced in many parishes with a eucharistic day, which begins with Exposition of the Blessed Sacrament after the last morning Mass and offers several hours of individual and communal prayer before our eucharistic Lord, often ending with Vespers, procession, and Benediction. This is a time of great grace for a parish, bringing all together in a unique way — as a parish family — to petition Jesus in the Sacrament of His Body and Blood for those things we need to be His Body in the world.

A pagan feast

Q. *One of my sisters has left the Church and joined a Fundamentalist sect. I was surprised to hear her say they do not celebrate Easter because it is supposedly a pagan feast. She says they prefer to emphasize the great truth of the Resurrection instead.*

A. What does your sister think we do on Easter, if not "emphasize the great truth of the Resurrection"?

The group she has gotten involved with obviously has a problem with Christian events having a history. Let me explain. It is true that the word "Easter" comes from an old English word which was used for a pagan spring festival commemorating the rebirth of Mother Earth. When the Gospel was preached to English-speaking peoples, a name was needed to describe the day of the Lord's resurrection. Looking through their culture, missionaries zeroed in on a name that could provide linkage between their past religious experience and their newfound Christian Faith. Something similar happened in regard to the observance of the Lord's Nativity, as we noted in the November-December 1987 issue of *The Catholic Answer*. This was likewise the procedure followed by St. Paul when he tried to preach the Gospel to the Athenians (cf. Acts 17:16-34).

I should mention that the first Christian feast to be celebrated was Sunday, precisely as the day of the Resurrection. Only later did Easter emerge as a distinct Sunday among them all when the liturgical year evolved in such a way that the life of Christ was spaced out over the entire year.

Washing feet

Q. On Holy Thursday I noticed that several women had their feet washed. Is this permissible? I thought that only men could participate in that ceremony since Jesus washed the feet of the Twelve Apostles, all of whom were men.

A. You are quite correct; however, I've heard a great deal about this kind of thing happening this year. This is all the more strange because in January of 1988 Cardinal Augustin Mayer, then prefect of the Congregations for the Sacraments and Divine Worship, sent out a circular letter on various aspects of the liturgical services of Holy Week. In discussing Holy Thursday, he specifically repeated that it was men's feet that were to be washed. In case the English could cause doubt, the Latin says "*viris*," meaning male persons; if the document envisioned males and females, the Latin would have been "*hominibus*."

Why all the fuss about who gets his or her feet washed? It is not a matter of indifference; in fact, it is critically important. Those who have carefully studied the Gospel of John know that John does not record the institution of either the Eucharist or the priesthood in the context of the Last Supper; instead, he substitutes the foot-washing ceremony. You will recall that Jesus notes that this is precisely the way his apostles will be admitted to a share in His ministry (cf. Jn 13:8f). Now, unless we are prepared to admit the possibility of the ordination of women, we cannot legitimately wash women's feet.

It is sad that a beautiful rite has become so politicized, with its significance being totally twisted beyond any connection with its origins. I know of at least three very fine bishops who engaged in the washing of women's feet this Holy Thursday, due in large measure to immense pressure. If this is what has happened to the rite (which is completely optional), then my suggestion would be to retire it to the liturgical dustbin for another moment in history when we can pray without giving everything we do a political slant, which is so divisive of unity in the Church.

Washing of feet again

Q. I have always thought that it was not permitted for women's feet to be washed on Holy Thursday, but for the past three years it has been done in our parish. What is the story here?

A. Yes, we are getting around to that time of year again, so let me remind all of what I have noted in two earlier editions: Under no conditions may women's feet be washed in the liturgy of the Lord's Supper on Holy Thursday. For a more detailed explanation, please see the question and answer immediately preceding this.

Tenebrae

Q. What is Tenebrae, and how is it conducted?

A. "Tenebrae" is the Latin word for "shadows" or "darkness." This service was very popular in the preconciliar era, went into disuse for some time, and now appears to be on the rebound. Originally, this service was a combination of the ancient Offices of Matins and Lauds as recited on the last three days of Holy Week. In the revival of Tenebrae, the ceremony is conducted on any day of Holy Week. This is a Liturgy of the Word, consisting of readings (especially from the Lamentations and the Fathers), as well as psalms. The most conspicuous feature of Tenebrae is the gradual extinction of the fifteen candles in the triangular candlestick called the Tenebrae Hearse, until only the center candle remains lighted, a symbol of our Lord; artificial lighting is also eliminated in stages. During the singing of the Benedictus (Zechariah's hymn of praise as recorded in Luke), the six altar candles are extinguished and the Christ Candle is hidden. Psalm 51 and the prayer of the day are then recited in total darkness.

After a brief pause a noise is made symbolizing the earthquake at the time of the Lord's resurrection. The single lighted candle is then restored to its former position as a symbol of the Risen Christ, and all depart in silence.

As you can see, this is a ceremony which is rich in symbolism, drama, and emotion. Some of the finest sacred music has been composed for this service over the centuries; composers like Victoria and Palestrina come to mind immediately. We brought back this rite in my parish last year, using both Latin and English chants; the people were deeply moved, and it is now a permanent fixture in our Holy Week schedule.

Lenten practice

Q. On Ash Wednesday all the holy water was removed from the fonts in our church and was replaced with sand. What is the reason for this? It really upset many people in the parish.

A. I have never heard of the practice you cite. Frankly, it sounds rather bizarre, especially since Lent focuses so much on baptism for the catechumens and on recommitment to one's baptismal promises for believers.

The Church does direct, however, that holy water be removed from the church for the Paschal Triduum, until the new water is blessed at the Easter Vigil Liturgy.

The Lenten season

Q. I find your answer on the days of Lent either incorrect or in need of further clarification. I was always under the impression that the Sundays of Lent were not to be calculated in the count.

A. A very good question. Christians of the second century engaged in a two-day fast; in the third century, that was extended to all of Holy Week; by the time of the Council of Nicea, the Quadragesima Paschae as a forty-day period of fasting and penance was known to all, but it originally began on the sixth Sunday before Easter and lasted until Holy Thursday, when the solemn restoration of penitents took place in the Roman Church. Because there was no fasting on Sundays, an effort was made in the fifth century to increase the actual number of fast days to forty.

This was done in two stages: (a) Good Friday and Holy Saturday were separated from the Paschal Triduum and added to preparatory fast, thus raising the number to 36; then the four weekdays before the first Sunday were added, thus bringing the season to 40. (b) In the sixth century the three Sundays before Ash Wednesday were included as a preparation for the Lenten season, but using round numbers to speak of 70, 60, and 50 days before Easter.

As you can see, the Lenten season has had a rather checkered history. The Church has always desired to link it to Christ's desert experience, but not in an absolute manner; after all, the use of the number forty in the Bible itself was never interpreted exactly. An excellent explanation of the history of Lent can be found in Adolf Adam's *Liturgical Year*, published by Pueblo Books in 1981.

Lent

Q. Enclosed is the set of Lenten regulations printed in our archdiocesan paper. You will see that it states that "Lent begins on Ash Wednesdays and ends before the Mass of the Lord's Supper on Holy Thursday." I always thought Lent ended just before or even during the Easter Vigil Liturgy.

A. Count up the days in Lent, and you will notice that the final days of Holy Week are not reckoned in the forty days. The beginning of the Mass of the Lord's Supper marks the onset of the Paschal Triduum, culminating in the celebration of the Easter Vigil Liturgy.

Different Mass

Q. What is the difference between a Mass of Christian Burial and a Mass of the Resurrection?

A. Although some priests refer to the Mass of Christian Burial as the Mass of the Resurrection, that is inaccurate: the only Mass of the Resurrection is Easter. What they are trying to stress is the Easter element in our Faith as we encounter the fact of death. Often associated with this is the use of white vestments and frequent strains of "Alleluia."

While these are noble sentiments to foster, it is also important to allow people to engage in the very normal process of mourning — all within the framework of a Christian belief in the Resurrection, of course. Furthermore, at times the joyous aspect is so highlighted that some people forget that the purpose of the Mass of Christian Burial is to pray FOR the deceased and not TO the deceased.

Liturgy of the Hours

Q. Recently our parish has been praying the Liturgy of the Hours before Mass. The only problem is that it seems that the psalms end up taking the place of certain Mass prayers. Can this be done?

A. Many monasteries combine the celebration of the Liturgy of the Hours with the Mass on occasion, and there is a definite form for this kind of service. However, I do not think it advisable for the average parish congregation. Why not simply celebrate Morning Prayer twenty minutes before the regularly scheduled Mass?

Mass titles

Q. What is the origin of phrases like "Mass in Honor of Pope Paul V" and "Danish Amen Mass" in the monthly missalette?

A. Throughout history, Masses have been composed in honor of various mysteries of the Faith, the saints, or the patrons who commissioned the works. Sometimes a sung Mass takes its name from a prominent musical feature in its composition (hence, the Danish Amen Mass). The titles you note place them in that tradition.

Saturday Mass

Q. I thought that Mass on Saturday night (when it was first allowed) was only for those who worked on Sunday and that everyone else had to attend on Sunday proper. It seems like some people no longer even make an effort to go to Church on Sunday morning. What's the position of the Church on this?

A. The liturgical day for a Sunday or solemnity begins the evening before with the praying of First Vespers for the day. This practice is an inheritance from Jewish liturgy. In the postconciliar years, this was expanded to include the possibility of an evening Mass of anticipation or a vigil Mass.

No legal preconditions must be met to fulfill one's Sunday Mass of obligation on Saturday night; however, it is clear that the original intent was to be of special assistance to workers, vacationers, or travelers — and this has been a great blessing to many such people.

At the same time, honesty also compels us to admit that many others have abused the privilege and now never attend Mass on Sunday proper, leading one to ask just what they are doing to sanctify the entire Lord's Day. The resolution of the problem lies in better catechesis and preaching, which stress that Sunday Mass is the high point of one's week and not an annoying obligation satisfied as quickly as possible.

Statues

Q. Where can I find in any official document a teaching that duplications of statues is forbidden for a church? The new priest in our parish says this is so and has acted accordingly by removing the second statue of the blessed

Mother. Can a priest just change anything in a church because he doesn't like it?

A. While very positive about images, the General Instruction of the Roman Missal states that "there should not be too many . . . images, lest they distract the people's attention from the ceremonies, and those which are there ought to conform to a correct order of prominence. There should not be more than one image of any particular saint" (n. 278).

Of course, problems of sensitivity, good taste, and liturgical propriety all come into play in this area. No, a priest cannot do simply as he pleases, but it does not seem out of order for him to have the final say; after all, he is (or should be) the expert on such matters. That having been said, there is no substitute for prudence in matters like these; at times not a few priests have won the battle of the statues and lost the war, especially in terms of parochial trust and affection.

Honesty also forces one to admit that all too often some sacred images are, objectively speaking, terrible art. A respect for the liturgy and for the sacred would suggest the destruction of such works and their replacement with other more worthy representations.

Going without

Q. When our pastor goes away for vacation each summer, a visiting priest substitutes for him on the weekends, while a layperson leads a Communion service for the weekdays. Some people think this is an abuse and is unnecessary. What is the Church's position on this?

Q. In my diocese a few times a year all priests are required by the bishop to attend a diocese-wide meeting. At such times deacons conduct liturgies. What should those "liturgies" consist in? May the deacon, for example, recite the whole eucharistic prayer and just omit the words of Consecration?

A. I am not comfortable with making substitutes for Mass too readily available. If I were a pastor who had difficulty finding a priest to celebrate daily Mass in my absence, I would encourage the faithful to gather for the Liturgy of the Word and then experience the hunger for the Eucharist which so many people around the world must know for months on end because of priest shortages. Let them then pray for an increase in priestly vocations and, at the same time, thank Almighty God that they miss out on the Eucharist for only one week a year.

As far as "priestless celebrations" of Holy Communion, no one (not even a deacon) may recite the eucharistic prayer, even omitting the words of Consecration. The approved rite calls for the Liturgy of the Word to be followed immediately by the Communion Rite (that is, beginning with the Lord's Prayer and concluding with the distribution of Holy Communion and the final prayer).

The Lord's Prayer

Q. Why is the "Amen" dropped from the Lord's Prayer, even when it is said apart from Mass?

A. It shouldn't be. The only reason for omitting the "Amen" from the Lord's Prayer at Mass is that it is followed by another prayer, directly related to it. At all other times, it is still presumed that one recites the concluding word. In the public recitation of the Rosary, for example, one finds the strange situation in which people say "Amen" after each "Hail Mary" or "Glory Be," but fail to do the same with the "Our Father," obviously an unconscious carryover from Mass.

Crucifix

Q. Is the cross with the Crucified Christ being phased out as a symbol of our Faith?

A. No, it is not. The General Instruction of the Roman Missal indicates that a crucifix must be on or near the altar during the celebration of the eucharistic sacrifice to stress the connection, of course, between the action historically commemorated by the crucifix and the action being sacramentally reenacted on the altar. Some people argue that the cross is a more fitting symbol since the absence of the Lord's Body proclaims His resurrection; that may or may not be the case. However, it is clear that in His risen Body, the Lord Jesus used as definitive proof of His identity that even in His glorified state He bore the wounds of His saving passion and death — the signs of His deep and abiding love for us.

Proper administration

Q. On the Sunday before the feast of St. Blaise, our parish had the blessing of throats, done by the pastor, another priest, and a nun. Is it legitimate for a nun to confer a blessing? Also, is it proper for a layperson to distribute ashes on Ash Wednesday?

A. My first comment would be that I do not approve of offering the blessing of St. Blaise on a day other than the feast itself, for a variety of reasons. First, it detracts from the centrality of Sunday and gives the impression that the memorial of a saint (even so minor a one) is of such importance as to preempt the Sunday liturgy. Second, it caters to the American tendency of the religious version of "one-stop banking." By that I mean, this strange desire to accomplish all one's religious obligations in one handy trip to church. It seems to me that if the blessing of one's throat is so important to one's spirituality, then one should be willing to come to church on the correct day.

That having been said, lay people and non-ordained Religious may not confer blessings. For an explanation of this, see the next question and answer ("Blessings").

Regarding the distribution of ashes, in some dioceses extraordinary ministers of Holy Communion may be deputed to administer ashes. Frankly, I would be far more restrictive about who distributes Holy Communion rather than ashes, but the thinking appears to be that ashes are connected to a call to repentance and hence linked to the Sacrament of Penance in some way. Following that line of thought, however, it would not make sense to allow deacons to distribute ashes, since they cannot grant absolution in the Sacrament of Penance.

Blessings

Q. Who may bless what nowadays? Are the rules different for a transitional deacon and for a permanent deacon?

A. Blessings are conferred by those in sacred orders, as put forth in the Book of Blessings, which was issued in Latin in 1984, but only now making its appearance in English. There is no distinction between permanent and transitional deacons, in terms of the powers conferred in ordination since the rite is the same.

As I read the new directives, a priest may bless any person or thing at any time. A deacon may bless persons during a liturgical rite which calls for such a blessing and things at any time. The new ritual adds a third category — a kind of "lay blessing," which does not declare something blessed but merely asks for God to accomplish this; if a layperson administers such a blessing (in a "priestless parish," for example), he or she does not make the sign of the cross over the person or object, but rather blesses himself when the Trinity is invoked.

Clarifications will have to be made as the new rites are used and questions arise from their use.

The Hail Mary

Q. Since when have the "thee's, thy's and thou's" been taken out of the "Hail Mary" and replaced with "you's and your's?" Who gave the permission for this?

A. No permission has been granted for such a switch. As a matter of fact, some years back the International Commission on English in the Liturgy had proposed a whole series of such updatings to the National Conference of Catholic Bishops (the only body authorized to make such changes), and the project was defeated. Simply put, then, whoever is inserting such changes is doing so on his/her own authority and is infringing on the rights of the rest of the community in so doing.

'Thee' vs. 'You'

Q. In reference to your answer on the replacement of the "thee's" and "thou's" of the Hail Mary: How can you say that such a substitution is not permitted when in the Divine Office the text of the Hail Mary, prepared by

the International Commission on English in the Liturgy, approved by the Episcopal Conference of the United States, and confirmed by the Apostolic See reads, "Hail Mary, full of grace, the Lord is with you."
A. I do not wish to imply that this makes the change mandatory, but it is clearly permitted if one should choose to use it.

Please realize that the original questioner was not talking about the Liturgy of the Hours but the recitation of the Rosary in her parish. What is approved for a liturgical text (done, by the way, to keep the style consistent with the rest of the translations) does not apply across the board. Hence, my disagreement with you. If you doubt the validity of what I say, simply consider the point I raised in the original response, namely, that the very change you suggest is legitimate was voted down by the very episcopal conference you mentioned. To repeat, then, it is not permissible to eliminate the "thee's" and "thou's"' until that action has been approved by the National Conference of Catholic Bishops and the Holy See.

Solo

Q. I have two liturgical questions for you: (1) Is it permissible for a priest to offer daily Mass with no one in attendance? (2) Is it proper to interrupt the Mass after the Gospel to say the Rosary?
A. First, liturgical law carries the expectation that at least a server would be present for Mass. Exceptions are possible when a priest would be denied the opportunity to celebrate Mass for lack of a congregation. The prayers of the Mass are clearly designed to have a dialogue between celebrant and congregation; however, they are equally a dialogue between the priest (acting on behalf of the Church) and Almighty God. Neither aspect should be forgotten too readily. If those understandings are in place, no priest will celebrate a private Mass casually, nor will others assume that such celebrations are, *ipso facto*, improper.

Second, nothing should ever interrupt the proper flow of the Mass. To insert the Rosary into the Mass is an aberration of the first order. I know of many parishes where the Rosary precedes daily Mass by fifteen minutes or follows it, but I have never heard of what you relate.

Not convinced

Q. Our little parish had used the Paluch missalette for years, but I noticed some time back that the Gospel verse given for the Fifth Sunday in Ordinary Time said: ". . . I will make you fishers of my people." However, the lectionary says: ". . . I will make you fishers of men." When I wrote to Paluch, I got back the very convoluted letter which I have enclosed. The bottom line seems to be that the editor says that this change and others like it are legitimate because we are getting a new lectionary and sacramentary soon. I am not convinced.

A. The expression "fishers of men" occurs twice in the New Testament (Mt 4:19 and Mk 1:17). I have checked both passages in the revised edition (1987) of the New American Bible, on which the lectionary is based. In both instances, "fishers of men" is retained. Therefore, the missalette company is engaging in arbitrary changes of texts, which have no basis in any approved text of the present or of the future. I have consulted with some people who do liturgical translation work, and they assure me that what I am sharing with you is correct and that what you were told is not.

While we are on the subject of text changes for alleged sexism, I might as well put in my oar on a related "pet peeve": missalettes which accord themselves the right to change the words of old hymns, without the permission of the authors. If a hymn is so irremediably sexist in language, why not just drop it from the repertoire? To change the language is as ignorant and arrogant in this instance as it would be to attempt to produce a better English for Shakespeare's plays.

Clowns, dance, and puppets

The following responses have come from the Congregation for Divine Worship on these topics:

1. *Clowns at Liturgy (February 27, 1987):* It is strictly forbidden that any form of clowning should take place in a church at any time. The Bishops' Committee on the Liturgy (USA) has already issued a statement forbidding such behavior during the liturgy. We should like Your Excellency to take measures to ensure that the liturgy is carried out in every detail according to the prescribed norms.

2. *Dance (April 27, 1987):* The second matter concerns a "Liturgical Dance Workshop" organized under the auspices of the Diocesan Liturgy Office for May 6, 1987. We should like to draw attention to the "Note concerning Dance in the Liturgy: published in *Notitiae*, no. 11 (1975), pp. 202-205, where it is stated that dance is not permitted during the course of the celebration of the liturgy.

3. *Puppets (June 8, 1987):* During the past few months the attention of this Congregation has been brought to a number of cases concerning the celebration of Masses for Children in which the celebrant resorts to theatrical props as didactic aids. These include puppets and toys. Such means were never envisaged by the Directory for Masses for Children. The position of this Congregation in this regard is that the use of puppets, toys, and other theatrical props during the course of the celebration of the sacred liturgy is not permitted under any circumstances. In schools and other places such didactic aids may be employed usefully.

Liturgical dance

Q. Is liturgical dance permitted? I have seen it on many occasions but have been told that it is not allowed by Rome.

A. Dancing during the sacred liturgy is not permitted by ruling of the Congregations for the Sacraments and Divine Worship, at least not in western cultures. I have seen liturgical dance done in Africa, and it was quite moving. However, in that culture, dance is associated with sacred realities, which is not the case in the West, hence, the reason for the ruling. Sometimes a kind of "sacred dance" is performed in non-liturgical prayer services. Of course, in those instances, liturgical law does not apply.

Sacred music

Q. Is sacred music assigned for Mass or not? If so, how can we condone such things as "Polka Masses"?

A. Yes, the music used in the liturgy is supposed to be sacred, that is, composed specifically for divine worship and used only in that context. In various postconciliar efforts at forging some kind of vernacular music, standards often went by the boards, so that in all too many churches sacred music is neither sacred nor music. I suspect it will take a great deal of time to produce music worthy of the sanctuary; of course, we do have a tremendous patrimony of beautiful music available to us, especially in Gregorian Chant and in the hymnody of various Anglican and Protestant communities.

In regard to phenomena like Polka Masses, all I can say is that I thought liturgical silliness like that went out with the '60s.

Liturgical abuse

Q. Enclosed is a "liturgy sheet" used during Lent in our seminary. You will notice that it calls for the celebrant to begin the Mass in the rear of the chapel, as well as many other bizarre practices. Are these things permissible? If not, what should I do to correct them?

A. It gets rather tiresome to see liturgical silliness perpetrated year after year, especially in seminaries. As I have said before, one would have thought that kind of thing died a decade or so ago. I can only answer that the "liturgy sheet" to be followed is not the creation of any committee but the General Instruction of the Roman Missal.

The fact that this kind of nonsense goes on in a seminary makes it all the more deplorable. Again, I would have thought that the seminary evaluation process which took place over the past few years would have gotten rid of such things. Not only are young men being exposed to poor liturgy (because it is not the Church's approved form of worship), but they are being educated in an attitude of disobedience and rebellion.

What should you do? Volunteer to work on the liturgy committee and make your voice heard. If that does no good, speak to your bishop about the situation, in the hope that he will take corrective action. At any rate, keep these experiences stored and resolve now that when you are ordained you will never inflict your own liturgical idiosyncrasies on the rest of the people of God, who have a right to the celebration of the liturgy according to the approved rites of the Church.

Omission

Q. The priests in our parish always omit the Penitential Rite and Creed. They recite the Gloria only on Christmas. I am very conservative, and these things bother me. Am I wrong? Can anything be done, short of going to another church?

A. To place this problem in its proper context, it is necessary to consider Vatican II's Constitution on the Liturgy, which indicates that no single individual, "not even a priest, may add, remove, or change anything in the liturgy on his own authority" (no. 22).

On, then, to the specific matters you mention. The Penitential Rite is only omitted when some other similar acknowledgment of sin has taken place (e.g., the sprinkling of the congregation with holy water). The Creed is required on all Sundays and solemnities. The Gloria is likewise called for on all Sundays (except in Advent and Lent), solemnities, and feasts. If your priests are deleting these prayers, they are violating liturgical law.

Many people have compared the liturgy to a drama, in which each actor has a specific part. I would suggest you discuss these issues with your clergy from this perspective — doing so charitably but firmly — and remind them that their role as celebrants is to play the part assigned them by the Church. Failure to do so is a nasty form of clericalism, which denies the laity their right to a liturgy sanctioned by the Church, one in which they can experience the presence of God in a calm and undisturbed manner. If such a conversation gets nowhere, appropriate action should be undertaken with diocesan authorities. However, only after attempts at a parish level have failed should higher authority be engaged.

Finally, let me caution you against referring to yourself as a "conservative" Catholic, as though membership in the Church admitted of political parties — thus giving legitimacy to incorrect actions. If you are with the universal Church, you are Catholic, pure and simple — no other labels are needed or desirable.

Men only

Q. As I travel around, I notice that some priests will not allow women to function as lectors, eucharistic ministers, and altar servers. Why?

A. In 1973, Pope Paul VI reformed the minor orders with the decree *Ministeria Quaedam*, eliminating the orders of porter and exorcist, as well as clerical tonsure, leaving in place the ministries of lector and acolyte. Generally speaking, young men were admitted to these minor orders as a part of their preparation for the priesthood. Because of their connection with the priesthood, Paul VI did not feel he could open up these ministries to women.

Therefore, only men may be officially installed in these ministries. Certain functions of these ministries, however, can be performed by women at times. For example, when installed lectors (or readers) are lacking in a parish, a pastor may assign the task to other lay people — male or female. In the same way, that part of the office of acolyte which involves the distribution of Holy Communion under conditions of grave need may be committed to lay people (male or female) as well. Serving Mass (another function of an installed acolyte), however, is limited to males, precisely because of the intimate link between service at the altar and the subsequent call to holy orders.

The phenomenon of altar girls has surfaced in some places, but it is clearly forbidden by liturgical law and the revised Code of Canon Law. Hence, pastors permitting or encouraging the practice are in violation of ecclesiastical law. The problem emerges, then, of how to halt a procedure (which was never allowed in the first place) without hurting the feelings of little girls who now must be told they can no longer serve. Pastoral sensitivity never should have made them "political footballs" to begin with. The most honest approach may well be for the pastor to admit that he (or his predecessor) acted in disobedience and now needs to correct the situation, at the same time reminding everyone that all are equal in the Church but that not all have the same calling — which Vatican II referred to as a diversity of roles and ministries.

The lesson in all this should be evident — always to think and act with the Church, so that later corrections are not necessary.

Altar girls

Q. There seems to be an inconsistency between your statement on altar girls and the Code of Canon Law. Note what I have highlighted on the enclosed sheet.

Q. The code is not black and white on this matter [of altar girls]. There has been no instruction since the code was revised concerning altar girls. Hence, no legal basis at this time for excluding them.

A. Both writers cite as their authority the commentary on the Code of Canon Law produced by the Canon Law Society of America; however, that work is merely a collection of opinions or interpretations of various American canon lawyers. As such, it is not authoritative. For that, it is necessary to consult either the Roman Commission for the interpretation of the code or the appropriate Roman Congregation which handles a particular area of Church life.

My explanation in the last issue may not have been precise enough, so let me try again. The 1983 Code of Canon Law differs from that of 1917 in many ways, not the least of which is its intention to touch upon liturgical law only when absolutely necessary. And so, Canon 2 states: "Liturgical norms existing at present retain their force unless some of them are contrary to the canons of the code." Furthermore, the new code avoids simply negative statements, perhaps explaining the lack of a direct prohibition.

Therefore, what does liturgical law say about altar girls? The General Instruction of the Roman Missal, in speaking of liturgical duties given over to lay people, notes that "services performed outside the sanctuary may also be given to women at the discretion of the rector of the church" (no. 70). This obviously excludes service at the altar. Nevertheless, some interpreted that to mean that girls could carry in procession the cross and candles, for example, "dropping them off," as it were, and thus not violate liturgical norms. A 1984 (post-code!) response from the Congregation for the Sacraments and Divine Worship, however, determines otherwise: "Girls and women may NOT carry the cross, the books, the candles."

The recent synod on the laity in Rome also made it clear that this tradition remains in force.

With all this in mind, I stand by my statement in the last issue of *The Catholic Answer*: Altar girls are forbidden by Church law.

One final note. Someone has suggested yet another reason for this, even though females may fulfill other liturgical roles, seemingly of even greater importance: When a woman reads the Scriptures at Mass, her activity is a service directed to the community; a server's duties are directed to the priest.

Female servers

Q. Our church bulletin carried a notice that we have no female servers in our parish because our bishop has not made a decision yet, but that Rome has given all bishops that authority. Is that true?

A. Absolutely not. In truth, the Holy See has repeatedly reminded bishops that they have no authority to make decisions of a liturgical nature. The universal law of the Church forbids female servers for any reason and under any guise. This is eminently clear to anyone who is willing to read the documents from the Holy See.

Female lectors

Q. You have stated that a 1984 response from the Congregations for the Sacraments and Divine Worship indicated that "girls and women may not carry the cross, the books, the candles" in procession. I am a woman lector; in obedience to that decree, I have now abstained from joining in the entrance procession, carrying the lectionary. My parish priests disagree with me and say that the document you referred to had nothing to do with lectors. Could you shed some light on the question?

A. Your priests are correct; the document was addressing the question of altar girls, not lectors, and the books in question were the altar missal or the pontifical (the bishop's liturgical book). If I were you, I would rest at ease and rejoin the procession. I would like to note your obvious sense of loyalty and love for the Church which enabled you to make such a decision, albeit unnecessary, and I applaud that.

Female lectors revisited

Q. For over twenty years I have been a woman lector in our parish. Just recently I discovered that female lectors were not part of the changes made by Vatican II. If this is in violation of Church law, I do not want to be a part of it, but perhaps I am being overly scrupulous.

A. Lectors (male or female) were not a part of the agenda of Vatican II at all. As a matter of fact, most liturgical reforms were developed after the council, following up on the impetus put forth in the conciliar document on the liturgy, as has generally been the case throughout history, including the Council of Trent.

According to Church law, any baptized Catholic may proclaim the Scriptures in the liturgical assembly if he or she is properly prepared and is possessed of the proper attitudes toward the Word of God. This is considered a normal liturgical function of the laity (male or female), unlike that of extraordinary ministers of Holy Communion (which requires extraordinary circumstances for them to be legitimately used). The only stipulation on readers is that those who are officially installed as such must be male (since this is still viewed in some way as being connected with preparation for the priesthood). However, any Catholic can perform the task of reading the Sacred Scriptures — even habitually — without being formally instituted.

If your conscience needs to be set to rest, just watch the next telecast of a papal Mass coming from St. Peter's in Rome, and you will see women lectors.

The embolism

Q. Is it optional for a priest to skip the prayer between the Our Father and "for the kingdom. . ."?

A. The prayer to which you refer is technically known as the embolism, and the people's response ("For the kingdom, etc.") is called the doxology.

I am sure some readers get tired of reading the same remark issue after issue, but the answer is the same: No priest has the authority to make changes in the liturgical texts. They are the possession of the whole Church; he is merely their guardian.

All together now

Q. Is it permissible for the priest to invite the people to recite the second half of the eucharistic prayer with him? What about the concluding doxology?

A. The eucharistic prayer forms a unity; therefore, it cannot be divided up between priest and people. In the eucharistic prayer the priest functions most explicitly in the person of Christ, praying to the Father on behalf of the Church, and so it is the priestly prayer of the Mass. It is a grave abuse for a celebrant to invite people to speak those prayers with him; it reflects a confusion of roles and ministries in the liturgy. The Vatican II document on the liturgy notes that participants in the liturgy are to do "all those parts and only those parts" which are rightfully theirs. The part of the eucharistic prayer which pertains to the people is the Great Amen, which ratifies the prayer of the priest.

Breaking the Host

Q. Is it wrong for a priest to break the Host at the Consecration when he says, "He took the bread and broke it"? A friend says it is sacrilegious.

A. The Mass is not simply a dramatic rehearsal or mimicry of the Last Supper. The proper moment for the "breaking of the Bread" is at the Agnus Dei. The symbolism then concentrates on the Eucharist being broken, so that it can be shared. Performing that action at the Consecration would signify something entirely different, and so the liturgy calls for it to be done in the spot indicated above.

Is the performance of the rite at the Consecration sacrilegious? I think the correct word is "improper," not "sacrilegious." Once again, however, let me underscore the impropriety for priests to take upon themselves liturgical innovation.

A sung Consecration

Q. I recently attended Mass in another state and was surprised to hear the priest sing the words of Consecration. Is this permissible?

A. The entire Mass can be sung, if deemed appropriate by the celebrant. If you were to look at the back of the Roman Missal used at the altar, you would find musical settings for all the parts of the Mass, including the eucharistic prayer. Sometimes a priest will sing the words of Consecration to add solemnity to the occasion. Such a practice would be particularly appropriate on Holy Thursday, for example.

'He blessed it'

Q. Why did Vatican II drop "He blessed it" from the Consecration?

A. To be exact, one should note that Vatican II did nothing in regard to specifics like changes in translation; that was the work of the Church at the level of local conferences of bishops, like the body to which all the bishops of the United States belong. They, in turn, gave responsibility for the work of translation to a group known as the International Commission on English in the Liturgy.

In the process of translating, the individuals involved would have begun with the original Latin text of the Mass, discovering the word was "*benedixit*," which translated a Greek word used in the New Testament texts related to the Eucharist, meaning "to bless" or "to offer praise and thanks." In the context of the Last Supper, which was a Passover meal, Jesus would have been following the very carefully regulated order (seder) for that meal, calling for the head of the family to say the blessing over the food; in Judaism, that blessing was an act of offering praise and thanks to Almighty God who had given them that food. Our notion of blessing as an act of consecration was not the primary notion for Jews. Of course, what Jesus subsequently did was indeed a consecration, but the prayer He offered at "the blessing" was the equivalent of our grace before meals.

A glance over some of the relevant biblical texts might be helpful in this regard. See, for example: Matthew 26:26-28; Mark 14:22-25; Luke 22:19-20; 1 Corinthians 11:23-25.

'Noble simplicity'

Q. Why does the first group of saints in the Eucharistic Prayer I (Roman canon) end with Andrew, while James and the rest are optional?

A. If you are following the eucharistic prayer in the missalette, you know that the names to which you refer are placed in parentheses, indicating as you suggest that their recitation is optional. In the revision of the rites, one of the goals was what Pope Paul VI always referred to as "noble simplicity." To some liturgists that has meant streamlining of rites or prayers, so that the principal point or points stand out. For that reason, there exists the possibility to eliminate the long list of names and simply to indicate our communion with "all the saints." The list, however, is very ancient and contains the names of apostles, as well as saints especially significant to the early Church at Rome. My own pastoral practice in this regard is to read the shorter list, unless it happens to be the feast of one of the saints mentioned in the longer version; in that instance, I read the whole list and, by pause or voice inflection, give special attention to the saint of the day.

You will notice, by the way, that a similar situation prevails with the commemoration of the saints after the Consecration.

Liturgical changes

Q. Several questions for you — all on the liturgy: Is it proper for a priest to substitute the word "friends" for "disciples" at the Consecration? Why would a church have kneelers for the first three rows only? Why can a church not have a tabernacle in the main body of the church, instead of in another part of the building, through several doors?

A. Each matter you refer to is a violation of liturgical law, to some degree.

(1) As I have said constantly in these pages, no priest *ever* has the right to change the words of the liturgy, let alone the consecratory formula. Those words are not mine; they come from the Vatican II Constitution on

the Sacred Liturgy. What the priest's agenda2 is in the substitution, I have no idea.

(2) The Roman Missal for the United States indicates that the congregation is to kneel from the conclusion of the Sanctus to the end of the eucharistic prayer. Unless one has a congregation of athletes, the presumption is that kneelers are provided to facilitate the process, particularly for the elderly or infirm. Basic Christian sensitivity seems to call for this. The only other possibility would be to conclude that the pastor does not want his people to obey the liturgical directives.

(3) The Blessed Sacrament, if it is not reserved on the central axis of the church, must be located in a place which is "prominent, conspicuous, beautifully decorated, and suitable for prayer," says Canon 938.2. Being situated at the end of a labyrinth hardly seems to fulfill the requirement of the law.

Eucharistic prayers

Q. I believe you erred when you said that a priest who refers to Jesus' "friends" (rather than "disciples") in the eucharistic prayer was improvising illicitly. As a matter of fact, all three eucharistic prayers for children use that word, as does the first eucharistic prayer for reconciliation.

A. Thank you, and the other dozen priests who wrote in! I must say, however, that given the full context of the original letter, I do not think we were dealing with a children's Mass or a reconciliation Mass, inasmuch as the impression came across that it was a regular Sunday liturgy, with the substitution happening on a recurring basis. Surely a Mass with a preponderance of adults cannot have a children's eucharistic prayer used.

To set the record straight, however, the writer above is quite correct in noting that a celebrant may be using a completely approved eucharistic prayer with the word "friends" replacing "disciples."

More on eucharistic prayers

Q. I would like to know how many eucharistic prayers are approved for Mass?

A. Four eucharistic prayers are in general use; three others are for Masses with children as the majority of the congregation; two are prayed in Masses for reconciliation. These are the only approved texts in the United States.

Such nonsense

Q. Is the Mass valid if the celebrant washes his hands before (not after) the Offertory, and then offers the bread and wine together and not separately?

A. No, the validity of the Mass is not affected by these actions, but what's the point of such nonsense? Does an individual priest have so much pride that he thinks he knows the way the liturgy should be structured better than the Universal Church? And if he thinks he's being original in offering the bread and wine together, he isn't; the old Dominican rite did it in exactly that way.

Please, Fathers, let's stop torturing our people with our liturgical idiosyncrasies.

Offertory prayers

Q. In your booklet on the biblical roots of the Mass, you omitted the Offertory prayers. Is that because they are lacking in a biblical foundation? Or is it because they are the private prayers of the celebrant?

A. No, they are not unbiblical. In fact, they have roots in the most ancient Jewish prayers of blessing. Your second guess is really closer, in that most people do not hear those prayers at Sunday Mass since they are recited while the congregation is singing a hymn during the preparation of the gifts.

Offertory gifts

Q. I was under the impression that the Offertory gifts were to be taken up to the altar after the collection, and that the money and the gifts of bread and wine should all be part of the Offertory procession. That is not done in my parish. Why?

A. First of all, the Offertory procession is entirely optional. It is a lovely rite, going back to the early Church and recaptured in the liturgical reform of Vatican II, but it is not essential. I imagine that most parishes do follow the procedure which you suggest, but that is not necessary. Perhaps your priest feels that too much time is wasted in waiting for the collection to be taken; still other priests do not like the idea of having money brought to the altar. Whatever the rationale, there is no strict requirement for the procession to occur according to your outline.

Prayer of the Faithful

Q. Where do the prayers in the General Intercessions come from?

A. The Prayer of the Faithful (or General Intercessions) is a part of the Mass which can be constructed by a number of different persons: celebrant, lector, or liturgical planners. More often than not, the petitions you hear at Sunday Mass come from a booklet prepared by one of the missalette companies; there are also books of such prayers on the market.

A set format should be followed: introduction by celebrant; petitions by lector, cantor, deacon, or celebrant; concluding prayer by celebrant. The petitions should also follow a particular order: needs of the Church Universal, the local church, the world (including civil officials), the sick, the oppressed, and the faithful departed. What we use on Sundays is really a "stripped-down" version of the bidding prayers of Good Friday, the ten petitions for the Church and the world which are among the most ancient prayers of the Roman Rite.

Between the Middle Ages and Vatican II, the General Intercessions were lost to the Roman Rite but were recaptured in the period of liturgical renewal.

Proper procedures

Q. Is it right for a pastoral associate to read the Gospel and give a homily at either Sunday or daily Mass?

A. I imagine that you are referring to a person who is not ordained. If so, the answer is an absolute "no." Sometimes pastoral associates lead Communion services in the absence of a priest; in those instances, such a person would generally use the Liturgy of the Word from the day and, yes, read the Gospel, perhaps offering a brief reflection on the Scripture readings. At Mass, however, this is the exclusive right and obligation of a deacon, priest, or bishop.

Awful sermons

Q. Why do priests give such awful sermons? Must they preach every Sunday and always on the readings? Why not preach on subjects which might be more interesting? I'm also sick of the social-activist agenda of so many priests. Why can't we just hear about Christ?

A. When I taught high school, I required my students to write summaries of the homilies they heard on Sunday in their parish churches. While the students were generally positive about their content and even their style, at times they faulted the preachers for a less-than-stirring presentation. Such is to be expected from both sides of the pulpit; that is, priests will have "off days," and parishioners will know times when circumstances in their lives will make them closed to God's Word, even should it be preached by Fulton Sheen. To sensitize the students to the priests' side of the situation, I occasionally asked them to write a homily themselves and then deliver it in class. As a result of such experiences, they were usually less negative in their evaluation of their priests' homilies. I mention this not to excuse bad preaching but to "balance the budget." Now, on to the specifics of the questions you raise.

First, the Church considers preaching a fundamental right and responsibility of priests; it is the way they feed their flock with the Word of God. Practically speaking, it is the only major opportunity for adult education possible. Therefore, a priest (or deacon) must prepare himself well, so that his people will have a fruitful encounter with the Sacred Scriptures, which are often not self-explanatory but require clarification and application (cf. Acts 8:31).

Because of the importance of having the Word proclaimed, the Church mandates a homily on all Sundays and holy days of obligation; the Church also strongly recommends preaching on the weekdays of Lent and Advent, and even throughout the year. The norm envisions a homily which deals with the Scripture readings assigned to that particular Mass; however, the priest may also explain some aspect of the Mass itself or of the life of the saint of the day. On rare occasions, he may set aside any of the above and reflect on a matter related to living the Christian life (e.g., the moral evil of abortion on Right to Life Sunday or the necessity of charity to an annual missionary appeal). Ideally, "more interesting subjects" should be integrated into a well-thought-out homily — the producing of which involves hours of hard work, including prayer, research, and writing. Personally, I see my efforts for the Sunday homily as a serious obligation owed to my people as a matter of justice since it is their right to be instructed in the truths of the Catholic Faith.

Your concern with an overdose of the "social-activist agenda" leaves me with an ambivalent feeling. If you are being regularly treated to outright political partisanship (whether of the "right" or the "left") from the pulpit, something is wrong. On the other hand, the Gospel has a necessary component of social activism. After all, how can I talk about the fatherhood of God without addressing its concrete implications contained in an expression like the "brotherhood of man" — understood as the basic equality of all people in the sight of God and our need to respond to them as we would to Christ Himself?

The dignity of the human person, Catholic political responsibility (that is, voting according to an informed Catholic conscience), prayer, and work for peace all come to mind as legitimate elements of a homily rooted in the Church's social teachings. A distaste for having those issues raised would be an unhealthy sign that one wants to keep the Gospel divorced from daily life, something which is irreconcilable with the way Catholicism has been lived through the centuries.

Talk, talk, talk

Q. *What is the difference between a sermon and a homily?*

A. A sermon is a talk on any religious topic, while a homily is a talk devoted to an exposition of the Scripture texts of the day, with an application to daily life.

Wording of the Creed

Q. *Where has the word "men" gone in the line of the Creed which says (or said), "for us men and for our salvation"? In my area of New Jersey, parishes just say, "for us and for our salvation." However, on recent trips to Pennsylvania and Florida, the Creed was still being recited in the old way. Is the dropping of "men" a local option, left up to the discretion of the local bishop?*

A. No, there is no local option on Mass texts. And no, the text is the same as it has been since this translation was first accepted by the National Conference of Catholic Bishops. For changes in translations to occur, the whole episcopal conference must vote and then have their decision ratified by the Holy See. Undoubtedly, you will recall that some years back, "men" was dropped from the prayer of Consecration over the wine, so that it now reads, "for you and for all." That change was made by the bishops' conference and approved by the appropriate congregation in Rome. I am told that there was some agitation at that time to make the change you discuss, and that the Congregation for the Doctrine of the Faith specifically intervened and ruled out such a change. Why, you ask? Because the line "for us men and for our salvation" is intended to be a parallel and balance to an earlier line, "He became man." In other words, these two elements of the Creed are in dialogue with each other, in the same way that humanity and divinity are, precisely in and through the mystery of the Incarnation affirmed in the Creed. As you can see, liturgical translation work is a multifaceted endeavor, which cannot be engaged in lightly or by theological lightweights since the essence of the Catholic Faith can be at stake at times. Apparently, some priests in your area are so taken up with the alleged necessity of using "inclusive" language that they are prepared to be disobedient to the Church and even risk robbing the Church of the very doctrine which makes her life possible.

Stoles, chasubles

Q. Why do priests' stoles hang straight now, when they used to be crossed? Also, why do some priests wear their stoles over their chasubles?

A. Prior to the liturgical reforms, priests' stoles were crossed to symbolize the fact that their sacramental powers were dependent on the authority of the bishop. Since the stole was under the chasuble, that symbol spoke only to the priest and perhaps the altar boy. I suppose that was the reason for the change. Stoles are not intended to be worn over chasubles. The word "chasuble" means "little house" and should cover everything the priest wears.

Some priests maintain that since the stole is the sign of the priestly office, it should be clearly visible to all. This is incorrect, however, because the eucharistic vestment is not the stole but the chasuble, which is worn only for the Mass, whereas the stole is worn for any priestly function, whether preaching or in the administration of a sacrament.

Blue vestments

Q. My parish used blue vestments for Advent. The pastor said that was to show that it was no longer a penitential season. Another priest says blue is not permitted. Who is right? Oddly enough, I often see blue used for Marian feasts.

A. Blue is not a liturgical color in the Roman Rite, and so cannot be used for either Advent or the Blessed Mother. Centuries ago, the Sarum Rite in

England did use blue for Advent, and Spain had an indult to wear blue for Marian feasts.

The color for Marian feasts is white; at times you will see blue trim but not a blue chasuble. The color for Advent is violet or purple. The General Instruction of the Roman Missal notes that Advent is still to be considered a penitential season, characterized by a sense of expectancy and hope. Therefore, some priests use a lighter or brighter hue of purple for Advent than they do for Lent.

As recently as this past winter, the newsletter of the Bishops' Committee on the Liturgy in Washington noted that blue vestments may not be worn in place of purple for Advent.

Vestments

Q. We have a priest who wears what he calls a "chasualb," instead of a chasuble and alb. Is this permissible?

A. The liturgical books call for the following vestments to be worn — and in this order: amice (if necessary), alb, cincture (if needed), stole, chasuble. If a sufficient number of chasubles is not available, concelebrants may wear an alb and stole; the principal celebrant must always wear a chasuble, unless not celebrating Mass "in a sacred place" (that is, a church or chapel). Your description does not seem to fit any of these circumstances.

Vestments again

Q. Are the liturgical vestments based on Old Testament commandments?

A. Many of our vestments have their origins in the Old Testament, while others come from ancient Roman dress. The alb, common to all liturgical ministers, is described in the Book of Leviticus as the garb of the high priest. The miter, worn by bishops today, was the headdress of the high priest. The chasuble and stole, on the other hand, were garments worn by Roman citizens and gradually adopted and adapted for Christian liturgical use.

Vestments one more time

Q. Are the old "fiddleback" chasubles banned from use today? What about black vestments?

A. The style of vestments to which you refer is properly called "Roman," and they are not banned. However, long before the council they were going out of use under the influence of the liturgical movement of the preconciliar period.

The chasuble is the last vestment put on by the priest and is supposed to cover everything else; its name in Latin means "a little house." The Roman version of the chasuble was an abbreviation of the full Gothic style. Although the Roman chasuble is not forbidden, it does represent a kind of liturgical "minimalism" best put aside.

Black vestments may be worn for funerals or on All Souls' Day. The decision is that of the celebrant.

Bells at Mass

Q. The permanent deacon in our parish has said the Vatican now forbids the ringing of bells at Mass. Is this true?

A. The ringing of bells at Mass is optional. The General Instruction of the Roman Missal indicates that bells *may* be rung at the usual times (that is, the epiclesis, elevations, and Communion). The purpose of bells is obviously to attract attention; some liturgists have argued that since the Mass is generally in the vernacular, the congregation no longer needs to be alerted to these moments since the words are audible and completely intelligible. I am not so sure that this is the case.

By the way, far from forbidding the ringing of bells, the Vatican rings bells itself at the elevations, at least at Masses in which I have participated!

Incense

Q. Why does the priest incense the altar and the coffin at a funeral Mass?

A. Incense is a sign of respect or reverence. As such, it is used to show veneration for the altar (which represents Christ), for the book of the Gospels, for the gifts to be transformed into the Body and Blood of Christ, for the Eucharist itself. Incense is also used for people, who are made in the image and likeness of God and more especially for Christians, who are conformed to Christ through baptism and thus made temples of the Holy Spirit. That regard for the human body remains even after a person has died, and so the censing of the casket in the funeral rite.

Kissing the altar

Q. What makes the altar so special that it is kissed by the priest and other ministers?

A. The altar in every religion is viewed as special because it is the site of sacrifice. In the early Church the altar came to symbolize Christ Himself; at the same time, the eucharistic sacrifice was being celebrated over the tombs of the martyrs, those who continued Christ's passion in their own lives. This latter practice eventually evolved into the placing of martyrs' relics in the altar (a tradition still encouraged but no longer mandated). For all these reasons, the altar is kissed. You say that this is done "by the priest and other ministers." The only ministers who should reverence the altar in this way are bishops, priests, and deacons because of their relationship to the altar through the reception of holy orders.

Holy water

Q. What is the tradition around the use of the holy water upon entering and leaving a church?

A. The use of holy water is an act of purification, a prayer for protection, and an implicit renewal of one's baptismal promises.

More holy water

Q. *Some time ago, at our parish High Mass, the priest came down the center aisle and sprinkled the people with holy water. Is this an option only before High Mass today?*

A. In the "old days," incense and holy water and chanting could only be done at a High Mass. In the revised rites, the distinction between High Mass and Low Mass has been abolished — precisely so that these beautiful options can be used at any time they would be pastorally effective. Thus, the Sprinkling Rite (*Asperges* or *Vidi Aquam*) can be used as a replacement for the Penitential Rite at any Sunday Mass. The celebrant may chant as much or as little of the Mass as he desires. Incense can be used at any Mass and need not be restricted to the equivalent of the old "High Mass."

It is rather ironic that the liturgies eliminated the distinction in order to facilitate the use of the lovely symbols of water, incense, and chant, but many priests labor under the impression that the options can be employed only under the most solemn circumstances.

Concelebration

Q. *Does a priest still have to celebrate Mass every day? Can concelebrating fulfill the obligation? If a Mass is concelebrated, how many stipends can be accepted?*

A. Canon law does not mandate that a priest celebrate Mass every day; however, the priest would be so inclined. After all, does a good husband need a law requiring him to show signs of love and affection to his wife?

Concelebration has a long tradition in the Church of the East and was only restored in the West at Vatican II. It is a beautiful witness to the unity of both the Eucharist and the priesthood. At the same time, no priest can be forced to concelebrate and always retains the right to celebrate a private Mass.

Each concelebrant may accept a stipend (since each may have his own intention), presuming he has not already celebrated another Mass for which he has received a stipend.

Many liturgists feel that concelebration can be "overdone," so that it loses its significance. This can happen when priests routinely concelebrate, or when the vestments are shabby (ideally, all concelebrants should wear alb, stole, and chasuble, although the chasuble may be omitted by all but the principal celebrant in case of necessity), or when the group of concelebration is so large as to become unwieldy.

Common sense and pastoral need should be the determining factors. When concelebration does not seem appropriate, clergy should attend Mass in cassock and surplice and, if desired, receive Holy Communion like the rest of the faithful.

Genuflection

Q. When are Catholics obliged to genuflect?

A. Liturgical law directs that a genuflection be made when everyone passes before the Blessed Sacrament — whether in the tabernacle or exposed on the altar for adoration. Besides those occasions, the celebrant must genuflect during Mass after he elevates the Sacred Host, after the elevation of the chalice, and again just before his own Communion. Until about fifteen years ago, a double genuflection (on two knees) was required before the exposed Sacrament.

Genuflection is a beautiful sign of our belief in the Real Presence of Christ in one Eucharist. If St. Paul says that "at Jesus' name every knee must bend" (Phil 2:10), how much more should that be so when one appears directly before the Lord in the Blessed Sacrament?

Some liturgists have pressed to replace the genuflection with a bow. However, that is not the tradition of the West (although it is in the Eastern churches). In our age and culture, genuflection makes a particularly strong doctrinal statement; after all, people bow to one another all the time — one only bends the knee to God!

Kneeling at Mass

Q. Two parishes in our area have changed the custom of kneeling at the Consecration, and the priests now tell us to stand. I was told that Christ is in the Word, in ourselves, and in the Eucharist all equally — and that is why we stand. What is your opinion?

A. The original Latin of the General Instruction of the Roman Missal mandates kneeling from the Epiclesis (when the priest extends his hands over the gifts) to the Memorial Acclamation (e.g., Christ has died, etc.). The U.S. bishops called for that posture for the duration of the eucharistic prayer.

If your priests told you that the presence of Christ in you and in the eucharistic species is equal, they are quite mistaken. The Vatican II Constitution on the Sacred Liturgy clearly states that the presence of Christ unfolds gradually in the liturgy — first, in the congregation gathering for worship; then, in the priest celebrant; next, in the Word of God proclaimed and explained; finally, in the transformation of the gifts of bread and wine into the Lord's Body and Blood.

The presence of Christ under the appearances of bread and wine is a constant and effective sign which can never signify anything but the presence of Christ. The presence of Christ in us is, unfortunately, often ambivalent as we give "mixed signals" by sinful actions and sinful lives. To suggest otherwise is to fail to take seriously the greatness of God and His complete transcendence over sinful man.

Standing is a sign of respect (hence, the position for the Gospel), while kneeling is a sign of adoration (and thus required for that part of the Mass which effects the Eucharist). It should be noted that no priest (or local bishop, for that matter) has the right to change liturgical law. Therefore, it would be wise to discuss this with your parish priest and, if necessary, with your bishop.

Kneeling again

Q. Regarding your response on kneeling at Mass, I would like to offer the following thoughts. Over the past several years we priests in our parish have allowed standing in our daily-Mass chapel because there are no kneelers, first of all, but also because there is a strong liturgical basis to this posture during the Canon of the Mass. If kneeling is so superior a gesture of reverence, why don't priests kneel during the eucharistic prayer? In short, I feel your answer was misleading and erroneous. The best liturgical tradition seems to support standing as an attitude of praise and thanksgiving, and kneeling as an attitude of penance.

A. The first and most obvious suggestion is for the parish to purchase kneelers for the weekday chapel. However, let's consider some of the theology presented in this question.

I am unaware of "a strong liturgical basis" for standing during the Canon in the Church of the West. I trust you are being facetious when you ask why priests don't kneel, inasmuch as we all know that priests stand outside the community during the eucharistic sacrifice of the Mass, over against it, and at its head — in persona Christi. And that is why the priest stands, and precisely why the congregation should not do so. Kneeling is a posture of penance, true, but it is also a posture of adoration, which is the clear intent at this juncture in the liturgy.

Finally, as regards "the best liturgical tradition" and what it recommends, let me remind the reverend writer that obedience and respect for liturgical norms reflects "the best liturgical tradition." And the law requires the congregation to *kneel.*

Honoring the Eucharist

Q. Father Joseph Champlin, in his book "Preaching and Teaching about the Eucharist," says that a double genuflection before the exposed Blessed Sacrament is no longer the norm, lest people get the idea that the Eucharist is to be more greatly venerated outside of Mass than within the celebration of the sacrifice. Is this true?

A. Yes, it is. While I can see the arguments on both sides, the norms do indicate that a single genuflection is to be used. Liturgical documents are generally positive; hence, they do not tell what not to do but what to do. Therefore, the document in question does not explicitly forbid a genuflection on two knees, but it does tell what should be done, namely, a regular genuflection. The rationale is that a clear connection should be made between the bringing about of the Eucharistic Presence during the Mass and the subsequent adoration of the Sacred Species outside the Mass. When you think about it, there is indeed a logic operative here: If the celebrant is instructed to genuflect on one knee after the Consecration of the elements of bread and wine, why should a double genuflection be made at other times? Certainly, Christ is no more present later than He was at the very moment of Consecration.

The Divine Presence

Q. I often hear it said that our Lord is just as present in the Word as He is the Eucharist. While it is surely true that God is present in His Word, isn't this statement just a bit too broad to be true? Of course, often enough some people operate as though Christ is more *present in the Word than in the Blessed Sacrament; I mean that the lectionary is carried with great fanfare and incensed, while the consecrated Host is not even elevated, let alone incensed.*

A. Some people have gotten this notion from a misreading of a conciliar quote: "The Church has always venerated the divine Scriptures as she venerated the Body of the Lord, insofar as she never ceases, particularly in the sacred liturgy, to partake of the bread of life and to offer it to the faithful from the one table of the word of God and the Body of Christ" (*Dei Verbum*, no. 21).

Some commentators stretch the analogy too far because they fail to read far enough, that is, to the second clause which begins with "insofar as." In other words, the equation is made between the Church's reverence for the Word and her reverence for the Eucharist, insofar as she makes both available to the faithful and both come from the same loving God.

The presence of God in His Word is a true presence, of course, but qualitatively different from Christ's Presence in the Eucharist. And the Constitution on the Sacred Liturgy of Vatican II makes that clear by speaking of the various degrees of presence and the gradual unfolding of Christ's Presence in the celebration of the Mass, so that we find Him in the community gathered for worship, in the celebrant, in the Word proclaimed, in the gifts offered, in the gifts transformed, and in the gifts received — moving in symphonic style until we reach a crescendo in the Consecration and Communion (cf. *Sacrosanctum Concilium*, no. 7).

In previous eras, perhaps some Catholics did not have a sufficiently well-developed appreciation of the importance and power of God's Word; however, the budget is not balanced by negating the correct insight in regard to the unsurpassing and unsurpassed dignity of the Blessed Sacrament. Your point is well-taken in reference to external signs of reverence for the Word and Sacrament; to incense the book of the Gospels without later incensing the very One to whom the Gospels lead is, to say the least, bizarre. That is bad liturgy, reflecting bad theology.

Formulaic prayers

Q. The other day at Mass, I watched people around me during the Creed. They were just mouthing words, reciting from memory, with no real thought or conviction. It was so sad. What can be done to wake up these people?

A. Perhaps the first question to ask is why you were looking around at others during the Profession of Faith! One could interpret this inquiry as being somewhat rash or judgmental of others since we can never know what others are truly thinking or what their inner dispositions are. That having been said, you do identify a legitimate concern.

A creed is essential for any cohesive faith community. However, like any formulaic prayer, it has one serious drawback, namely, that at times we "mouth words," as you put it, without thinking or reflecting on their meaning. When people use traditional prayers (and there is nothing wrong with that — just think, Jesus gave us one to use, and He used the Psalms in just that way), they need not advert to every single word every time the prayer is said. Sometimes the words come together in such a way that a general mood is created, leading to an attitude or posture of prayer. This is very often the case with the Rosary, for example.

When a priest suspects that the vitality is being sapped from a particular prayer by its frequent use, an easy solution may be to preach on its significance or to highlight a key line before its communal recitation.

Since we are constantly changing through the circumstances of our lives, we can usually glean new meanings from a prayer which we have recited thousands of times. Our lives bring the necessary spontaneity to what could otherwise become dry formulas.

Mass revision

Q. Why did the Catholic Church have to hire six Protestant ministers to revise the Mass after Vatican II?

A. You have been reading literature from some right-wing schismatics, and there is no truth to the allegation.

Present at Vatican II were only non-Catholic observers (Protestant, Jewish, Islamic, and even nonbelievers), who attended the various sessions of the council and offered their own reflections on matters when asked to do so. When the postconciliar liturgical reform began, it was natural to consult with other Christians about such things; after all, one of the primary goals of the council was Christian unity, and no real unity could be achieved if division existed over something as basic as worship. Hence, the consultation process.

The implication made above is that the Protestants involved in the consultation "Protestantized" the Catholic liturgy. The charge is silly because one need only look at liturgies of the early Church and see how close today's is to those. Furthermore, the reverse has actually occurred in many instances. For example, twenty years ago the celebration of the Eucharist on Sundays was a rarity in most Protestant churches; today that is the norm for many. Our revised lectionary (the cycle of readings) was adopted by several denominations like the Anglicans, Presbyterians, Lutherans, and other mainline groups. Ironically, many Protestant laity have accused their clergy of "selling out" to Rome in becoming "too Catholic."

'Lefebvrites'

Q. In your last column you judged "Lefebvrites" rather harshly. Wouldn't you have to admit that liturgical abuses gave Archbishop Lefebvre and his followers a real "cause"?

A. I would take exception to your suggestion that I "judged Lefebvre rather harshly." In fact, I have always maintained a strong but sad sympathy for the prelate and his people.

The point you mention, however, is quite valid. Ironically, I alluded to it in the last paragraph of my response, but it was removed in the final editing stages because of space limitations. So, yes, I agree that if vernacular liturgical celebrations were conducted with dignity and decorum and if Latin Masses according to the revised rites were more generally available, the schismatic movement of Archbishop Lefebvre would have most of the steam taken out of it.

Defending Lefebvre

Q. I must say that I terribly resented Father Dimock's attack on Archbishop Marcel Lefebvre. Enclosed is a document produced by Cardinal Ottaviani for Pope Paul VI about the problems of the new Mass. What do you have to say to that?

A. I do not think Father Dimock was uncharitable in his handling of the Lefebvre question. That having been said, let me deal with your specific point.

I was a seminarian when the so-called "Ottaviani Intervention" was published and recall having studied it very carefully. Rereading it twenty years later, I find that I have the same mixed reaction: The cardinal made some very good points (which were taken into account by Pope Paul before promulgating the rite which we now have) and some rather unworthy observations.

My first complaint about the document is that it is authored "by a group of Roman theologians." I don't enjoy reading the works of nameless individuals (and yes, this also happens on the other side of the fence today, especially with some statements produced by anonymous committees purporting to speak for a whole conference of bishops). The only possible reason for not signing one's name to an academic paper is embarrassment over the content, and one finds a good deal of careless scholarship, innuendo, and needless nitpicking in "A Critical Study of the *Novus Ordo Missae*."

Interestingly, one should note that the rite we presently celebrate universally is not called the *Novus Ordo Missae* (New Order of Mass), but only the *Ordo Missae* (Order of Mass).

In terms of issues raised by the study, I would highlight but a few:

(1) The authors make quite a bit of the fact that the revised rite did not receive the endorsement of the Synod of Bishops, was never voted on by the worldwide body of bishops, and had never been requested by the faithful. Since when do "traditional" Catholics use such criteria?

(2) The document expresses dismay that the word "memorial" is used to describe the Mass, instead of "the unbloody renewal of the sacrifice of Calvary." In point of fact, a correct biblical theology of "memorial" means exactly that what happened on Calvary is "renewed" on the Church's altars — a point made several times in TCA in articles on the Mass. Besides, to allay such fears, Pope Paul VI directed that in several places where "Lord's Supper" or "memorial of the Lord" were used, the phrase "or sacrifice of the Mass" should follow — precisely to underscore the fact that we are talking about synonymous expressions. By the way, St. Thomas Aquinas specifically refers to the Mass as "*memoria*" in his beautiful hymn, "*O Sacrum Convivium.*"

(3) The charge is made that "the Real Presence of Christ is never alluded to and belief in it is implicitly repudiated." If that is so, what is one to make of lines like, "Grant that we, who are nourished by his body and blood, may be filled with his Holy Spirit. . ."? Or, "we offer you his body and blood, the acceptable sacrifice which brings salvation to the whole world"? Such examples could be multiplied ad infinitum.

(4) The authors make much about the fact that the new Offertory prayers say that the bread will become "the bread of life," the suggestion being that this expression is a denigration of the doctrine of transubstantiation. If that is true, then the theologians ought to question the author of the fourth Gospel, who says that this is exactly what Jesus called the Eucharist (cf. Jn 6:48).

(5) I agree that the practical abandonment of Latin was a mistake, but that cannot be laid at the doorstep of either Vatican II or Pope Paul VI's "*Ordo Missae*"; as a matter of fact, Pope Paul consistently spoke of the necessity of preserving Latin. Whatever one wants to say about the use or non-use of Latin, it should be clear that the Order of Mass used has nothing to do with that question. If one substantially accepts the Ottaviani intervention, it seems that one is asserting that the Holy Spirit left the Church when the Order of Mass of Pope Paul VI began to be celebrated. And if that is so, then one would logically be required to leave this Church. I do not think one need defend every element of the "new Mass," and I do

believe that improvements are possible (even bringing in certain elements from the so-called "Tridentine Mass"); however, it is necessary to hold that the doctrine reflected in the revised rites does indeed correspond to the Faith as we have always known it. My guess is that with the "generous application" (to quote Pope John Paul II) of the 1984 indult for the use of the 1962 Roman Missal, a healthy interaction can begin to take place, so that a more natural, organic development of rites can occur — under legitimate ecclesiastical authority, of course.

In summary, I feel it foolhardy to declare that everything that went before was either hopelessly useless or incapable of perfection; similarly, it makes no sense to argue that the new is either blatantly heretical or the apex of liturgical development.

Altar drama

Q. *Why did Vatican II order the altars to be turned around?*

A. Vatican II never ordered the altars to be "turned around," nor did any subsequent liturgical legislation at the universal level.

Interestingly enough, many places (especially Spain, France, and Germany) had Mass "facing the people" decades before Vatican II. The "old Mass" could always be celebrated that way, and the best proof of it is that the papal altar in St. Peter's Basilica in Rome was so constructed (in the sixteenth century) so that the Pope has people on four sides of the altar.

When the liturgical documents advocated a free-standing altar (one not attached to the back wall), the reason cited was to provide the celebrant with the possibility of completely circling the altar for the censings. Some would-be liturgists speak disparagingly of a Mass celebrated with "the priest's back to the people." A more accurate description is Mass "facing East," toward the rising sun. In that style, priests and people all face the same direction.

To have the priest face the people has advantages and disadvantages alike. The biggest liability is that a very clericalistic impression can be created, turning the Mass into a kind of drama with the priest as the principal actor or as a dialogue between priest and people. The Mass, however, is neither. To reap the assets of Mass facing the people (greater visibility, for example), a celebrant needs to be conscious of the difficulties and thus seek to minimize them (for example, by not staring into the congregation during the eucharistic prayer, but keeping his gaze fixed either on the altar or on heaven).

Although universal law does not mandate Mass facing the people, many bishops have called for the practice in their dioceses. This, however, should not lead to the destruction of old "high altars" (especially if they are true works of art). Much less should it suggest a cheap, uninspiring table stuck between the old altar and the congregation. If an altar is erected to face the people, it should be of the highest quality, befitting the worship of Almighty God.

Mass in Latin

Q. *It seems that many dioceses are now scheduling Latin Masses of both the old rite and the new, but I was shocked to hear recently from some friends that in other dioceses bishops have actually forbidden the celebration of Mass in Latin according to either rite. Is this possible?*

A. It is happening, I know, but when a bishop prohibits the celebration of Mass in Latin according to the revised rites, he is acting beyond his authority. Why do I say that? Because the Code of Canon Law says the following: "The eucharistic celebration is to be carried out *either in the Latin language* or in another language, provided the liturgical texts have been lawfully approved" (Canon 928, emphasis added). In other words, no permission is ever needed to offer Mass in Latin; permission is needed to use the vernacular, however. Of course, this canon merely reflects very accurately the position adopted by the Fathers of Vatican II in their Constitution on the Sacred Liturgy.

Liturgical renewal

Q. *In reading "The Ratzinger Report," I got the impression that liturgical reform has been taken much further in this country than was intended by Vatican II, particularly regarding the use of the traditional hymns and the use of Latin in certain parts of the Mass. Do you agree?*

A. Liturgical renewal is essential in every age if the Faith is to be properly communicated and celebrated through the Church's rites, and history gives strong witness to that process of ongoing liturgical development. One need only read a classic work like Father Josef Jungmann's two volumes on *The Mass of the Roman Rite* to see this. However, there is a difference between reformation and deformation. What Cardinal Ratzinger refers to and what so many Catholics in the United States have endured is the latter; this makes all liturgical renewal operate under a cloud of suspicion and gives fuel to those who oppose any legitimate and necessary change.

All too often some self-proclaimed liturgists in this country and elsewhere have taken it upon themselves to set a new course for the liturgy, not infrequently completely at odds with the Faith once received from the saints. Liturgy can never be a totally new creation, for as in doctrine, the developmental process must be organic. By that I mean that new forms must grow out of older forms and be in continuity with them; in nature we know that a frog can never give birth to a cat. Similarly, in the Church what is brought forth must always be recognizable in terms of its origins and in its contemporary dress; otherwise, we are not dealing with changes in keeping with the Catholic Tradition.

Cardinal Ratzinger has written movingly about the lost "sense of the sacred," which occurs when people try to politicize liturgy or use it for entertainment instead of the worship of the one true God. Reverence and respect in the house of God, good hymns, sacred language — all these things help to reinforce our doctrinal conviction that Christ is present in the Eucharist in a unique manner. When the external forms are hastily or unwisely discarded, disaster often ensues. It is probably no exaggeration to say that in many places an entire generation of young Catholics has been raised without a clear notion of the Real Presence, not because the doctrine has been denied in religion classes or from the pulpit but because the liturgy has often failed to teach this profound truth through the signs employed or because the symbols used contradict the teaching.

I should note that this is not the difficulty of the revised rites themselves but has been brought on by self-appointed "experts" who tamper with the liturgy and try to make it into something it was never intended to be.

For all these reasons and aside from considerations about obedience to liturgical law, I have always been a strong opponent of liturgical revision which is unauthorized and unwarranted. My own experience tells me that the younger priests coming up the line are usually rather sensitive to this point; having suffered the effects of liturgical silliness and confusion as young people, not a few of them are resolved not to repeat the same mistakes as leaders of the Church at worship.

I think this is what Cardinal Ratzinger is talking about, and I am in total agreement with him. I would refer readers to his wonderful book on the liturgy, *Feast of Faith* (Ignatius Press, San Francisco).

Vatican II

Q. How may I acquire a book that contains the changes brought about by Vatican II and those not changed by the council as well? I have the Code of Canon Law, but that doesn't seem to say too much about liturgy.

A. You are correct that the Code of Canon Law doesn't deal with liturgy very much; in fact, it avoids it because liturgical norms are generally found in liturgical books, not law books.

To assist you in your study, I would suggest the two-volume paperback (or one-volume study edition) which deals with all the conciliar and postconciliar changes in liturgy and all other areas of Catholic life: *Vatican Council II: Conciliar and Post-Conciliar Documents*, edited by Austin Flannery and published by Costello in Northport, New York.

The Last Supper

Q. In what language was the first Mass said?

A. I imagine you are referring to the Last Supper. If so, we are talking about a Passover meal, which was completely ritualized and, therefore, would have been in Hebrew — even though the language spoken in Palestine at that time was Aramaic.

The Mass

Q. Why is our eucharistic service called the Mass?

A. The name comes from a historical accident. As you may know, at the conclusion of the Mass, the priest (or deacon) says, in the Latin, "*Ite, missa est.*" Literally, that means, "Go, it (the Church or congregation) is sent." "*Missa*" (dismissal) gradually and eventually became the name for the entire service. That translates into English as "Mass."

6. CATHOLIC PRACTICES

Mormon marriage

Q. Can permission be given for a Catholic to marry a Mormon in the Mormon church? Once married in such a ceremony, is it possible for the Catholic party to receive Holy Communion?

A. According to Church law, a Catholic may marry a non-Catholic in the ceremony of another faith or in a completely civil ceremony, for serious reason (e.g., the family of the non-Catholic is adamantly opposed to a Catholic rite, thus causing family tension). Such an arrangement, when done with permission of one's bishop, constitutes a valid marriage in the eyes of the Church. Therefore, such a person may lead a full sacramental life.

That having been said, I would offer two cautions. First, if a Catholic ceremony is such a stumbling block for the other party or his family, this may well signal other serious faith-related problems on the horizon. Some honest discussion and a good deal of prayer and reflection would seem to be in order.

Second, specifically regarding the Mormon marriage, the questioner should know that although a Mormon can marry a non-Mormon in his local church, only a ceremony in the Temple at Salt Lake or other recognized temple is considered a "sealed" marriage, that is, enrolling the couple in the celestial marriage rolls — and that rite can be performed only between two practicing Mormons.

Israel

Q. Exactly what is the Vatican stand on Israel, and why is it so?

A. The Holy See's position on the State of Israel is quite simple, but often gets garbled by anti-Catholic people in the media. The Vatican does not question Israel's right to exist as a nation, and the popes have consistently and unequivocally affirmed that right. The controversy surrounds the issue of diplomatic recognition of Israel.

The Vatican, as a secular state and recognized as such in international law, enters into relations with other nations in varying degrees. Formal diplomatic relations are always the result of the initiative of the other state. When the Holy See evaluates such a request, it does so with certain moral objectives in mind.

The problems relevant to Vatican-Israeli relations come down to the following, from the Vatican perspective:

1. The Holy See never formally recognizes any nation which is involved in an unresolved border dispute. For this reason, the Church "recognizes" neither Israel nor Jordan.

2. The Vatican insists on some sort of international status for Jerusalem, guaranteeing access to the holy shrines for Jews, Christians, and Moslems alike — unbeholden to any national government's whims, Israeli or otherwise.

3. The Holy See is determined to represent the rights of the Palestinians in Israel. In fact, the Vatican sees its continued refusal to establish full diplomatic ties with Israel as a "bargaining chip" in the endeavor to secure justice for the Palestinian people.

Therefore, it is not a one-sided refusal. On the contrary, the Holy See would gladly enter into full diplomatic relations with Israel if Israel did not refuse the Vatican conditions. Diplomacy has very special rules; intimately connected are the norms for recognition and non-recognition of nations. When the Holy See comes on the diplomatic scene, it can never forget that it is not just a secular state but preeminently the Church of Jesus Christ, which must reflect His values in all areas of life, including the world of diplomacy and maybe even *especially* there.

Gargoyles

Q. Enclosed are several snapshots of the outside of our parish church. At the top you will find a rather grotesque figure; what is its significance on a church building?

A. From what I can gather, the figure you are referring to is a gargoyle, used in medieval architecture at the top corners of churches, symbolically designed to scare away demons from the sacred precincts. The tradition survives in some contemporary buildings. Certainly one should not take it for anything more or less than it is: Some see it as superstition at its worst, while others prefer to view it as a prayer in stone for God's house to be preserved from the presence of the Evil One.

Christian burial

Q. As an elderly Catholic, I find myself going to a lot of funerals. I am amazed that the priests never discuss anything about sin, judgment, hell, or purgatory. It seems that they presume (and sometimes even declare!) that all the dead just go to heaven automatically. Did I miss something at Vatican II?

A. When I hear funeral homilies like those you have described, I often joke with the celebrant afterwards by asking him, "Did you take a stipend for that Mass?" He usually looks puzzled at that point, so I go on: "If you are certain that the deceased is truly in heaven, then you had no right to take a stipend to offer Mass asking God to take him to Himself. However, if you're not sure, then you had no right to canonize him."

I think much of this unofficial "canonizing" at funerals in recent years is an overreaction to some of the excessive "fire and brimstone" sermons of a bygone era, in which one could have gotten the impression at times that just about everyone in the universe was headed for hell in a handbasket. But the budget never gets balanced by going to the opposite extreme.

The homily at a Mass of Christian Burial should deal with the following: the resurrection of the dead; the need to pray for the dead; the importance of being prepared to meet Christ, who is at once a just and merciful Judge; and the Communion of Saints. In no case should this homily devolve into a eulogy.

Cremation

Q. A friend of mine says she thinks burial wastes a lot of space, better given over to the living, and that she wants to be cremated. I told her the Church does not permit cremation, but she insists that has changed. Can you resolve this debate?

A. I would agree with your friend that many American customs related to death and dying are ridiculous at best. I would not, however, be as cavalier as she seems to be about the human body after death. The Church has always accorded the body great reverence in death (e.g., incensing the body during the Mass of Christian Burial) because that body was, as St. Paul put it, the temple of the Holy Spirit; every time that person received Holy Communion, he or she became a tabernacle. Therefore, the body is deserving of special honor — even after death.

At the time of the Enlightenment, some skeptics considered the Christian doctrine of the resurrection of the dead to be an absurdity; to emphasize their point, they willed their bodies to be cremated, challenging God, as it were, to put a body together from those ashes on the last day. Cremation, for them, was the final and lasting mockery of the Christian Faith. For that reason, the Church forbade any Catholic from submitting his body for cremation. Since no one seems to have such thoughts today, the Church has lifted the ban, and the Code of Canon Law (revised in 1983) says that "the pious custom of burial (should) be retained; but (the law) does not forbid cremation, *unless* this is chosen for reasons which are contrary to Christian teaching" (emphasis added).

Cremation again

Q. If a person is cremated, can the ashes be brought to the church for the funeral Mass and must the ashes then be buried? Can they be scattered over the ocean, for example?

A. As already noted in these pages, the 1983 Code of Canon Law permits cremation when this is not done so as to cast doubt on the resurrection of the dead. Since this permission is relatively recent, all its implications have not been worked out in detail.

Canonists would seem to indicate that the body can be brought to the church and cremated afterwards. If cremation occurs first, however, the ashes may not be treated like the body; that is, they may not be blessed with holy water or incensed. Although the ashes need not be interred, they may not be scattered.

Cremation clarification

The following is a clarification on cremation as presented in the September-October 1988 edition of The Catholic Answer. *It is written by Most Reverend Joseph A. Ferrario, Bishop of Honolulu.*

According to canon law and Church practice, the body was to be brought to the Church before cremation if a family wanted the full burial rites over the remains. In cases when the people insisted on bringing the cremains to Church, the canonists interpreted the law to direct the placement of the cremains near the bereaved family on a table or on the church pew and all rites were to be omitted over the cremains.

However, some dioceses throughout the world sought and obtained a rescript to allow full rites over the cremains. The dioceses of Canada sought and obtained this permission. One of the New England bishops whose diocesan boundaries were contiguous to Canadian dioceses brought the permission to the attention of the American bishops in a plenary session. There was not that much interest in it.

Since cremation has always been a part of the Asian tradition here in the state of Hawaii and therefore much desired among our Catholics with an Asian background, I petitioned Rome for this rescript and permission, and received it. So, in the Diocese of Honolulu, if the people plan for cremation we can have the complete burial rites over the ashes.

The law is not clear about the scattering of ashes. It does not actually forbid such a practice. However, our Catholic tradition would call for an interment of some sort.

'God bless you'

Q. Why do we say, "God bless you" when a person sneezes? Is it a custom, habit, tradition, or what?

A. Believe it or not, it seems that when we move beyond Chicago, the expression is not all that common! The practice does go back at least to medieval England when it was thought that sneezing released demons from a sick person; therefore, the "God bless you." It is a lovely and charming custom, which should be preserved, in my opinion, simply because it gives a religious witness in an increasingly secularized society.

Prefers silence

Q. Why do we have to listen to foreign priests preach in our church every week? Wouldn't it be better if one of the Americans on the staff spoke? They're so difficult to understand that I think a ten-minute period of silence would be better.

A. It would seem to me that you should be grateful that some parents somewhere in the world are still producing Christian families which foster priestly vocations, and that some men are willing to come to a foreign land to serve your spiritual needs. While cutting through a foreign accent might be burdensome at first, it might be just the penance to offer so that we Americans can begin again to raise up a generation of native clergy here.

Over the past decade I have written and spoken often on the shortage of priests in the United States. In my estimation, it might be well for bishops to leave parishes without priests if they haven't produced a vocation in a particular period of time. Perhaps then our people would wake up to the fact that priests do not drop from the sky but must be "home-grown," with all that this implies.

Votive candles

Q. *As a recent convert, I am interested in some background on why Catholics light votive candles.*

A. First of all, welcome to the Church!

Many Catholics have "foggy" notions on this topic, too, so don't feel strange about the question. The lighted candle serves as a kind of prolongation of one's personal prayer. Unable to remain physically in prayer beyond a particular time, the person lights a candle which does remain and symbolizes the desire for the prayer to continue. This practice is not unlike that of Orthodox Jews who, when praying at the Wailing Wall in Jerusalem, jot down their petitions on scraps of paper, which they then place in the cracks in the wall, enabling their prayer to be present to God even when they cannot be completely attentive to their petition.

Conciliar works

Q. *You have recommended the two-volume work on the conciliar and postconciliar documents, but with no address for the publisher. Could you please provide it?*

A. Costello Publishing Co. may be contacted by writing to Box 9 in Northport, NY 11768.

Use of churches

Q. *Is it now allowed to have Christmas programs in church? Formerly, we had them in the school gym, and the seating was adequate. This year, however, the program was held in the church. Even though it was only singing, there was a good deal of loud socializing, too.*

A. Last year the Holy See issued a document on concerts in churches, the point being that only sacred music could be performed and that no admission charges could be levied. Since you give no particulars about the concert you attended, I cannot say anything more about it. However, if there was "loud socializing," that indicates to me that the people have not been trained to have the proper reverence for the church building as the house of God and especially for the Blessed Sacrament. My guess is that you probably have similar behavior at other times, and this is the kind of situation that requires constant vigilance on the part of pastors, ushers, and others concerned with the sacred liturgy.

Flags in church

Q. When we received a new pastor a few years ago, his first order of business was to remove the American and papal flags from our church. This really caused quite a furor. We now have a new pastor and would like to approach him about returning them. What is the position of the Church on this matter?

A. Liturgical regulations indicate that flags do not belong within the sanctuary. Aside from that, nothing else is mentioned. Many churches hang the flags from the choir loft or place them in the vestibule or in the back of the church. The reason is not to be unpatriotic but to keep our focus — which is the worship of Almighty God.

If the flags are so important to so many parishioners, why not talk to your new pastor about returning them to the church, but in a place where they would not detract from the liturgy?

RENEW

Q. Can you please explain the Church's attitude toward a program called "RENEW"? I've heard bad things about it, but my pastor says we're going into it.

A. The program to which you refer began over a decade ago. It was designed to be, as the name implies, a program of parish renewal, combining prayer and study to deepen the faith-life of the parish community. It placed great stress on small groups as a means to achieve its goals. All that is quite praiseworthy, anyone would agree.

The problem surfaced in two areas. First, the methodology of the study groups was such that leaders were to function simply as "facilitators," so that any answer offered by anyone in the group should be valued as much as any other. Needless to say, when one is dealing with matters of faith and revealed truth, one answer is not as good as any other. Second, for a program which extended over many months, one could rightfully expect a presentation of the Catholic Faith in all its fullness. However, many critical elements of Catholic doctrine were missing. Thus, participants could emerge from the program with a less than complete appreciation of Catholicism.

As a result of numerous complaints about RENEW, the Bishops' Committee on Doctrine was asked to conduct a study to determine if the objections raised were justified. The final report praised many aspects of the program, but did identify the two areas cited above as requiring remediation from the program directors. Presumably, the changes called for by the bishops will be made.

Spirit-filled churches

Q. I know some Catholic churches that are truly Spirit-filled places. How can every parish "catch the Spirit"?

A. I must confess that this question makes me distinctly uncomfortable because it smacks of an elitist mentality which is destructive of genuine Christian community.

The Church teaches firmly that anyone who has been baptized has received the gift of the Holy Spirit. That initial relationship is then strengthened in confirmation. In fact, the Holy Spirit is operative in every sacramental encounter. Therefore, every Catholic parish is "truly Spirit-filled."

That having been said, two different situations emerge. The first involves people who do not respond to the promptings of the Spirit and so do not live like "Spirit-filled" people. That problem has been with the Church from her first days and is an indication that the Church is every bit as human as she is divine. The appropriate response is not complacency but an attitude of understanding which seeks to deal with the problem effectively.

The second concerns an approach to the Christian life which endeavors to make one's personal standards of Christianity those of the entire Church. This is unfair when the particular issues are not faith-related but merely external matters (like styles of prayer or preferences in music). This would also extend to a desire to have all believers "speak in tongues" or engage in "faith healing," both sometimes used as acid tests for determining if an individual or community is "Spirit-filled." St. Paul saw things differently and encouraged his readers to seek "the greater gifts" (1 Cor 12:31), namely, "faith, hope, and love, and the greatest of these is love" (1 Cor 13:13).

Finally, one does not " catch the Spirit" but is caught by Him. The distinction is not an exercise in theological "cuteness." It reminds us that almighty God always takes the initiative and that our task is to be open to His action and to respond accordingly.

Masons

Q. I live in a town where the Masons are very powerful. For years I resisted joining because Catholics were forbidden to do so. Some years ago when I learned that the law had been relaxed, I finally joined. Now someone tells me membership in the Masons is not permitted for Catholics again. What's the story?

A. It appears that some confusion existed for some time on this point, requiring the Congregation for the Doctrine of the Faith to formulate a definite response. That reply was in the negative, for the following reasons.

Freemasonry (its proper name) is a secret society, demanding the total adherence of its members. Its history is marked by open hostility to the Catholic Church and to organized religion in general. Its philosophy is relativistic and naturalistic, and its theology flies in the face of traditional Judaeo-Christian concepts of God, truth, and the human person. Because of the basic incompatibility of Freemasonry and Catholicism, the Congregation for the Doctrine of the Faith has clarified and restated the ban on Catholic membership in the organization.

It is good to realize that other Christian bodies also forbid their members to belong to the Masons. Even the elitist exclusivity you describe in your question should be ample reason to refrain from membership, never mind the doctrinal difficulties.

School prayer

Q. Does the Catholic Church fear a school prayer amendment? If not, what if a prayer contrary to Catholic teaching were chosen?

A. The Church, as such, has no formal position on the question of prayer in government schools, presuming that it would be voluntary and nondenominational. These two concerns would also be part of the constitutional question.

As someone who has studied the First Amendment religion clauses very carefully, I must say I am most ambivalent on this matter. Certainly no one can argue that the First Amendment, in the minds of its drafters, was designed to prevent voluntary school prayer. After all, for nearly two centuries government schools began class with a prayer, and there is not the slightest hint anywhere that anyone imagined it violated the law.

That having been said, I do have two objections to such prayers in the context of contemporary public education. First, given the lack of values which has become a part of the landscape of government education, I would not want to give the impression that simply opening the day with a prayer can heal that severe wound, which has crippled the educational process in this country for several decades now. Second, whose prayer would be used (as you note in your question)? And what about children who do not opt to pray, for any number of reasons? Nearly seventy years ago my own father was kept back in the fourth grade because of a refusal to recite the Protestant version of the Lord's Prayer.

Many people of good will think that prayer would be a good way to begin to put education back on track in the governmental school system. I am not sure if that isn't putting the cart before the horse. Frankly, my own preference is that the United States join the rest of the free nations of the world by giving parents the opportunity to choose religiously oriented schools for their children without financial penalty; then pluralism is more properly served in a way consonant with the best in the American tradition of freedom and democracy.

Shroud of Turin

Q. I have just read a book which seems to make a good case for the fact that the Shroud of Turin is a forgery. If that is so, why have so many popes seemed to believe in it? Also, why doesn't the Church crack down on fraudulent relics?

A. I am unaware of any papal declaration about the authenticity of the Shroud. Pope John Paul II has followed the lead of Pope Paul VI in submitting the Shroud to further scientific investigation. Science will never be able to say with total assurance that it is in fact the burial garment of our Lord. The most we could expect is a narrowing of the gap, which eliminates many other possibilities.

The Church is very careful with relics. The problem often occurs at the popular level, where pious people can be manipulated by unscrupulous individuals.

It must be recalled, however, that our Faith is centered in Christ. Relics, like any other sacramentals, should lead to a deeper faith in Him; when that fails to happen, they have become counterproductive and need to be put aside.

Good godparent

Q. When I was a nonpracticing Catholic, I became a godparent for a Methodist baby. In light of your recent answer on a similar question, I am wondering if I should inform the parents that now, as a practicing Catholic, I would have serious problems of conscience in living up to the promises I made at their child's baptism. Please advise.

A. I think it would be prudent to discuss this matter with the parents, lest they assume that you would still be inclined to raise their child as a Methodist, should anything happen to them. Very often less fervent people might be happy simply to have their child reared in any Christian denomination, and that is what they might tell you. Your concern for your role as a godparent is laudable.

Godparents for Protestants

Q. Can Catholics become godparents for a Lutheran baby whose parents left the Catholic Church?

A. First of all, Catholics cannot be godparents for any non-Catholic ceremony. What sense would it make for a practicing Catholic to say that he or she would rear a child in a faith which we believe to be deficient in one or more areas? It is important to stress that being a godparent should never be viewed as a mere social convention or social honor; it carries with it serious responsibilities, which is why the Church always insists on *practicing* Catholics for those who undertake this role for Catholic babies.

The situation you describe has an added difficulty attached to it, and that is that the parents involved have left the true Church (for whatever reason) and now ask Catholics to give implicit approval to their action by participating in this ceremony. For them to ask for this is a tremendous display of insensitivity; for a Catholic to acquiesce is a serious breach of faith and loyalty to the Church. The Catholic needs to remind this couple of the Vatican II statement: "Hence they could not be saved who, knowing that the Catholic Church was founded by God through Christ, would refuse to enter it, or to remain in it" (*Lumen Gentium*, no. 14).

Pagan feasts

Q. My daughter is a Fundamentalist and insists that Christians should not be celebrating Halloween because it is a pagan holiday, as well as sinful and anti-Christian. Just what does the Church teach about this holiday?

A. I imagine your daughter is a convert to Fundamentalism from Catholicism. Maybe she has forgotten her holy days of obligation. November 1 is the Solemnity of All Saints, also known in the British Isles as All Hallows. The night before is therefore called All Hallows Eve, that is, Halloween.

Undoubtedly, many pagan cultures had celebrations dealing with ghosts and goblins, but Halloween began as a day on which children dressed up as various saints (who would be honored the following day). I think any reasonable person would view this as a relatively harmless activity. Of course, the truth is that many Fundamentalists have difficulty with any kind of feasts or ceremonies and so look for excuses to condemn them. Naturally, if one looks hard and long enough, he can usually find something offensive in anything — just what the Scribes and Pharisees did with our Lord's teaching and Person.

Proselytizers

Q. How do I handle Seventh Day Adventists, Assembly of God people, or Jehovah's Witnesses who come to my door proselytizing?

A. People who are so committed to their beliefs that they seek to make converts are to be admired. Problems surface, however, when they are either misinformed or bigoted.

It seems to me that Catholics should welcome anyone as Christ, but that also suggests that the guest is acting in Christlike charity. My own father always relished opportunities to engage in dialogue with door-to-door missionaries, because he saw such moments as opportunities to share his Faith with them. I know of at least one visitor whom he led into the fullness of Christian Faith found in the Catholic Church.

Dialogue is one thing; harassment is another. When individuals become offensive, they have ceased to act in a Christlike manner; they have thus worn out their welcome and should be shown to the door.

It is a good idea always to have on hand some good Catholic pamphlets on a variety of topics to offer non-Catholic missionaries, especially designed to answer the most common questions regarding Catholicism. A Catholic who does not know his or her Faith well should do two things: first, keep the door closed; second, remedy the deficiencies.

In-family proselytizing

Q. What should I do when I discover my Fundamentalist in-laws indoctrinating my children in their beliefs?

A. The problem you identify is one reason why the Church has always discouraged "mixed marriages." Religion is such an important part of life that it automatically impels a believer to share it with others.

Presuming that your in-laws are people of goodwill who love your children, they undoubtedly feel they are loving their grandchildren by imparting their version of the Gospel to them. All the goodwill in the world, however, cannot justify an attempt on the part of anyone (relative, teacher, or government official) to interpose himself between a parent and child. It is both your right and responsibility, then, to make it known to your in-laws that they are engaging in what you consider reprehensible action, which you will not tolerate. If they will not agree to cease their proselytizing of your children, they should be told that they will not be allowed to see them.

All this naturally presupposes that your husband sees things your way. If he does not, you have a most serious problem on your hands, perhaps calling for family counseling. Let's hope and pray that the difficulty can be settled in a spirit of true Christian charity.

Mixed marriages

Q. Can a Catholic validly married to a Jew raise their children as Jews and still receive the sacraments?

A. I am presuming that the Catholic party has freely chosen not to raise the children as Catholics, and not that the Jewish party has forbidden it. If that is so, why would the Catholic be bothered with attending Mass and receiving the sacraments; that seems like so much of a charade to me. Don't you agree?

More mixed marriages

Q. I have been asked to participate in a Roman Catholic/Greek Orthodox wedding. The Catholic says her pastor will be there, and that it is completely approved of by the Church. I realize there are unity talks going on between the Churches, but I wonder about participation in their liturgy. What about receiving Holy Communion?

A. Yes, it is possible for a Catholic to marry a Greek Orthodox in an Orthodox ceremony, and to do so licitly and validly, provided the proper dispensation has been obtained. I presume that is the case here since you say the bride's pastor will be present.

As a matter of fact, many Catholic theologians and canonists say that it is better to have the wedding in the Orthodox Church because some Orthodox question the validity of our marriages for a most interesting reason: They believe the priest is the minister of the sacrament, while we hold that the spouses administer the sacrament to each other. If the Catholic priest does not see himself as the minister, they reason that he cannot have the intention to administer the sacrament, and hence it is invalid. Therefore, the simplest procedure is to obtain a dispensation from the Catholic form of marriage.

Since I do not know what you are expected to do in the wedding, I cannot answer you any more completely. Neither the Orthodox nor the Catholic Church permit intercommunion, so that is out of the question.

Greek Orthodox

Q. My daughter is married in the Greek Orthodox Church. Can she receive the sacraments of the Catholic Church?

A. That depends.

Generally speaking, most Catholic priests advise an Orthodox wedding ceremony, done with the permission of the Catholic bishop, thus allowing the marriage to be recognized in the eyes of the Catholic Church. For well over a decade now, Catholics have been able to obtain a dispensation to marry in the Orthodox Church.

The only hesitancy I have about your question is that you do not indicate that your daughter did obtain a dispensation (but even that can be rectified). As long as there was no previous marriage for either of them and the marriage is indeed recognized by the Catholic Church, there would be no problem with her maintaining a fully sacramental life in the Catholic Church.

Mixed marriage again

Q. How is the marriage of a Lutheran and a Catholic looked upon by the Church?

A. I am not sure of precisely what you mean. Because the Church believes, based on two thousand years of experience, that the best chances for marital success exist when spouses share a common faith, the Church frowns on all mixed marriages.

In recent years, however, especially under impulse from the ecumenical movement, the Church has relaxed her discipline for mixed marriages. While such a marriage was always possible, the newer norms make it a less distasteful event for all concerned, especially in terms of the liturgical ceremony. Presently, a non-Catholic person is informed of the necessity to participate in the Church's marriage-preparation programs, of the promise to be made by the Catholic partner to raise all children as Catholics, and of the advisability (and in some dioceses, obligation) for the non-Catholic to study the Catholic Faith — at least for purposes of information and deeper understanding.

For the celebration of the sacrament, a non-Catholic minister may be invited to participate, but only the Catholic priest or deacon actually receives the vows. The couple may be married at either a simple ceremony or at a Mass. If family problems make a wedding in a Catholic church problematic, the parish priest can petition the diocesan bishop for the couple for a dispensation "from form," which means the possibility of being married before a non-Catholic clergyman or even a justice of the peace. Truly grave reasons must exist for this option, however, and where Catholicism would be so negatively viewed, it seems the Catholic party should think twice before making a permanent commitment.

The bottom-line answer, I suppose, is that the Church is not enthusiastic about mixed marriages, but tries to be as helpful as possible to those entering into them. All Catholic couples should have a good priest-friend to rely on, especially for the early years of marriage. I think this is particularly important for ecumenical or mixed marriages.

Marriage preparation

Q. Are the various dioceses around the country all requiring certain mandatory preparation periods for marriage? Ours now calls for a four-month notice and either an engaged encounter or pre-Cana conferences.

A. Most dioceses now require a period of four to twelve months notice to the parish before marriage, lest a couple rush into a union without proper consideration and preparation.

Similarly, various programs are offered and mandated to ensure that the couple have the best information possible available to them, so that they can make an intelligent and informed judgment on their suitability for marriage in general and to this partner in particular. While such programs may seem like an annoying and unnecessary obstacle to young people head over heels in love, they are usually rather grateful later on, if the formation either causes them to understand each other better or brings them to a decision that marriage is not right for them at the present moment, or at any time.

The Church exercises pastoral care for couples when she provides such programs, and likewise protects the sanctity of marriage from unthought-out celebrations.

Holy days

Q. I recently visited Canada and learned that they do not observe August 15 as a holy day of obligation. This puzzled me, since I thought all Catholics observed the same six days in every country.

A. In addition to every Sunday, the Church also observes the following days with special solemnity: the Nativity, Epiphany, and Ascension of our Lord, as well as the commemoration of His Body and Blood on Corpus Christi; the motherhood of Mary and her Immaculate Conception and Assumption; St. Joseph, Sts. Peter and Paul, and All Saints' Day.

Of these ten days of observance, the national episcopal conference must select at least two — Christmas and one Marian feast. The holy days of obligation in the United States are six (Epiphany and Corpus Christi are transferred to the nearest Sunday, while St. Joseph and Sts. Peter and Paul remain as weekly observance without a Mass obligation).

Readers may recall an effort afoot some years back to reduce the number of holy days of obligation in this country, but the move met with great resistance from laity and hierarchy alike, who saw in it an attempt to desacralize yet further an already profane existence for all too many Christians.

Dispensation from holy days

Q. How can a bishop waive the obligation of a diocese to attend Mass on a holy day of obligation if that day falls on a Saturday or Monday?

A. Diocesan bishops do have the faculty to dispense from a holy day Mass obligation when the appropriate conditions prevail. Please recall that the six holy days observed as days of obligation in the United States are not divinely appointed; hence, dispensation is possible. However, it is important to notice that I said a bishop can dispense "when the appropriate conditions prevail." What does that mean?

The dispensation is given in view of alleviating an overwhelming burden. Usually, this would involve priests more than lay people. For example, there are far-flung dioceses in this country where a priest has charge of several missions separated, literally, by hundreds of miles. To expect a priest to drive, let us say, five hundred miles between Friday night (the vigil of the holy day) and Saturday morning, and then begin all over again on Saturday night for the Sunday obligation, would be a tremendous strain, leading to physical and/or emotional difficulties. That is the kind of situation a dispensation should alleviate.

Granting such dispensations too freely has two negative effects, in my judgment: (1) It removes the place of good, healthy sacrifice from the lives of clergy and laity alike. (2) It reduces religion to a matter of convenience.

Confession and the deaf

Q. I am seventy-seven years old and totally deaf, but do attend Mass regularly. I was told recently that it was not compulsory for a deaf person to receive the Sacrament of Penance, which pleased me because I haven't gone to confession in many years. However, I am also concerned because I have received Holy Communion on a number of occasions when not in the state of grace. As a result, I have just stopped going to Communion. I don't lip-read well or use sign language. Please advise.

A. The law of the Church requires every Catholic to receive the Sacrament of Penance at least once a year if conscious of serious sin. That obliges all, without distinction.

Someone who is hearing-impaired may have a particular difficulty in observing this precept since, under normal circumstances (regular Saturday afternoon confessions, for instance), louder speech on the part of the confessor and/or the penitent would violate the seal of confession.

I would suggest making an appointment with a priest, so that your special needs can be met. Any priest should be more than happy to give the extra consideration which your disability demands. Furthermore, receiving the Sacrament of Penance is not simply fulfilling an ecclesiastical law; it is a means of grace and consolation which you should not be denied.

At the same time, I cannot stress enough the necessity of being properly prepared to encounter our Lord in Holy Communion. Receiving the Eucharist in the state of mortal sin is a sacrilege, strongly condemned by St. Paul (1 Cor 11:26-29).

Mass attire

Q. One of our pastors has caused quite a stir by forbidding people to attend Mass in shorts and the like. I understand the archbishop has disciplined him and told him he can't do this. What is your opinion?

A. For years, as a weekend assistant, I worked at parishes at the Jersey Shore. The attire could be abominable: tank tops, shorts, bikinis, bare feet! Invariably, pastors had to post signs with a dress code and also post ushers at the doors of the church to ensure that the church would not be used as an extension of the beach. However, this problem is not limited to resort-type parishes. In fact, inappropriate attire seems to be pandemic in parishes across the country.

Part of it comes from what is at best a relaxed attitude toward worship among Catholics or at worst one of "couldn't care less." Yet another major aspect of the difficulty arises from priests' reluctance to set standards out of fear that they will experience a strong reaction from either their people or their bishops, if not both. The end result, however, is that thousands of Catholics across the nation appear in church on Sundays in outfits they wouldn't wear to the local bar or mall.

Let's be honest: What we wear tells others what we think of what we are doing, and just as much, it influences how we act. Protestants and Jews could teach us Catholics a great deal about the value of dressing up for worship, not in the sense of engaging in a fashion contest but as a sign of recognition that we are worshiping and meeting the King of the Universe.

Regarding the legitimacy of setting standards of dress, I would simply note that the dress code outlined by the pastor you mention is the very one posted on the doors of all the basilicas of Rome, and anyone failing to meet that standard is denied entrance. How the priest in question explained or enforced it, I do not know; that he had a code is completely legitimate and, in my judgment, praiseworthy. May his tribe increase!

Intercommunion

Q. *Is it a sin to attend a non-Catholic church with your children who are members there and to participate in their Communion service? I could not get to a Catholic church.*

A. The degree of sinfulness of the action would depend on a number of facts missing from your letter. However, I think the sin of bad example would surely have been committed, as well as the sin of disobeying Church law which forbids Catholics from receiving Communion in non-Catholic services.

Since I have written before on intercommunion, I shall not belabor that point now, but I would like to reflect on the bad-example aspect. Obviously your children have left the Catholic Church to join some other Christian community; the Second Vatican Council speaks of such an action in the harshest of terms. Your participation in their worship gives tacit approval to their act of infidelity to the Catholic Faith. In my judgment, it would have been far better to worship alone on that particular Sunday than to attend services with children who have apostasized from the one true Church. Your refusal to attend church with them would have spoken volumes about your continued disapproval of their action; your participation, on the other hand, could only be interpreted as understanding or even total acceptance. I don't think that is what you wanted to communicate since you seem upset now.

The greatest act of love you can render your children now is to let them know how much their present state concerns you because their eternal salvation is at stake (see Vatican II, *Lumen Gentium*, no. 14), and the essence of Christian love (and parental as well) is rooted in the firm desire for the salvation of the beloved. Try to share that insight with them in a way which is both convincing and loving at one and the same time.

Forced attendance

Q. *What stand can a Catholic mother justly propose to her children over the age of eighteen who live at home but refuse to go to Sunday Mass?*

A. The solution to me is quite simple: If your children are dependent enough to live at home, they are dependent enough to live by your values, an essential element of which is Sunday Mass attendance.

Wouldn't it be better for young people to go to Mass because they *want* to do so, rather than because they are forced to do so? Of course, but that begs the question. Parents must set policies and standards for their children. When they give up on basic issues like this, their offspring often get the impression that the matter really can't be too important to them; otherwise, they would be fighting over it. At least, that's what high-school and college students have told me for years.

The task of parents is to share their values with their children. When that is carefully done in childhood, those values are gradually assimilated into the lifestyle of the young people, unless some unfortunate intervention occurs. By and large, however, parents simply need to reinforce these basics consistently and lovingly for them to take hold. Will they get opposition from their adolescents or young adults? In all likelihood, that will happen from time to time, but one should not mistake questioning for rejection; very often, young people pursue issues only to hear convincing arguments. It is only when they are not forthcoming that true rejection creeps in.

My advice, both as a priest and educator, is to challenge your children and hold them to it. They will end up respecting both you and your value system, which is the goal of parenthood, isn't it?

Parental responsibility

Q. At what age does a parent's responsibility for a child's going to Sunday Mass end? Is "forcing" a good practice?

A. In a certain sense parental responsibility for children never ends, especially where their spiritual welfare is at stake. In a more narrow sense, however, I imagine it would be reasonable to say that when children have left home, a parent's potential for "forcing" anything is well-nigh gone. Of course, a parent always hopes that what has been stressed as a value will have been integrated into an adolescent or adult child's permanent way of life.

The value of "forcing" is that it is a very strong manner of indicating what is of significance to a particular family, in just the same way that children are "forced" to eat three meals a day or go to school.

Catechesis

Q. Who has the primary responsibility for passing on our Faith to the next generation?

A. According to the Second Vatican Council, parents are the primary educators of their children. That means that the fundamentals of the Christian Faith and family prayer should be a part of their lives long before they ever come near a formal educational program run by the Church.

That having been said, it must be recalled that children do belong to circles of relationships outside the home or "domestic Church." The Church and society also need to offer their resources to parents. The Church at Vatican II reminded parents of their responsibility to use Catholic schools wherever and whenever possible. Catholic schools not only provide systematic catechesis, but also a total environment of faith and Christian values, in addition to the opportunity to learn in an atmosphere which sees truth as one — with no false dichotomies between faith and science.

It seems to me as a priest and educator that Catholic schools were never more valuable than they are today, especially to help parents counterbalance the negative influences of a neo-pagan society and consistent and forceful attempts to inculcate its anti-Christian worldview.

For Catholics, then, parents, Church, and Catholic educational institutions work together for the good of the children, so as to lead them to Christ.

Mass for non-Catholics

Q. May Masses be said for non-Catholics? If so, why?

A. Yes, they may. Your question seems to suggest some confusion between praying for someone and that person's reception of Holy Communion, which is problematical for non-Catholics.

When Mass is celebrated for someone — living or dead, Catholic or otherwise — the Church merely prays for that person's welfare, especially spiritual. To be restored to health or to obtain the gift of eternal salvation is not something limited to explicit membership in Christ's Church.

Converts

Q. How does my daughter go about converting to Catholicism?

A. If you are a Catholic, you would be the biggest help in her conversion process. If not, some Catholic friend might introduce her to a local priest, or she could simply go to the rectory and introduce herself.

If she is not baptized, she would have to begin instruction in the Catholic Faith and participate in the restored Rite of Christian Initiation of Adults. If she is a member of some Christian denomination, participation in the RCIA is not required.

During her time of catechumenate, she should read as much about the Church as possible and obtain as broad an appreciation of Catholic liturgy and Church history as possible, all the while living according to the Catholic moral code. If all this makes sense to her, she should then ask to be received into full communion with the Catholic Church, receiving the Sacraments of Penance, Confirmation, and Eucharist from the priest responsible for her reception into the Church. If she is not baptized, she will probably be baptized, confirmed, and communicated at the Easter Vigil Liturgy in her new parish.

It should be observed that "converting" to Catholicism is not a personal choice; on the contrary, it is the recognition that God has chosen me and not that I have chosen Him! Therefore, we are concerned with a process of discerning the truth of Catholicism and the voice of Christ at one and the same time. The process is essentially a communal one, with various members of the Church helping the convert to hear and to understand.

RCIA program

Q. Like your questioner from a few months back, I too am having problems being admitted to the Catholic Church because of an inability to attend the RCIA program.

I am an Anglican, originally baptized as an Evangelical and Reformed, but with no baptismal certificate. What do you suggest?

A. You are asking two different questions. Let me deal with each.

First, dozens of letters came to me from all parts of the country because of my response on the RCIA, mostly from people in similar situations as the original writer. Some came from RCIA directors who questioned the correctness of my reply. My answer was correct, as given, and faithfully reflects the National Statutes for the Catechumenate, approved by the National Conference of Catholic Bishops in 1986. Simply put, catechumens are the unbaptized and they must participate in the RCIA, which is a program of rites and instructions in preparation for the sacraments of initiation (baptism, confirmation, Eucharist). Christians (that is, baptized persons) from other faith communities, desirous of entrance into full communion with the Catholic Church, may be invited to participate in certain aspects of the RCIA, but may not be forced to do so, nor should their participation give the impression that they are catechumens. Hence, the document frowns upon their being received into the Church at the Easter Vigil, lest the congregation be confused about just who is a catechumen and who is not (cf. no. 33).

Second, your own particular situation is somewhat complicated by the absence of a baptismal certificate. If you became an Anglican as an adult, I imagine you were confirmed in the Anglican Church. If so, the Anglican priest must have obtained some kind of assurance of your baptism. If the church of baptism cannot produce the document, a reliable party who knows you were baptized can attest to it. In that case, no baptism should be performed and you should be treated as any other convert from another Christian communion.

Baptism dilemma

Q. I've wanted to have my children baptized but have been regularly denied by my parish priest because my husband and I were not married in the Church. Is there any right of appeal that we have?

A. It is always dangerous to attempt an answer to a question like this because so many factors can be involved. For example, were either you or your husband previously married? Is there any impediment to your being married now in the Church? I don't know these answers and so my response would have to be rather guarded.

Your pastor is trying to safeguard the dignity of the Sacrament of Baptism, which can only be administered to children whose parents give evidence that they intend to rear their children in the practice of the Faith.

In fact, in the course of the baptismal liturgy, the priest specifically asks the parents if they will do so. Parents who are not living a full sacramental life would have difficulty in making such promise, or so it would seem.

If you are not married in the Church because either or both you and your husband were involved in a previous valid union, have you sought out an annulment? If that process is now going on, I would take that as a sign of goodwill on your part if I were your pastor and would proceed with your children's baptisms. On the other hand, if you have simply chosen not to marry in the Church, then I would agree with your pastor's decision. If you feel an injustice has been done to you and your children, you should contact your diocesan office and seek an opinion there.

The correct procedure in these kinds of delicate situations is not for the priest to deny baptism but merely to postpone it until parents demonstrate their willingness to live according to the Gospel. This, then, should be viewed as a waiting period and time of decision to respond to God's offer of grace; it is a "teachable" moment for all.

Parish registration

Q. The liturgical nonsense in our parish all too often reaches fever pitch. To what extent is a Catholic obliged to register at the parish in which he resides?

A. The 1983 Code of Canon Law is much less restrictive on where a person must register. The 1917 Code considered registration in the parish within whose boundaries one lived to be necessary unless one belonged to an ethnic parish, for example. The new law envisions the possibility for people to have specific needs which cannot be met within the geographical bounds of a particular parish.

In your place, I would approach the pastor and tell him why you are not comfortable with membership in his parish and indicate your intention to register elsewhere. Then go to the pastor of the church with which you wish to associate yourself and ask him to register you there.

While you are within your rights to do this, I would caution against the practice of "parish hopping" or "shopping around for a parish," which often takes place for less than noble reasons (e.g., a desire to avoid hearing the Gospel in all its fullness or an effort to sidestep parish support).

Byzantine Rite

Q. We are Latin Rite Catholics by birth. In our quest for a parish which upholds orthodoxy and is faithful to Rome, we have been attending the local Byzantine Catholic Church, and I have some practical questions: (1) Is it permissible to attend this church on Sundays for an extended period of time, without obtaining a "change of rite" from Rome? (2) May my children receive their First Confession and First Communion in the Eastern Rite? (3) May we become "bi-ritual"?

A. I should comment at the outset that it is sad that people have to go shopping for a parish for the reasons you cite. The answers to your well-thought-out questions, however, are rather straightforward: (1) Any Catholic may attend liturgy in any other Catholic church or rite for any length of time with no difficulty. Of course, such attendance fulfills one's Sunday obligation. (2) If you want your children to receive First Penance and First Holy Communion in the Byzantine Rite, you should obtain the permission of your Latin Rite bishop-pastor and present that document to the Byzantine Rite priest, who can then accommodate you. (3) It is not possible for a layperson to be "bi-ritual"; in fact, it's even a misnomer for priests. What it means in reality is that a priest is, let us say, Latin Rite, but for pastoral reasons would also like to function liturgically in the Ruthenian Rite. With the approval of his Latin Rite bishop and that of the Ruthenian Rite bishop, the request is sent to Rome, which grants the petition if the rationale is compelling. In truth, however, the priest does not change rite or hold a kind of "dual citizenship." Obviously, such a permission could not be granted to laity since they already can attend divine liturgy in the particular rite in question with no problem. If you are irremediably unhappy in the Latin Rite, you can petition the Holy See to change rites.

Inclusive language

Q. *We have a nun in our parish who has taken it upon herself to blacken out every noun referring to the male gender in the missal, lectionary, and book of the Gospels. She has inserted her version of inclusive language. The lectors are upset, but the pastor has done nothing about the situation. Is she within her rights?*

A. No, she is not. Vatican II's Constitution on the Sacred Liturgy notes clearly that no individual and not even a conference of bishops has the authority to tamper with the liturgy, let alone the Scriptures.

The issue of "inclusive" language in the liturgy is a non-issue for most people in the pew, and when others try to hammer away at this, especially in the context of the liturgy, it is tantamount to a politicizing of the liturgy.

The English language is somewhat defective in this regard, and certainly we should be sensitive to language which could give the wrong impression. However, the solution is not to take the law and the language into one's own hands. That is why the bishops' conference has a liturgical committee, which is deputed to study such matters and make appropriate recommendations to the Holy See. Anything less is an improper arrogation of power to oneself and an infringement on the rights of the entire Catholic community.

Exclusive language

Q. *A former issue of TCA dealt with the question of "exclusive language" in reference to God and the liturgy. I liked your answer and thought you* *might enjoy the enclosed article by a linguistics scholar, which reinforces what you said.*

A. Thank you for the article, which is indeed excellent. The author makes the point that "only God can name God" and that arbitrary linguistic changes "proposed by feminist theologians do not merely add a few unfamiliar words for God, as some would like to think, but in fact introduce beliefs about God that differ radically from those inherent in Christian faith, understanding, and Scripture." For anyone interested, I recommend "Language for God and Feminist Language: A Literary and Rhetorical Analysis" by Roland Mushat Frye, Professor Emeritus of Literature at the University of Pennsylvania, appearing in the January 1989 issue of *Interpretation*, which is a journal of Bible and theology, published by Union Theological Seminary at 3401 Brook Road, Richmond, VA 23227.

Female roles

Q. In your last issue of TCA, you said that girls could not serve at the altar; I am a twelve-year-old altar girl. I do not want to do anything that the Pope doesn't like, so I am thinking about resigning, but what else could I do for my church if I don't serve?

A. What a sensitive and precocious young lady! God bless you.

In God's plan there are many ways that people can serve. Some tasks are reserved to women, some to men; some functions are performed by males and females alike. Serving at the altar is so closely connected to the priesthood that the Church insists on male servers. Young girls can read at Mass; they can greet people at the door of the church or take up the collection; they can work in the sacristy; they can sing in the choir or lead the singing. Consider doing one of these things.

If I may digress at this point and address priests: Do you see what happens when we go off on our own and do what the Church does not authorize? Surely there is more pain in asking someone to resign from a position held over a period of time than in simply saying from the outset that it is not an option.

Salvation and wealth

Q. As a layman who is reasonably "well off," I often wonder about what I need to do to be saved, in light of Mark 10:17-30. Does Jesus require one to sell all his assets and give all to the poor, literally?

A. The passage to which you refer contains our Lord's call to discipleship. As such, it serves as the ideal toward which all Christians should strive: A refusal to rely on material possessions and a determination to have God's providence as one's only protection.

Not everyone has the vocation to live a life of evangelical poverty; if one has that calling and does not heed it, then his or her eternal salvation is jeopardized. The Vatican II Decree on Religious Life notes that Religious who embrace this radical form of lifestyle serve as a challenge to all others in the Church to be similarly reliant on Almighty God.

Some people, however, are called to live in the world with their wealth, which our Lord never condemned. In fact, it appears in several Scripture passages that both Jesus and the apostles depended on the generosity of just such individuals for their own needs.

In the Christian scheme of things, neither wealth nor poverty are guarantors of a particular station in the afterlife. Rather, it is a question of what is done with them. The rich who advance the Kingdom of God will be rewarded; the poor who rebel against their status and curse God for it will be condemned.

Cash gifts for Religious

Q. Years ago certain collections remained in the parishes for rectory expenses. How is it done now? On occasion I wish to give a cash gift to a priest or nun. How do I present it, so that he or she may keep it for personal use?

A. Procedures differ from diocese to diocese in terms of local finances. However, I think what I shall say is fairly representative of most situations. In general, rectory upkeep (including food and salaries for housekeeper, cook, etc.) is considered a part of overall parish maintenance. As such, it is one line in the parish budget. Diocesan clergy receive a subsistence salary (usually around $500 a month), in addition to room and board. From their salary, priests must pay for their clothing, cars, and auto insurance; health and life insurance (and also a retirement policy) are the responsibility of either the parish or the diocese. Priests who belong to religious orders do not receive a salary, and all their material needs are met by their communities.

As far as giving monetary gifts to clergy and Religious, again a distinction must be made between priests in vows and secular clergy. Religious priests (like brothers and sisters) take a vow of poverty, which precludes personal ownership of things or personal bank accounts. Not infrequently today, Religious may accept financial gifts from people, inform their superior of the gift, and the superior generally tells them to use it for necessities or perhaps toward a vacation or the like.

If the gift is connected with the administration of a sacrament, some dioceses have very strict policies in that area. For example, in some places "stole fees" (stipends for baptisms, weddings, funerals) must go into the parish fund; in others, they are the property of the celebrant; in still others, they go into a "kitty" and are divided up among all the priests at the end of the month. This was an important source of income for priests many years ago when salaries were as low as a dollar a day; stipends (whether for Masses or sacraments) are much less needed today due to moderate increases over the years. It should be noted, however, that Catholic clergy are the lowest paid in the United States, even when counting in all the benefits.

Tuned out

Q. One of our parish priests gives homilies excellent in content, but his delivery is so terrible that people tune him out. This is unfortunate since his problem could be so readily cured. He has a pleasant voice, but apparently has never learned how to use it. What can a parishioner do to help?

A. Your question reveals a great deal of understanding and sensitivity, which is already a tremendous help to your priest. So often priests hear only the negative reactions to their ministry and very little positive feedback.

If I were you, I would approach the situation in this way. Ask the priest for an appointment (between Sunday Masses is hardly an apt moment for such a discussion). When you get together, affirm him in all the areas possible, as you have already indicated here. Then tell him the one problem you perceive, without claiming to represent a cast of thousands. Acknowledge the fact that you realize public speaking is difficult. He will probably indicate that he has one of two problems — lack of sufficient training or nerves. Therefore, you should be prepared to offer him concrete sources of help. Leave him with the assurance that even if he cannot become another Fulton Sheen (who, by the way, said he was on pins and needles every time he spoke in public), that you will appreciate who he is and all he does for Christ and His Church.

You say that you think "his problem could be so readily cured." That all depends. My experience with teaching high-school students public speaking for many years led me to the conclusion that truly excellent orators are born and not made. Other forensics coaches dispute that opinion. I would say, however, that if the priest's content is good, you should make a concerted effort to garner what you can since he is obviously making a significant effort within his own personal limitations.

Priests reading this should take note of how seriously their people regard the Sunday homily, and hence how serious a responsibility we have to make it a salutary encounter with God's Word.

Laicization

Q. Have there been any changes made in how priests are laicized?

A. Laicization is that process whereby a priest is permitted to leave the active ministry and return to the lay state — all the while remaining a priest since the character of ordination remains forever. It is a concession granted as much for the good of the Church as for the individual priest, since an unhappy priest could do a great deal of harm to the Church.

When Pope John Paul II took office, he expressed his concern that this procedure had been used too cavalierly, and so he tightened up the process considerably. In general, the rescript of laicization dispenses a priest from his promise of celibacy and his obligation to recite the Divine Office daily. However, the man may not function in any liturgical capacity (not even as a lector), nor may he teach religion at any level (elementary, secondary, or college), nor administer a Catholic school. The Church does not impose these restrictions to be vindictive, but for the good of the Church. After all, backing out of a serious commitment like the priesthood is not a praiseworthy action, and such a person cannot be held up to the rest of the Church as a model for emulation. This does not judge the individual but is simply an objective and dispassionate evaluation of the situation.

It should be noted that in an emergency, a laicized priest can exercise the priestly ministry. Also worth mentioning is that some men who have left the active ministry have petitioned to return; the Holy Father studies each case on an individual basis. The rescript presupposes no return, but theoretically, the door is never completely shut.

Priests' problems

Q. It's very hard for me to go to confession anymore when I think about all the problems priests are having with sex and everything else. How can they help me when they're so confused themselves?

A. To begin with, it is important to recall that the principal celebrant in every sacrament is Jesus Christ; the priest is merely His human instrument. Because a priest is human, he is weak and, yes, sinful. That should come as no news to anyone. The validity of a sacrament never depends on the holiness or worthiness of the individual priest; if that were so, we would never have any assurance of having celebrated a valid sacrament.

That having been said, I can understand your dismay when the foibles of priests come to light, as it is distressing for Catholics who show their priests such great love and trust, as well as embarrassing for the entire Church. The solution is not to be judgmental but to pray for them — that they would indeed practice what they preach. Our Lord dealt with this same issue in Judaism by reminding the people that the scribes were the lawful teachers of the Chosen People and, as such, deserved respect and obedience; however, he went on to say that they should not follow their example. Thankfully, the number of priests who do not live according to their vocational commitment is relatively small (granted, even one is too many). Do not allow a small number to obscure your vision of the vast majority who struggle, with God's grace, to live as they should.

Religious orders

Q. I am a divorced Catholic, never married in the Church. Are there any religious orders for women who wish to enter religious life after having raised a child and having had a spouse?

A. Many congregations of women accept candidates who were previously married and are now either divorced (with an ecclesiastical decree of nullity) or widowed.

You can write to the various religious communities or contact your diocesan director of vocations for a listing of sisters to contact.

Some people think that virginity is necessary for entrance into the convent, but that is not the case for all orders. A classic example is that of St. Elizabeth Ann Seton, who was the widowed mother of several children.

Virginity and sisters

Q. If one is interested in becoming a sister, is it necessary that she be a virgin?

A. Some congregations of women will not accept into their communities women who have been married. I am not aware of any who would even ask the question of whether or not one is a virgin.

The Church does, however, have a specific rite for the consecration of a virgin. Obviously this would be for a woman who is indeed a virgin and intends to remain so, publicly vowing herself to that state as a special sign.

Proper procedures

Q. I have been separated from my wife for two years and want to become a religious brother. Can I do this without getting divorced first?

A. If you were married in the Church, a civil divorce would have to be followed by a canonical declaration of nullity. If the marriage was not in the Church to begin with, a civil divorce would still be required and an ecclesiastical decree noting that the marriage was invalid because the Catholic form of marriage had not been heeded. Were the Church to accept a candidate for religious life without such matters taken care of, the particular order could readily be sued for alienation of affection; even worse, were the marriage valid, it would be allowing a man to back out of his commitment to his wife, which is a sacrament.

Religious garb

Q. I would like to commend you on printing Father Dimock's article on religious life. It was excellent. I would like to know, however, why Religious in the United States get away with not wearing their habits. In our parish the nuns do so when the bishop comes.

A. First of all, let us be clear that Church law requires *all* Religious — male and female alike — to wear the habit. Sometimes the issue is framed in such a way as to suggest that the law is being unfairly applied to women, while men are allowed to do as they please. That is not the case.

Canon 669 clearly states: "Religious are to wear the habit of the institute made according to the norm of proper law as a sign of their consecration and as a testimony of poverty." As you can see, the law is not at all ambiguous. Hence, I find it difficult to comprehend how Religious (as individuals or communities) can justify disobedience or disregard of the law of the Church. After all, religious life obtains its meaning from the Church, thus qualifying the Church to define the appropriate characteristics of the life.

When congregations of Religious submit their constitutions to the Congregation for Religious in Rome, one of the items noted is whether or not the document calls for the wearing of the habit. Failure to do so results in the rejection of the constitution. For that reason, the documents of many American communities have been rejected repeatedly over the years, and some congregations have begun to question if they want approval from the Holy See at all. Others have put into their constitutions what they know is required but have tacitly agreed not to enforce the rule on garb; this is obviously dishonest and unworthy of mature believers, let alone Religious.

One final point should be made: bishops have the ultimate authority to legislate for all Religious working in their dioceses; therefore, a bishop could decide that he would allow no Religious to function in his diocese who failed to observe the law on the habit.

While it is certainly true that the habit does not make the monk, it does do a great deal to help foster identity, especially in terms of one's connection with the Church one serves. As Pope John Paul II has put it on several occasions, it is also a powerful way of "keeping God on the streets" of the secular city.

Late vocations

Q. How much education must a man have to become a priest after having a full career in the secular world?

A. Let me answer in some detail, to cover all situations.

Some dioceses and orders still have high-school seminaries for boys disposed toward a priestly vocation; these can be "live-in" or commuter institutions. Most priests, however, entered the seminary after high school, enrolling in a college seminary program, most of which today are associated with a regular Catholic college, with a special residence for the seminarians. At that level, the young men obtain a bachelor's degree, usually in philosophy or classical languages, in order to prepare them for the next level of education.

After graduation from college, seminarians begin their formal study of theology, which includes at least four years' worth of courses in Scripture, dogmatic and moral theology, Church history, canon law, counseling, and homiletics. At the conclusion of this process, they are ordained deacons and usually function as such in parishes for about a year. Upon successful completion of the internship, the deacons are ordained priests.

Older men who already possess a bachelor's degree often have to take at least a year of "pre-theology," to make up for lacks in their education, most especially in areas like philosophy or Latin. When those gaps are filled in, they then proceed along the road as described above. Dioceses differ in their approach to "late vocations," so it is best to ascertain the policy from the vocation director of the diocese in which you are interested.

Vicar

Q. What is a vicar?

A. The word vicar comes from the Latin word "*vicarius*," which means a representative or "stand-in."

In ecclesiastical usage, one finds the word in many different situations, but always with the notion presented above. Hence, we speak of the Pope being the "Vicar of Christ," meaning that he represents Christ for and to us. Or, one reads about the "Vicar General" of a diocese; this priest is deputed to speak and act for the diocesan bishop in certain circumstances outlined in canon law or by the express wish of the bishop. An expression which is new on the scene comes about as the result of the 1983 Code of Canon Law, as we hear about "parochial vicars," previously known by a variety of titles over the years: curate, assistant pastor, associate pastor. The new code envisions this priest as the representative of the "*parochus*" or parish priest (pastor).

The title 'Father'

Q. Why do Catholics call priests "Father," even though the Bible forbids it?

A. Does the Bible forbid it? I don't think it does. My reading of Matthew 23:9 and its context lead me to some very different conclusions.

Jesus does not condemn the use of titles as such; He condemns their use when they suggest equality with God. St. Paul (who obviously was in touch and in conformity with the will of Christ) did not hesitate to speak of His ministry as "fatherhood" (cf. 1 Cor 4:15). The author of the Johannine epistles addressed his remarks to the "fathers" of the community, by which he meant the spiritual leaders (cf. 1 Jn 2:14).

Strangely, some Christians who get upset by hearing priests called "Father" refer to their own ministers as "Doctor" (which means "teacher"), a title equally ruled out by a literal interpretation of the same Matthean passage.

The title of "Father" does not place a priest on a pedestal, creating distance between him and his people. On the contrary, it serves as a reminder of the depth of the relationship that exists: that because of Christ, His Gospel, and His Church, all relationships in the Church are essentially familial.

'Reverend Mr.'

Q. Why are transitional deacons addressed as "Reverend Mr." and permitted to wear clerical garb, while neither is so with permanent deacons?

A. In point of fact, transitional deacons are *required* (not permitted) to wear clerical garb. When Pope Paul VI restored the permanent diaconate, many questioned the exact role and identity of such men; not a few theologians argued that they should serve as a kind of "bridge ministry" between the priests and the laity, having a foot in both worlds, as it were. For that reason, they maintained that permanent deacons should not be given any special form of address or garb which would distinguish them.

The new Code of Canon Law acknowledges this division of thought on the matter by exempting permanent deacons from the obligation to wear clerical garb, where the local bishop has decreed otherwise (which is the case in most American dioceses). However, I have noticed in the past few years that some bishops and pastors have begun to look twice at this policy, particularly when deacons are engaged in hospital or prison chaplaincies, or when they must conduct wake or graveside services. Not being identifiable as a cleric can be detrimental to their ministry, making them less effective and minimizing the overt presence of the Church in such cases. The longer the permanent diaconate is around, the more questions of a practical nature will surface and require resolution.

As far as transitional deacons go, their wearing of the Roman collar is generally no more than an official cutoff date, beyond which lay clothing is no longer permitted at all. In most seminaries students must wear clerical garb in formal settings (like liturgy, class, meals, parochial work), precisely as a way of helping them to grow into their vocation and making them comfortable with their identity as "marked men."

Married priests

Q. *How come the priests of the Byzantine Rite can marry while those of the Roman Rite cannot? Are Greek Orthodox priests Catholic? Do they consider the Pope their head?*

A. Clerical celibacy is not a matter of divine law. However, our Lord strongly counseled it (cf. Mt 19:29; Lk 14:26; Mk 10:29), as did St. Paul (cf. 1 Cor 7:7). Therefore, its practice can be regulated by the Church.

From earliest days, celibacy was so highly esteemed in the Church of West or Latin Rite that we find evidence of its being mandated as early as the fourth to sixth centuries. In the East, celibacy was demanded only of monks, from whose ranks the bishops have always been selected.

Recently, Pope John Paul II has permitted certain Anglican (Episcopalian) clergy to seek priestly ordination in the Catholic Church even though they are married. This is a dispensation given due to the exceptional circumstances involved.

Byzantine Rite priests are Catholic and thus accept the Pope as the visible head of the Church. Orthodox priests are validly ordained but do not accept the primacy of the bishop of Rome and so are not Catholic. The question of the papacy is the single most significant divider between clergy and the Eastern Churches, thus calling for our fervent prayers that this "sticking point" would be resolved, so that full ecclesial and eucharistic communion car be attained.

The very fact that priests of different rites within the one Catholic Church live under varied disciplines (including different approaches to celibacy) is an indicator of the genuine pluralism which has always existed in the Catholic Church.

Married clergy

Q. Why does the Church allow other married clergy to convert and function as priests, while not allowing Catholic priests who left to get married to return, especially since we need priests so badly?

A. Even before Vatican II, Pope Pius XII and Pope John XXIII made provisions for non-Catholic clergy coming into full communion with the Catholic Church to continue on as clergy, even if they were married. Pope John Paul II simply followed that pattern. As I read your question, however, you do not object to the fact that these men are married but that Catholic priests who have left the active ministry to marry cannot function as priests. Let me explain the rationale behind the difference in treatment.

Various Christian denominations permit a married clergy. Thus these ministers were merely engaged in accepted practices within their former ecclesial communities. Once they became convinced of the truth of the claims of the Catholic Church, they desired to enter. At the same time, they also wished to exercise a ministerial role. Since the law of celibacy is not of divine origin, the Church may dispense, for good reason, with the law she made. The situation is not at all the same with Catholic priests who have left the active ministry. These men had many years to study and pray before making a final commitment to a priesthood which they knew required a celibate lifestyle and which, in fact, involved the making of a solemn promise at subdiaconate (formerly) or diaconate (presently). Their decision to enter the priesthood was free, as was their decision to leave.

The non-Catholic clergy are being granted a dispensation, so as to facilitate their coming into the Church. Our own priests are being done no injustice by being allowed to do just what they asked of the Church in the rescript of laicization — to return to the lay state because of an inability to function in a healthy manner according to the wishes of the Church. It should be noted, however, that celibacy is not the only reason men leave the active ministry and, in fact, may not be the most common reason at all.

Married deacons

Q. Are married deacons permitted to have normal sexual relations with their wives?

A. Yes, they are. Your question may arise from some confusion regarding the traditional concerns for "ritual purity." Among the Jewish priests (who were married), abstinence from sexual intercourse was required when they were on duty in the Temple. It was considered improper for them to offer sacrifice after having had intercourse with their wives; therefore, for the duration of their duty, they actually lived at the Temple away from their wives. In fact, a careful study of world religions demonstrates a rather consistent pattern of linking priesthood and sexual abstinence in some form.

At any rate, this practice carried over into Christianity, so that in the early Church married priests also abstained from intercourse the night before they were to offer the eucharistic sacrifice. As daily Mass became the norm, priests found themselves abstaining more and more, with the result that celibacy became the norm and eventually the law in the Western Church, as it is to this day.

That was never the case with married deacons, however, since deacons (whether married or celibate) do not offer the Eucharist but merely assist at it.

Chaplains

Q. I have often noticed stories covering chaplains to the police, the military, and so on. One of the subjects was a nun. Correct me if I am wrong but does not canon law forbid women this task: "A chaplain is a PRIEST to whom is entrusted in a stable manner the pastoral care. . ." (Canon 564)?

A. You are correct. Sometimes our common parlance gets sloppy and does not adequately reflect our theology. This same phenomenon has surfaced in the application of the word "minister" to all kinds of people. Technically speaking, only one who has been ordained (deacon, priest, or bishop) can be called a minister, a point stressed at the Laity Synod in Rome in 1987.

May non-clerics teach seminarians?

Q. The seminary I attend has two sisters teaching us. One teaches liturgy, and the other teaches preaching. Is this permitted?

A. Yes, it is permitted for non-clerics to teach in seminaries, provided they have the appropriate background for the courses they are teaching. The courses you mention could be taught by any qualified person from an academic point of view; I would have questions about practical aspects.

For example, can a sister convincingly teach seminarians how to baptize or anoint, inasmuch as she has never done these things? Similarly with preaching; although a layperson or Religious might have much to offer in terms of public-speaking techniques, being incapable of preaching oneself hardly adds credibility to one's presentation.

Aside from considerations about the seminarians' education, I would also wonder about the advisability of placing people in positions which could set them up for frustration. It seems to me that it would take an extremely rare person to prepare young men to perform actions which one is unable to do oneself. While any qualified person may teach in a seminary, spiritual direction is limited to priests. Apparently, some American seminaries were not observing this norm and Rome was required to intervene, reminding all of the limitation.

Latin and priestly formation

Q. Is Latin required learning for priests?

A. As most people know, in "the old days" Latin was a staple of the curriculum for any college seminarian; of course, that was pretty much the case for most educated people. For future priests, however, it was crucial because theology classes were taught in Latin, all the source books and even textbooks were written in Latin, and the future priest would have to pray the Divine Office and celebrate Mass in that language as well for the rest of his life.

With the widespread use of the vernacular in the late '60s, some seminary faculties began to question the wisdom and necessity of a Latin background. It would not have been uncommon in the late '70s to come upon newly ordained priests who could say they had never studied a day of Latin. As time goes on, however, many bishops and theology professors have discovered that the loss of Latin training has been quite detrimental to a serious study of theology and has also resulted in a loss of a grip on the Catholic Tradition. Furthermore, one would have to admit that it is at least a little bit ridiculous that a man could be ordained for the Latin Rite, not know a word of the language, and be completely incapable of celebrating liturgy in that language. For all these reasons, Latin seems to be making a return in most college seminary programs; Roman guidelines also require its inclusion in the curriculum.

Unholy Fathers

Q. Does the Church admit that there have been unspiritual popes?

A. The Church does not have to "admit" to the charge; history amply documents it. That having been said, we shouldn't blow all this out of proportion. After all, the balance sheet of history records far more virtuous popes than lascivious ones. The simple truth, however, is that the Church does not rise and fall on the morality of individual popes but on the truth of the doctrine they taught.

Certainly the witness of their teaching is magnified many times over when their lives and their words are in total correspondence, but the Scriptures provide us with at least three examples of something less than the ideal. First, our Lord dealt with this very question in the context of the leadership of the Judaism of His own day: "The scribes and the Pharisees have taken their seat on the chair of Moses. Therefore, do and observe all things whatsoever they tell you, but do not follow their example. For they preach but they do not practice" (Mt 23:2f). Second, the Risen Christ did not hesitate to give to Peter the position of "substitute shepherd" in the

Church in the same moment as He reminded him of his threefold sin of denial (cf. Jn 21:15-19). Finally, Paul notes his confrontation with Peter, not because the Prince of the Apostles had taught error but because he was not living up to the implications of the correct teaching (cf. Gal 2:11).

Popes, like all other human beings, are sinful persons, in need of the Sacrament of Penance as much as any other Christian. However, we would be remiss if we failed to mention how fortunate we have been in modern times to have the saintliest of popes, particularly in this century. Their goodness is not the illusion of pious imaginations but quite obvious; after all, with all the enemies of Christ and His Church on the horizon, nothing could offer more grist for the mill than scandalous successors of St. Peter.

Cardinals

Q. *In addressing letters to the various ranks of Catholic clergy, all titles precede the personal names, except for that of a cardinal, in which we say "Thomas Cardinal Smith." Why this procedure?*

A. Some of these traditions are shrouded in mystery, but the standard explanation offered for the mode of address for a cardinal is this: The title comes from the Latin word *cardo* (hinge), underscoring the fact that a cardinal serves as a "hinge" between the Pope and various other sectors of the Church. That aspect of his ministry is highlighted even in his name as the title serves as a "hinge" between his Christian name and his surname.

Increasingly, this practice applies only in formal situations (such as in letters). "Cardinal Thomas Smith" is now a common way of addressing cardinals, but the old form is still preferred.

Roman collars

Q. *Please comment on the various styles of Roman collar. Is this merely personal preference? What is its history? Why do Protestant ministers wear a Roman collar, inasmuch as this seems to refer to Rome and the Pope, with which they are not in union?*

A. Let me back into this question by going through some of the history first. Once clergy began to dress in an identifiable manner, the black cassock became the standard garb of the secular priest. One of the many tasks performed by clergy in the Middle Ages was teaching, so that all teachers eventually adopted the cassock as the academic gown still used for formal academic events.

When the Protestant Reformation occurred, even those reformers who did not consider clerical garb as desirable maintained it to the extent that they used it for preaching and teaching (hence portraits of Luther and others so attired). When priests found themselves in hostile environments, they stopped wearing the Roman cassock (with the buttons down the front) in public and produced a kind of abbreviated version of it in what we in the

United States know as a clerical suit (and that explains the name "Roman collar").

The various styles of collar are matters of personal preference. Most commonly worn today is the black shirt with a slip-in tab collar; for more formal functions, many wear a black shirt-front with a full collar and a white French-cut shirt underneath. Some younger priests and seminarians seem to be leaning toward an older style of collar (current until the 1950s), which has often been regarded as a Protestant form of dress; in reality, it was the only kind of collar worn by all priests for almost a hundred and fifty years in this country.

As far as non-Catholic clergy and the "Roman" collar go, most would simply refer to it as a "clerical" collar, leaving out the Roman connection. As an aside, it is interesting to observe how many non-Catholics have taken up clerical garb in the past twenty years, obviously seeing in it a valuable witness and means of evangelization. Finally, black is still the required color for Catholic clergy in the United States, decided on by the American bishops in the late 1970s, in response to requests to add other colors to the wardrobe. In Europe and even in Rome, however, gray and dark blue are permissible. I suspect that the American hierarchy were hesitant in this regard because of a concern that our clergy not be confused with those of other denominations, a question which does not generally surface in Europe because countries tend to be more religiously homogeneous.

'Decked-out' prelates

Q. I am a nineteen-year-old convert and have a question regarding the hierarchy, asked with all respect: In their official garb, they look like they're worth a million, dripping in jewels and the like. Did Christ really intend this?

A. I think you've been reading too many novels!

I deal with bishops day in and day out, and I've yet to see one "dripping in jewels." The normal insignia of a bishop include a pectoral cross and a ring, both usually of gold or silver. I find it amusing that some people who object to a bishop's wearing of such objects are themselves often "dripping" in gold chains and bracelets. The pectoral cross symbolizes the bishop's willingness to die for the Church, as did our Lord. The episcopal ring proclaims his marriage to the local church or diocese. Beyond that, he generally just wears the regular clerical garb of any other priest. For ceremonial occasions, the bishop wears either a black cassock with red piping or a purple cassock and a purple zucchetto (skull cap). Additional insignia for liturgical events include the crozier, or shepherd's staff, and the miter, the hat worn in Old Testament times by the high priest. Clearly, then, these special signs of office are not intended to be lavish but simple reminders to the man himself and to the people he serves of who and what he is by God's grace and, therefore, what he is supposed to be.

If we viewed a bishop as a successor of the apostles and as Christ in our midst in a unique way, I do not think we would have any problem with these symbols.

Monsignor

Q. Is the monsignorate obsolete? Monsignors seem to be an endangered species in many dioceses. Do you think this is for the better or worse?

A. The monsignorate is a man-made honor of relatively recent origin in the Church (the nineteenth century). It is a title conferred on a priest by the Holy Father, usually at the recommendation of the priest's local bishop, to acknowledge his exceptional work on behalf of the Church. The priest is permitted to wear either a black cassock with red piping and purple sash or a purple cassock, depending on his rank. The monsignor becomes an honorary member of the papal household.

Some dioceses eliminated the monsignorate for all practical purposes after the Second Vatican Council. In the past decade or so, however, it seems to be on the rebound in many places. Ideally speaking, a priest should seek no honor, except to further God's Kingdom here on earth, but psychologically viewed, the monsignorate can serve as a healthy "pat on the back."

Sometimes the monsignorate reached the point of the ridiculous in some dioceses as upwards of twenty-five percent of the clergy eventually attained that rank, leading everyone to ask what it could possibly mean in such situations. When the honor is given out sparingly and justly, I think it can be a positive thing. When priests perceive it as a perpetuation of the "old boy system," it becomes divisive and problematic.

'Wealth' of the Church

Q. After many years, my husband is finally interested in the Church again. However, he finds the Church's wealth a tremendous stumbling block. He says the Church should emulate St. Francis of Assisi and be less concerned with buildings, artwork, and ornate vestments. How does the Church respond to his objections?

A. Anyone who has read the papers lately knows that excessive wealth is not a problem of the Church and that, as a matter of fact, the Holy See is operating at a deficit of $65 million.

Ask your husband to consider these possibilities. Without buildings, how would the Church carry on the work of evangelization or catechesis? The Catholic school system in the United States is the most extensive nongovernmental educational network in world history — what a clear statement of Catholic priorities that is. Our schools, hospitals, nursing homes, and services rendered by Catholic Charities are concrete demonstrations of concern, based on the Gospel message. Such efforts cannot even be attempted without the necessary delivery systems in place — all of which take money.

The Church's ownership of priceless artwork likewise makes some important and powerful statements: (1) It is a testimony to the primacy of the spiritual over the material and an indication of the beauty of which man is capable when inspired by faith; (2) It enables art to be available to all and not just to the rich who can afford to maintain such works in the privacy of their homes. Recall that artworks in the Vatican are available for all to appreciate and not a select few; such works are also an invitation to faith for nonbelievers. Sometimes people argue that the Church should sell these things and give the money to the poor. Be warned in advance: Judas was the first to make that proposal. While that sounds like a grand gesture, it would be nothing more than mere tokenism. Someone has determined that were that done, each poor person in the world would receive approximately thirty-two cents.

Finally, what about ornate vestments and other liturgical appointments? It is significant to realize that a priest's everyday street clothing is a simple black suit. He "dresses up" only for the liturgy, when he "puts on Christ" in a wholly unique and marvelous way. This is our feeble human endeavor to accord God the glory due His name; this also has the effect of raising our own minds and hearts beyond what we normally encounter, to consider a world and life beyond. For all these reasons, St. Francis, whom you rightly cite as the saint of the poor, was the first to demand nothing but the finest for use at God's altar. Mother Teresa of Calcutta operates on the same principle.

Often enough, people who speak like your husband mean well but fail to evaluate the situation completely from a perspective of faith. Involuntary poverty is an evil to be combatted, especially when it is caused by human selfishness or greed. However, a far greater evil is a failure to offer fitting public worship to the Creator. When clear indications of the genuine love of God are in place, love of neighbor is never far behind.

Vatican 'wealth'

Q. Why does our Pope live in such splendor and glory while so much of the world's population lives in poverty? I find it hard to believe that the Lord Jesus would have surrounded Himself in such luxury. If the Catholic Church sold even one quarter of the riches in Vatican City, the proceeds could easily feed a great many of the world's hungry.

A. Having just returned from a trip to Rome, I found your question interesting for a number of reasons.

First, have you ever been inside the papal apartments or even seen pictures? I have, and splendor is certainly not the word to describe them. As a matter of fact, they are typical of homes built in the sixteenth century, and I, for one, would prefer not living in the dampness you describe as splendor.

The furnishings are modest, and the Pope's food is substantial but unpretentious — surely nothing like that consumed by other heads of state and perhaps likewise by other religious leaders.

Second, to talk about selling off Vatican "wealth" reveals a certain naïveté, which I have discussed before in this column. The wealth is in intangibles, for the most part. The artwork belongs to the whole Church, indeed the whole world; it not only stands as a testimony to the Faith which produced it but also serves as a vehicle of evangelization. Assuming that all these "treasures" could be sold and the proceeds given to the poor, what concrete results would ensue? Someone has calculated that such a sale would net each poor person in the world approximately thirty-two cents. This would obviously do nothing to assist anyone's hunger problems and could be seen as little more than a grandstand gesture or tokenism.

Perhaps the Catholics of America, the wealthiest members of the Church, would do better to be more concerned and generous toward the poor from their own resources, which outstrip those of the Holy Father many times over.

Kissing the ground

Q. *Why did the Pope not kiss the ground upon disembarking from the plane at his unscheduled stop in South Africa? Surely he's not implying that because of its policy of apartheid that South Africa is not "good enough" to earn this gesture? If that is the case, it's a stumbling block to me because many of the countries he has visited in the past are much more repressive of human rights. Plus, one could mention the Kurt Waldheim visit.*

A. I think you answered your own question. My guess (and that's all it is) is that the Holy Father did not tender his now-familiar gesture of kissing the ground of a country on his first official visit precisely because it was unscheduled and hence an unofficial visit.

As far as the remark on the Waldheim visit, I intend to respond to that in considerable detail in an upcoming issue of TCA because so many malicious, slanderous, and erroneous comments have been made in that regard.

'PP'

Q. *When the Holy Father signs his name, he does so in Latin: Ioannes Paulus PP II. What does the "PP" stand for?*

A. That stands for "*Papa Pontifex.*" Both titles were held by the ancient Roman high priest. The first means "father," while the second means "bridge builder" (between heaven and earth). If the pagan Romans considered those names appropriate for their high priest, how much more so for the man who is the Vicar of Christ on earth?

Papal blessings

Q. Over the years I have received two papal blessings, the first from Pope Pius XII and the second from Pope John Paul II. The wordings are entirely different. The first seems to do more for the recipient: "Granting the sacred papal blessing and absolution of all sins in the moment of death, even in the case that you cannot go to confession or receive Holy Communion, and only after making an act of contrition and pronouncing with your lips and heart the holy Name of Jesus." The second just says, "I give from my heart a special papal blessing to you." Why the change? Is the first one still valid for me?

A. The first does not ring true, not because the content is wrong but simply because it is not the style of papal blessings; that sounds much more like an explanation of what is involved with receiving an apostolic or papal blessing. And thus your second text is best explained by the first.

Vatican II digest

Q. Is there a pamphlet which, in digest form, communicates the sixteen documents of Vatican II to clarify things for those who are confused?

A. A handy booklet, just such as you describe, came out a few years after the council. The work is entitled, "Outlines of the 16 Documents: Vatican II." The cost is $1.50 for a booklet of a little more than one hundred pages. It is available from *The Long Island Catholic*, Box 700, Hempstead, NY 11551.

General Index